Whatever Happened to Frank and Fearless?

The impact of new public management on the Australian Public Service

Whatever Happened to Frank and Fearless?

The impact of new public management on the Australian Public Service

Kathy MacDermott

THE AUSTRALIAN NATIONAL UNIVERSITY

E PRESS

Published by ANU E Press
The Australian National University
Canberra ACT 0200, Australia
Email: anuepress@anu.edu.au
This title is also available online at: http://epress.anu.edu.au/frank_fearless_citation.html

National Library of Australia
Cataloguing-in-Publication entry

Author:	McDermott, Kathy.
Title:	Whatever happened to frank and fearless? : the impact of the new public service management on the Australian public service / Kathy MacDermott.
ISBN:	9781921313912 (pbk.) 9781921313929 (web)
Series:	ANZSOG series
Notes:	Bibliography.
Subjects:	Civil service--Australia. Public administration--Australia. Australia--Politics and government.
Dewey Number:	351.94

Cover design by John Butcher.

Funding for this monograph series has been provided by the Australia and New Zealand School of Government Research Program.

John Wanna, *Series Editor*

Professor John Wanna is the Sir John Bunting Chair of Public Administration at the Research School of Social Sciences at The Australian National University. He is the director of research for the Australian and New Zealand School of Government (ANZSOG). He is also a joint appointment with the Department of Politics and Public Policy at Griffith University and a principal researcher with two research centres: the Governance and Public Policy Research Centre and the nationally-funded Key Centre in Ethics, Law, Justice and Governance at Griffith University. Professor Wanna has produced around 17 books including two national text books on policy and public management. He has produced a number of research-based studies on budgeting and financial management including: *Budgetary Management and Control* (1990); *Managing Public Expenditure* (2000), *From Accounting to Accountability* (2001) and, most recently, *Controlling Public Expenditure* (2003). He has just completed a study of state level leadership covering all the state and territory leaders — entitled *Yes Premier: Labor leadership in Australia's states and territories* — and has edited a book on Westminster Legacies in Asia and the Pacific — *Westminster Legacies: Democracy and responsible government in Asia and the Pacific*. He was a chief investigator in a major Australian Research Council funded study of the Future of Governance in Australia (1999-2001) involving Griffith and the ANU. His research interests include Australian and comparative politics, public expenditure and budgeting, and government-business relations. He also writes on Australian politics in newspapers such as *The Australian*, *Courier-Mail* and *The Canberra Times* and has been a regular state political commentator on ABC radio and TV.

Table of Contents

Author Profile

Dr Kathy MacDermott has taught in universities in Australia and the United States. More recently, she has worked in the senior executive service of the Australian Public Service in industrial relations policy and public sector governance, and has published in these areas. Her responsibilities have included managing evaluations of how the APS Values and Code of Conduct have been applied in practice and the conduct of the annual *State of the Service* report.

Acknowledgements

I would like to thank Andrew Podger for reading and rereading the manuscript and providing valuable and patient commentary, John Nethercote for his thorough comments and suggestions, and David Webster for his persistent contribution to quality control. Thanks too to the two anonymous reviewers whose comments and suggestions have contributed to shaping the final product. I would also like to thank the *State of the Service* team for the important research that they have made publicly available. More generally, I would also like to acknowledge the influence of many public servants with whom I have worked, who continue to struggle with these issues every day and who care about personal and public integrity. Discussions with these people lie behind the hypothetical cases raised in the book. Discussions with Amy Webster and Sarah Webster lie behind the desire to write it in the first place. I am also grateful to ANZSOG and, especially, to John Wanna and John Butcher for their advice throughout the process and to Anne Gelling for her editorial assistance.

Foreword

Dr Kathy MacDermott's monograph sets out a series of controversial arguments that challenge some widely and strongly held views.

Many, like me, continue to regard the New Public Management reforms of the 1980s and 1990s in Australia as groundbreaking, demonstrating how the public sector can deliver efficient and effective services in an internationally competitive economy. Many also of my vintage and older continue to view favourably the Coombs Royal Commission's other two emphases on responsiveness to the elected government and community participation in government, reinforcing democratic principles and breaking down the hegemony of the public service. And there are strong adherents of the more recent emphasis on performance management and workplace reform.

MacDermott does not oppose these reforms, but questions how some have been applied in practice and how they have cumulatively re-positioned public servants and their relationship with the political arm of government. In doing so, some leaders of the reforms will no doubt feel somewhat uncomfortable about aspects of MacDermott's analysis.

This monograph is important. It does not suggest turning back the clock, but seeks reconsideration of some of the effects of the reforms of the last 25 years. Have some gone too far? Have we lost sight of the idealistic aspirations behind some of the reforms? Have there been unintended consequences from some initiatives? Have we let the rhetoric run away from the reality?

Importantly, MacDermott looks at the reforms from the perspective of public servants down the line, not just departmental secretaries. What is the context in which they now operate and what behaviours do they believe the system expects of them today? In particular, are they encouraged to be responsive to the point where they compromise their duty to be apolitical and impartial and concerned for the public interest?

Some of the challenges MacDermott identifies are:

- the extent to which contestability of policy advice is improving the contest for ideas or enhancing the ability of governments to find the advice they want;
- the extent to which performance management is improving organisational performance or reinforcing pressure to conform;
- the extent to which devolution has enhanced flexibility to deliver better results or has involved a trade-off of policy influence for managerial control, with public servants subject to closer direction by both managers and by ministerial advisers and ministers;

- the extent to which workforce reforms in the public sector have increased flexibility and enhanced employees' capacity to identify with and contribute to organisational objectives, or have disempowered employees, discouraged teamwork and reduced innovation and professional autonomy;
- the extent to which outsourcing has improved efficiency and effectiveness through competition or has undermined altruism and concern for the public interest both within the public service and amongst the non-government sector.

I do not agree with all of MacDermott's conclusions, although I know of real instances that are consistent with almost all of her hypothetical cases and I know well that the APS Commission survey data confirm widespread unease amongst public servants. In a few cases, however, I think that unease is just misplaced; in other cases, there is indeed supporting evidence reinforcing the need to revisit current practice, for example in performance management and workplace relations.

More generally, MacDermott's plea for a firmer focus on public value strikes a chord with me. Public servants do want to serve the elected government, but they want to be recognised by government and the public for their contribution to the public interest by their professionalism. The opportunity to serve the public remains the greatest attraction to join the public service, and the greatest motivator to perform. If not managed appropriately some of the reforms, notwithstanding their intrinsic merits, do present a danger of undermining this fundamental value which drives the public service.

Andrew Podger

Overview

Under s.10(1)(a) of the *Public Service Act* 1999 (hereafter referred to as the *Public Service Act*) the Australian public service (the APS) is required to be 'apolitical, performing its functions in an impartial and professional manner'. Under s.10(1)(f) it is required to be 'responsive' in advising government and in implementing its policies and programs.

In recent times—but not, certainly, for the first time in recent Australian history—doubts have arisen about the ability of public servants to maintain the balance between these functions. Much has been written about a perceived politicisation of the public service. Two separate, but interrelated, sets of circumstance have fed these debates. The first of these is a cluster of events at the political level, in which the role of Australian public servants has been criticised or questioned. The second is the introduction into the public service of new models of organisation, administration and behaviour, known collectively here as New Public Management or NPM.

Though the implementation of NPM has been tailored by different governments to their differing requirements, its underpinning principles have been broadly supported by Australian political parties since its emergence in the 1980s. The overall aim of NPM is to make the public service more flexible and efficient, and more responsive to government. Key components of NPM at the Commonwealth level in Australia have included making the work of public servants contestable; the introduction of performance management, including individual performance assessment and pay; the devolution of centralised managerial controls to individual agencies; the restructuring of public sector industrial relations according to contract-based models; and the outsourcing of service delivery to third-party service providers (including profit-based and not-for-profit entities). Most people working within and writing about the public service during the implementation of NPM reforms have accepted that these disciplines have improved its flexibility and efficiency. However, the disciplines associated with NPM have also provided the means to reshape relations between government and the public service in less benign ways.

The aim of this monograph is to analyse a number of key NPM systems with regard to their involvement—individually and in aggregate—in such changes to the relations between government and the public service. It is thus about the expression of public service governance and frameworks in the Australian body politic rather than about how the public service has operated in specific recent events. It is focused on the public service at the Commonwealth level, although this does not mean that a similar analysis of state public sectors could not be undertaken.

The overall conclusion is that the NPM reforms have been internalised by the public service in ways that leave it much less protected against pressures towards politicisation than in the past. This is not to deny its increased efficiency[1] nor does it mean that it is necessary to turn back the clock and undo what has been done in the interests of public sector reform. There are, however, ways of recalibrating the drivers of the system so that public servants are better able to distinguish their role from that of ministerial advisers. Some of these issues and options are considered in chapter seven.

ENDNOTES

[1] See, for example, Public Service and Merit Protection Commission, *Re-engineering People Management: From Good Intentions to Good Practice* (Canberra, 1997), Ch. 1; http://www.apsc.gov.au/publications96/reengineering.htm, viewed 14 Feb. 2008; Australian National Audit Office Audit Report, *Managing People for Business Outcomes: Year Two, Across Agency*, ANAO Audit Report No. 50 2002-2003 (Canberra, 2003), part of a longitudinal study of the effectiveness and efficiency of all aspects of people management in 13 agencies, covering some 36% of APS employees. The study assessed each people-management practice area against four criteria: quality, HR integration, effectiveness and efficiency, and business contribution.

Chapter 1. A failure of public administration?

Introduction

Debate in the press about the politicisation of the APS has intensified in recent years. Undoubtedly these debates are not new. As will be seen, debate about the 'proper' role of the public service has continued virtually unabated since the Whitlam Government introduced ministerial advisers following its election in 1972. Nevertheless, commentators on both sides of politics have reflected on both the number and profile of recent controversies involving perceptions of public service politicisation.[1] These include the 'Children Overboard' affair (known to the Senate as 'A Certain Maritime Incident') involving the Departments of Defence, Immigration and the Prime Minister and Cabinet; the cases of the detention of Cornelia Rau and the deportation of Vivian Solon, involving the then Department of Immigration and Multicultural and Indigenous Affairs (DIMIA);[2] the payments made by the Australian Wheat Board (AWB) to the regime of Saddam Hussein in order to obtain contracts for the sale of Australian wheat to Iraq, involving the Department of Foreign Affairs and Trade (DFAT); the detention of Dr Mohamed Haneef, involving the Australian Federal Police; and the role of a senior public servant in the Employment and Workplace Relations portfolio as the face of the Howard Government's *WorkChoices* media campaign.

Debate around most of these cases has tended, particularly in media analysis, to focus on issues of 'who knew what and when'. All except the last have resulted in some form of formal inquiry.[3] Each involves allegations or suppositions about the degree of direct or indirect complicity between public servants and politicians concerning the communication or management of politically sensitive information. It is not the intent of this monograph to pursue what is known or can be inferred about the involvement of individual public servants in these cases. Rather, it explores how changes made to the administration of the public service over the past 30 years have had the effect of progressively blurring the differences between what professional public servants do and what politicians might want them to do.

The chapters that follow argue that a number of the core 'traditional' principles of public administration that have applied in Australian, as in other Westminster systems of government,[4] have been compromised following New Public Management reforms. Australian NPM, it will be argued, brought about a number of distinct and mutually reinforcing institutional reforms embedded in a number of distinct and mutually reinforcing systems. Like all system changes, they were introduced gradually, applied unevenly, and have been the work of many hands. The formal intention was to introduce new disciplines to the public service, making it more efficient, effective and responsive to government. Over time, however, some of those disciplines have been ratcheted up to the point where responsiveness tips into complicity.

The following description and analysis of how this happened, and is continuing to happen, is intended to inform broader debates about the role and function of the public service in the early twenty-first century. The examples cited are recent and in the public domain, but it should be understood, as a former Public Service Commissioner has observed, that 'insiders know better than anyone … that the concerns have been mounting in the Commonwealth since before 1996, and have been evident equally if not more so at state level under both Labor and conservative governments'.[5]

The terms of the debate

In 2006 the then Secretary of the Department of the Prime Minister and Cabinet, Dr Peter Shergold, described the 'Children Overboard' affair and the mistreatment of Cornelia Rau and Vivian Solon as 'failures of public administration', unfortunate 'mistakes' that have nothing to tell us about public service culture or the relation between the public service and the Government:

> I do not accept that the failures represent the collapse of the Westminster tradition or the diminution of public service values or a sad decline in ethical standards. More profoundly, the mistakes are failures of public administration not instances of government conspiracy. The government did not direct public servants to provide false information or fail to correct the record or act outside the law. Nor did it intimate that such behaviour was acceptable. Nor did Ministers put impenetrable barriers around themselves.[6]

This representation of the present state of the public service is significant for a number of reasons. The language suggests that, so long as the Government did not explicitly direct, or intimate, that public servants should act unethically or unlawfully, then there were no broader institutional issues and the problems were simply local. That is not, however, how the system works or is meant to work. Public servants are meant to serve ministers and act in their name. The Public Service Act calls for responsiveness to ministers (s.10(1)(f)), responsiveness that anticipates as well as implements their requirements. It calls for a performance culture with a focus on 'achieving results' sought by government (s. 10(1)(k)). Responsiveness is hardwired into service-wide legislation, service-wide policies, and agency arrangements to support them. Without an understanding of how this overarching framework positions individual public servants who are making (or failing to make) administrative decisions, there is always going to be an increased risk of 'failures of public administration':

> We look to previous instances, such as the 'certain maritime incident' or children overboard affair; the illegal detention of Australian citizens by the Department of Immigration and Indigenous Affairs, the problems revealed by the so-called 'travel rorts' affair, and difficulties with trust fund monies in the land transport development fund. Any one of these in isolation would be a problem that could be attributed to one-off failings on the part of individuals. Taken together, they begin to amount to a pattern—a systematic lack of capacity to identify problems, keep accurate records, and draw these uncomfortable problems to the attention of ministers.[7]

The real questions to ask about these failures are:

- can a system that privileges responsiveness be tipped into complicity?
- what are the circumstances that turn individual lapses of judgement into systems failures?
- can the cause of these failings properly be labelled as politicisation?

Critically, these questions are often about the changing meanings of the terms in which the questions themselves are posed. Over time and across contexts the meanings of even key words like 'politicisation' and 'responsiveness' alter, as do those of more obviously slippery terms like 'performance culture', 'contestability', 'managing for results', 'organisational alignment', 'partnerships'—and even 'New Public Management' itself, which is subject to ongoing debate and redefinition.[8] All of these terms are embedded in and changed by the history of their use.

Take 'responsiveness', for example. The need for increased responsiveness was identified by the Royal Commission on Australian Government Administration (RCAGA) in 1976. As will be seen later in the chapter, RCAGA used the term to refer to a more adaptive approach to service delivery as well as a sensitivity to government objectives that included a more efficient approach to implementing them. Over time, the latter became the dominant meaning of 'responsiveness' for the APS. Looking back in 1993 on the broad pattern of the Dawkins reforms in the 1980s, Prime Minister Paul Keating reflected that:

> Central to our reforms of the public service was the desire to ensure that the government of the country belonged to the elected politicians. We stated at the outset that a key objective was to make the Public Service more responsive to the government of the day, more responsive in the sense that it would be better able to recognise and achieve the Government's overall policy objectives.[9]

In 1999 'responsiveness' acquired a legal definition as one of the APS Values established in the Public Service Act to guide the conduct of public servants. The initial Public Service Bill 1997, presented by Peter Reith, included the bare clause (s.10(f)): 'the APS is responsive to the Government in providing timely advice and implementing the Government's policies and programs'. This emphasis on both advising and implementation was broadly consistent with the overall thrust of RCAGA, but the definition itself lacked a number of critical qualifiers that had been recommended to the Government. The Bill was referred to the Joint Committee on Public Accounts (JCPA), which urged a strengthening 'in relation to the provision of frank and honest advice'.[10] Fearlessness, it appears, was not even on the agenda. Senate amendments unacceptable to the Government were made and the Bill was allowed by Minister Reith to lapse. The next Minister Assisting the Prime Minister for the Public Service shepherded an amended version through Parliament which read: 'the APS is responsive to the Government in providing frank, honest, comprehensive, accurate and timely advice and in implementing the Government's policies and programs' (s. 10(1)(f)).

Section 10(1)(f) of the Public Service Act has since been elaborated by the Public Service Commissioner in *APS Values and Code of Conduct in Practice: A Guide to Official Conduct for APS Employees and Agency Heads*. The guidance still links operational efficiency with strategic attainment of government goals, and emphasises 'a close and cooperative relationship with Ministers and their employees':

> Responsiveness to the Government demands a willingness and capacity to be effective and efficient. Responsive APS employees:
>
> * are knowledgeable about the Government's stated policies
> * are sensitive to the intent and direction of policy
> * take a whole-of-government view [and] are well informed about the issues involved
> * draw on professional knowledge and expertise and are alert to best practice
> * consult relevant stakeholders and understand their different perspectives
> * provide practical and realistic options and assess their costs, benefits and consequences
> * convey advice clearly and succinctly
> * carry out decisions and implement programs promptly, conscientiously, efficiently and effectively.

> Responsive advice is frank, honest, comprehensive, accurate and timely (APS Value (f)). The advice should be well argued and creative, anticipate issues and appreciate the underlying intent of government policy.

Responsive advice is also forthright and direct and does not withhold or gloss over important known facts or 'bad news'.

Responsiveness demands a close and cooperative relationship with Ministers and their employees. The policy advisory process is an iterative one, which may involve frequent feedback between the APS and the Minister and his or her office.

Responsive implementation of the Government's policies and programs (APS Value (f)) is achieved through a close and cooperative relationship with Ministers and their employees. Ministers may make decisions, and issue policy guidelines with which decisions made by APS employees must comply. Such Ministerial decisions and policy guidance must, of course, comply with the law and decisions by APS employees must meet their responsibilities for impartiality and efficient, effective and ethical use of resources.[11]

Adjusted or alternative definitions of what 'responsiveness' should mean have been posed by academics, media commentators, and members of the Opposition.[12] What it means in practice to working public servants, when disciplined by the contestability of policy advice (see Chapter 2), inserted in a performance management system (see Chapter 3), experienced through devolved relations with specific ministers' offices (see Chapter 4), aligned with ministerial priorities through individual contracts (see Chapter 5) and re-expressed through a cooperative partnership (see Chapter 6), can shrink to 'what have you done for the minister that's special'?[13]   This is not the normative meaning of 'responsiveness', but it can be the operational one.

Or take 'politicisation'. A recent article by Richard Mulgan offers a useful and much-needed account of the concept as 'understood within the context of the APS Values associated with a professional public service':

> In order to be able to offer the same degree of loyal service to governments of differing political persuasions, professional public servants are expected to maintain a certain distance from concerns of their political masters. 'Politicisation' is the term used to describe the erosion of such distance. It marks the crossing of a line between proper responsiveness to the elected government and undue involvement in the government's electoral fortunes.[14]

For the public service, the legislated equivalent of this is the requirement under section 10 of the Public Service Act to be 'apolitical, performing its functions in an impartial and professional manner'. As in the case of 'responsiveness', this definition has been elaborated by the Public Service Commissioner:

The role of the APS is to serve the Government of the day: to provide the same high standard of policy advice, implementation and professional support, irrespective of which political party is in power. This is at the core of the professionalism of the APS.

The APS works within, and to implement, the elected government's policies and outcomes. While it is not independent, it is well placed to draw on a depth of knowledge and experience including longer-term perspectives.

Good advice from the APS is unbiased and objective. It is politically neutral but not naïve, and is developed and offered with an understanding of its implications and of the broader policy directions set by government.

APS employees have a role to assist Ministers with their parliamentary and public roles, such as drafting speeches.

In the course of their employment, however, APS employees should not engage in party political activities such as distributing political material, nor should they use office facilities or resources to provide support of a party political nature such as producing political publications or conducting market research unrelated to programme responsibilities.[15]

These definitions are altogether consistent with that proposed by Mulgan. Like his, however, they remain 'slippery in meaning because the line [between proper responsiveness to the elected government and undue involvement] itself is often blurred and hard to draw and because charges of politicisation are often part of adversarial political rhetoric'.[16] One of the most common defences against a charge of politicisation, for example, is to treat the word as an indicator of the personal or party agenda of whoever used it.[17] Another means of neutering the concept—described by Mulgan as 'singl[ing] out the more overt form of direct instruction'—is to reduce it to whether or not a government 'issued … direct instructions to falsify the record'.[18] Consistent with this strategy, analysts who hypothesise the existence of less overt forms of politicisation lay themselves open to being criticised as conspiracy theorists. In any event, to confine an analysis of politicisation to 'who said what to whom, when' simply shifts attention away from institutions to individuals. While there is much to be said at this level, it is often associated with histories of specific events or interactions, generally between individual public servants and their ministers and ministerial advisers. These histories assume that, whether or not specific interactions were proper, there is a normative version of such relationships, one in which the proper line between responsiveness to the elected government and undue involvement is respected. Such an assumption incorporates a further assumption that both public servants and ministers and their advisers clearly understand their different roles. This has not always been the case.

Ministerial advisers were added to the machinery of government by Labor following the 1972 election. RCAGA itself 'did not generally favour policy advisers in ministers offices'.[19] It recommended instead that where a minister felt the need for additional policy advice, 'it will frequently be more helpful to him if the resources of the department are more effectively mobilised or stimulated to be responsive to his needs'.[20] Nevertheless, the Fraser Government did not abolish the institution, although it did cut back on its numbers. The Hawke Government in its turn decided to greatly increase the number of ministerial advisers, which it presented as a trade-off for not proceeding with an election commitment to politicise 10 per cent of the senior executive service.[21] This trade-off effectively clarified a difference in role between public servants and ministerial advisers. Ministerial advisers would protect public servants from pressure to become politicised by providing those services themselves, from within the minister's own private office. Thus, 'the partisan policy role that had been so controversial and fiercely resisted in the Whitlam period was asserted and legitimised from the outset of the Hawke Labor period'.[22] Over time, the policy capacity of the ministerial office was strengthened[23] and the work of the senior public servant became more managerial.[24] These changes have continued to test the roles proper to public servants and ministerial advisers, secretaries and ministers, and with them the definitions proper to 'responsiveness' and 'politicisation'.

State of the Service and other data

When asked about their own understanding of their roles, departmental secretaries reported themselves to be mainly 'relaxed and comfortable' about their relations with ministers:

> The confidential surveys of Secretaries conducted in recent years by Professor Patrick Weller provide little evidence that 'Australia's mandarins' are intimidated. Every departmental secretary 'declared that the new contract conditions made no difference to the fearlessness of their policy advice' [although, a footnote advises, 'several noted that some of their colleagues were more cowed']. Similarly a confidential questionnaire undertaken by Professor Bob Gregory of 22 Secretaries and Commonwealth government CEOs in late 2003 found that just three agreed with the statement that politicians were improperly involving themselves in the business of public servants. Gregory concluded that 'in the minds of current APS departmental heads the conventions of "traditional ministerial responsibility" are very much alive and well ...'[25]

Just how much reliance can be placed on this kind of confidential research is open to question. As far as those further down the line are concerned, a survey conducted in the same year found that, of those public servants who had had contact with ministers and their advisers over the previous two years, 35 per cent had encountered a 'challenge in balancing the need to be apolitical, impartial and professional, responsive to the Government and openly accountable (as per the APS Values) in dealing with ministers and/or ministers' offices', and a further five per cent were unsure.[26] The findings of subsequent surveys have remained remarkably consistent with these perceptions.[27] The questions put to secretaries and to public servants were differently worded: those put to secretaries concerned the behaviour of politicians generally, and those put to public servants were confined to their own ministers and their advisers. More importantly, the question of possible impropriety is differently put in each survey. The point is, however, that if you are interested in whether systems unduly restrain the provision of frank and fearless advice, you do not look only at those who are at the top of the system. Bureaucratic decision making occurs all the way up (and down) the line.

There are factors other than management systems that constrain decision making, and some of these have a disproportionate impact on lower-level staff. With respect to the challenges to public servants posed by ministers and their advisers, it is undoubtedly the case that the considerable growth in the number of ministerial advisers has increased the penetration of contact between ministers' offices and agencies. According to the *2003–04 State of the Service Report*, at 1 May 2004 the total number of ministerial personal staff was 392, an increase of 89 per cent from the 207 at April 1983,[28] following the Hawke Government's decision to appoint political advisers to ministers' offices. There are some simple logistical reasons for this increase, including ministers' needs for additional support following changes in information and communications technology used by media commentators, and the sheer physical size of the office space available following the move to the new Parliament House. The simple fact that numbers of ministerial staff have increased means, however, that there is more scope for interaction between this group and public servants. Technological change—email, mobile phones, SMS, etc.—means that there is increased scope for this contact to be direct, bypassing conventional channels of approach down through the hierarchy, and that the expectation is for short turn-around times.

While the increase in the numbers of ministerial advisers is known, there are no pre-2003 data available on the corresponding increase in the numbers of public servants who are responding to their requests. However, there are relevant data on the classification levels of those public servants being contacted by ministers and their advisers, and the extent to which public servants at different levels have 'experience[d] a challenge' during one or more of those interactions. In 2004–05, 73 per cent of Senior Executive Service employees surveyed reported having had direct contact[29] with ministers and/or their advisers in the preceding year. 35 per cent of their immediate subordinates (executive level employees) and 15 per cent of the lower grades (APS 1–6) also reported having had direct contact with the minister's office. Given the actual numbers of employees in each of these groups (the APS generally exhibits a pyramidal structure), it appears that individuals in the lower grades who experienced this direct contact outnumbered senior executive staff by a ratio of about 10:1.[30] This is contrary to the conventional view of how the system works.

Not surprisingly, executive-level public servants were less likely than departmental secretaries to report being comfortable and confident during such interactions. In 2004–5 one-third of public servants who had been in direct contact with ministers or their advisers in the last 12 months reported that they had only moderate (22 per cent) or very low (10 per cent) levels of confidence that they could appropriately balance the legislated public service values of being apolitical, impartial and professional, responsive to government and openly accountable.[31] This group is more likely to be on the receiving end of difficult questions than APS-level staff, and less likely to be familiar with the conventions for managing them than the senior executive staff. While confidence in balancing the APS Values was found not to be correlated with age, sex or size of agency, it was correlated with awareness of agreed written and unwritten processes in place in an agency for resolving staff concerns about the nature of requests from ministerial offices.[32] This may go some way to further explaining why public servants as a group are less confident than their departmental secretaries in their interactions with ministers and their advisers: they are less likely to be familiar with any conventions or protocols that apply to such interactions—and have less power to assert any such knowledge.

There are some data on the availability of such protocols. For example, many agencies require the purport of oral briefings to ministers or ministerial staff on key issues to be confirmed in writing (including emails or follow-up minutes). Nine large agencies reported in the *2004–05 State of the Service* agency survey that they had this protocol in place—a fact unlikely to have escaped their agency heads—and yet between 37 and 66 per cent of their relevant employees were not sure whether their agency had such a protocol in place.[33] These people may not have known whether they should be keeping records of their oral advice any more than new or untrained ministerial advisers may have known whether they could ask that records not be kept. It is in situations like this that decisions can 'make themselves', and that the default response may become responsiveness, where responsiveness has lost touch with any countervailing requirement for apolitical professionalism. Advisers may ask that records not be kept and public servants may see it as their duty to acquiesce. Or, even if public servants are aware that they may be being asked to do something outside usual practice, they may find it more difficult to decline on the ground of a generalised public service 'professionalism' than on the ground of a formal protocol. In the absence of explicit guidance and responsible leadership, administrative failures may more readily occur, even when no direct pressure is being personally exerted on any individual public servant. However, there are indications that pressure has been exerted by some ministerial offices. Indeed, the *2004–05 State of the Service Report* found that between 12 and 52 per cent of employees in large agencies reported having faced a challenge during interactions with their political masters.[34]

Claims of 'politicisation' do not take us far into the nature of these interactions, and are counterproductive to the extent that they may be used to deflect or avoid analysis. Most public servants are 'political' to the extent that they understand and have conscious views on the political factors influencing government policies and their application. That may be why they joined the public service or it may be an effect of having joined it. Nearly all public servants are aware that they are bound by law to behave apolitically and accountably.[35] Public servants at DIMIA appear to have been particularly well informed in this area. In 2002–03 staff at DIMIA reported the highest levels of participation in training that included an emphasis on the APS Values.[36] Nevertheless, at DIMIA, as Palmer (2006) found, 'a strong government policy' flowed through 'rigid attitudes and processes' into poor individual decision making with the consequence that numbers of individuals suffered who should not have suffered.[37] To understand failures of due process—in relation to information flow, record-keeping, regulatory decision making or disbursing grants—particularly when such failures occur in politically sensitive environments, it is important to understand the intersection, over time, of the legislated public service values and the actual management systems in which they are applied. The fact that such failures are still largely the exception suggests that individual public servants understand what can happen to principles when they get caught up in administrative machinery, and are prepared to act to sustain what is principled. How long that can continue is unclear.

The purpose of this study, then, is not to probe for conspiracies but to study the present system of public administration: how it positions public servants in relation to the governments they serve, and how 'failures of public administration' can be the outcome. The system itself is presented in the context of the changes that have been made since the introduction of ministerial advisers by the Whitlam Government in 1972 and the tabling of the RCAGA report in 1976. RCAGA is the point that has been identified by previous and current Public Service Commissioners, the former Auditor-General and the former head of the Department of the Prime Minister and Cabinet as a 'watershed in administrative thinking and reforms' whose 'enduring themes have proved to influence greatly the reforms of the past 25 years'.[38] In retrospect, at least, there is agreement on the powerful and lasting influence of the report's three key themes:

- increased responsiveness to the elected government;
- improved efficiency and effectiveness, with devolution and stronger emphasis on results; and
- greater community participation in government.[39]

Without assuming the existence of a previous golden age,[40] the discussion is confined to those changes undertaken following RCAGA and consistent with NPM that were intended to enhance the efficiency and effectiveness of public servants and their responsiveness to government. A chronology of reforms between 1975 and 2003 prepared by the Parliamentary Library and included at the end of this volume as an appendix shows that both of the major parties have had a hand in driving these reforms, and that 'successive governments have generally consolidated, or at least tolerated, the changes of previous governments.'[41]

The reforms in theory

The Public Service Act provides Australian public servants with a set of principles and a code of conduct to guide their behaviour.[42] Because the APS Values are principles-based, their application in particular circumstances is broadly up to the public servant applying them; but there are sanctions for failing to conform to them. The *APS Code of Conduct*, at section 13 of the Act, includes a general provision that employees must 'at all times behave in a way that upholds the APS Values and the integrity and good reputation of the APS'. Agency heads and the senior executive service are required under the Act to promote as well as uphold both the APS Values and the Code.

The APS Values, in effect, constitute a professional code of ethics for public servants. Nevertheless, the APS Values are the artefact of legislation, and reflect the views of the executive and the Parliament at a particular point in time about the conduct of public administration. Their presence in the Act is indicative of a conviction, common when the legislation was being drafted and still widely held, that the processes and procedures of public administration could be made more efficient and effective if detailed rules were replaced by broad principles coupled with an emphasis on getting results. It was argued that principles-based decision making would enable public servants to remain focused on what is important—what the APS Value at s.10(1)(k) of the Public Service Act calls, comprehensively, 'achieving results and managing performance'—while providing procedural flexibility around how to go about doing it.

The groundwork for this approach was laid in 1976 when RCAGA tabled its report. The report used 'responsiveness' to refer to a public service that listened to community views; 'responsiveness' in the sense prescribed in the Public Service Act was a consequence of its recommendations. One of the 'persistent themes'[43] of RCAGA was the need to increase government efficiency, by which it meant both being attuned to government policies and implementing them cost-effectively. Accordingly, RCAGA saw a need to ensure that there was 'clarity in the objectives of the government and in the priority which is to be attached to them' (3.2.2); that 'staff identify themselves with the objectives to which their own efforts are directed' (3.2.9); that 'decision makers at various levels have the scope to exercise initiative within the range of work for which they are primarily responsible' (3.2.3); and that it is understood that 'performance will be assessed and ... officers at all levels are held accountable for their actions and decisions' (3.2.11).[44] Recommendations emerging from RCAGA and subsequent Commonwealth reviews progressively embraced concepts and practices from the private sector as a means of increasing efficiency, including contract management, corporate planning strategies, and independent evaluation and performance management systems. These systems made possible a transition from managing inputs into public services through centralised agencies such as the Treasury and the Public Service Board, to managing for outputs and outcomes by individual agencies and managers. This certainly meant that 'decision makers at various levels have the scope to exercise initiative' as recommended by RCAGA, but it also meant that they were to do so in the interests of government objectives:

> If targets could be set for efficiency, they could equally be set and assessed for attainment of government policy ... While the publicly stated reason for the adoption of the elements of the change was at least in part efficiency, more often than not the changes were an embrace by the political executive of a desire for greater responsiveness. In part, the proposed changes were forcing the political executive and the senior members of the public service closer together, something that had not previously been a central feature of Australia's Westminster system.[45]

In 1984, the Financial Management Improvement Program (FMIP) was introduced to implement management devolution, improved corporate and business planning, increased public accountability and increased emphasis on the evaluation of effective performance. Budgeting and financial accountability arrangements were adapted from private sector practices for government-based systems through mechanisms such as program budgeting (introduced in the 1980s) and the outcomes/outputs framework (introduced in the late 1990s). Reliance on market-based management systems was ratcheted up. Initially this meant increased use of purchaser/provider splits and market testing for many activities funded through the budget, and commercialisation and privatisation of many activities that were paid for by users (such as Telstra, for example). Some activities were moved out of the budget-dependent sector and into the non-budget sector as they became financially dependent on competitively-based decisions by government agencies.

The financial management changes were complemented by similar changes in personnel management, with progressively increased devolution of authority to departmental secretaries. The overall trend was to treat agencies as separate businesses and departmental secretaries as CEOs.[46] Between them, the *Financial Management and Accountability Act 1997* and the *Public Service Act* provided departmental secretaries with increased authority with regard to staff management, finances, assets, resources and technology, and performance management arrangements. Employment powers (including those of dismissal) were streamlined, and formal provision was made for secretaries to enter into collective and/or individual employment contracts and agreements pursuant to the Workplace Relations Act 1996. Departmental secretaries were expected to use these powers to put in place a performance management system covering all employees and guiding the movement of their salaries. Such systems were to be results-oriented. They were to be linked to organisational and business goals and to provide employees with a clear statement of what was expected of their performance together with an opportunity to comment on those expectations.[47]

While departmental secretaries were becoming CEOs to their staff, their own relations to ministers were taking on a number of features of private sector employment. In 1976, the Fraser Government had legislated to provide that appointments to the position of the head of a department were to be made on the recommendation of the Prime Minister following a report from a committee including at least two departmental heads and chaired by the Chairman of the Public Service Board. In 1984, the Labor Government legislated to give the political arm of government an increased role in managing and dismissing secretaries, and to remove the appointments procedures put in place by the previous Government on the grounds that they 'are gratuitous and they place inappropriate power in the hands of the public servants involved'.[48] Instead, departmental heads would be appointed on the recommendation of the Prime Minister, following a report from the Chair of the then Public Service Board. In the same year the Hawke Government amended the Public Service Act 1922 to clarify that department secretaries, no longer 'permanent' heads, were to manage their departments 'under the minister', and would be appointed to particular positions for a term of five years. Immediately after Paul Keating assumed the Prime Ministership in 1991, three senior departmental secretaries were replaced because ministers wanted someone else. The replacements were 'described as having impressed ministers as doers but two had also had close connections with the Labor Party in the past'.[49] In 1994, the Keating Government introduced contracts for secretaries, and encouraged consideration of contracts for the senior executive service. In 1996, six secretaries lost their jobs directly after the election of the Howard Government. In 1999, Paul Barrett was dismissed as Secretary of the Department of Defence. The reason given was that he had lost the confidence of the Minister, John Moore. Performance pay for secretaries was introduced in 1999.

Australia was not alone in legislating for a responsive and results-oriented management in its public service. Similar packages of financial and human-resource changes were also being embraced to varying degrees across a number of public sectors, particularly those in English-speaking countries. While many elements of NPM were the conventional wisdom of the World Bank and the OECD,[50] its implementation was not at all a single comprehensive program: it evolved incrementally and exhibited different emphases in different cultural and administrative frameworks. The OECD broadly characterised these changes as implementing a transition from a bureaucratic to a market model:

> The market model is based on market-type mechanisms, as opposed to the bureaucratic model, which operates the public service on a monopoly-provider basis. The aim is to let managers manage on terms similar to their private sector counterparts. To promote a performance orientation, the system is subject to market disciplines such as competitive tendering and contracting out, cost recovery, and accrual accounting (including capital costs). It may even go so far as to result in total privatisation of the activity. In some cases performance standards are enforced through individual or institutional performance contracts which exchange operational and/or resource flexibility for accountability for pre set results targets.[51]

In 1997 the OECD undertook 10 country case studies of public sector reform based on the presence of market and market-type mechanisms. On the basis of these studies, it prepared a map matrix positioning the countries along two continuums—a 'bureaucracy versus market orientation' and 'administrator versus manager orientation'—in order to reach a measure of relative degree of performance-oriented priorities (see Figure 1). The map located Australia's position at the end of the Hawke/Keating period as only somewhat less performance-oriented than most other English-speaking countries studied.

Figure 1

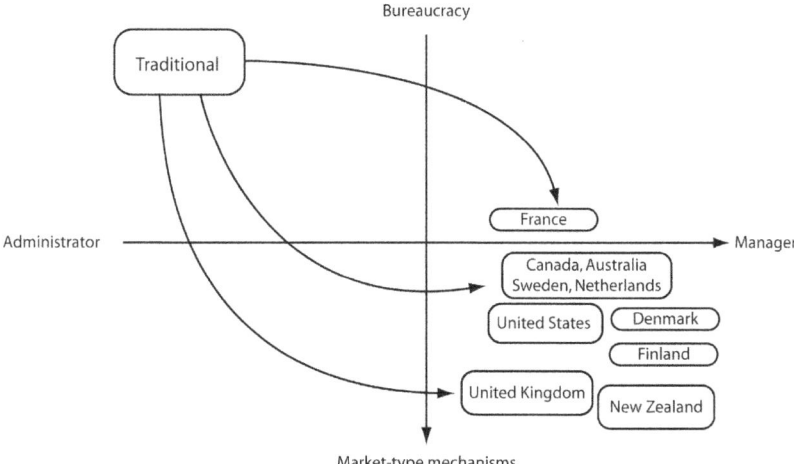

Source: OECD

As these paradigm shifts were taking place, there was increasing interest in articulating the APS Values and providing a legislative codification of standards of official conduct within the more devolved and flexible system. The Public Service Board had already published *Guidelines on Official Conduct of Commonwealth Public Servants in 1979*; but that was a consolidated reference document containing the rules and conventions governing ethical conduct. It did not seek to go behind those rules and conventions to articulate values, although of course it did exhibit their application. Some initial work on public service values had been pursued through RCAGA and the Institute of Public Administration Australia (IPAA), with more detailed work undertaken by the then Management Advisory Board and its Management Improvement Advisory Committee (MAB/MIAC). The first official articulation of what was likely to emerge from this process was provided in the 1993 Management Advisory Board (MAB) publication, *Building a Better Public Service*, which summed it all up as follows:

> These [public service] values or principles have traditionally stressed the centrality of merit-based staffing, probity and integrity, efficiency, and loyalty to government while providing frank and fearless advice. More recently, additional emphasis has been placed on the need for responsiveness to governments, managing for results and improving accountability.[52]

In 1994 the 'Public Service Act Review Group' expressed similar views, believing that a new public service act should be built around a mix of ethical and efficiency-oriented principles and values.

The work of the MAB and of the Review Group heavily influenced the APS Values articulated in the Public Service Act five years later. A number of the core 'traditional' principles of public administration that had applied in Westminster systems of government for over 100 years were included in the specific APS Values legislated by the Parliament in 1999 for Australian public servants:

- the apolitical nature of the APS (s. 10(1)(a);
- accountability within the framework of ministerial responsibility to the government, the parliament and the Australian public (s. 10(1)(e);
- impartial, as well as fair, effective and courteous service (s. 10(1)(g);
- the merit principle governing employment decisions (s. 10(1)(b); and
- the highest ethical standards (s. 10(1)(d).[53]

The influence of NPM can be found, in particular, in sections 10(1)(f) mandating responsiveness to government—although an attentiveness to government objectives has always been expected of public servants—and 10(1)(k), which reinforces responsiveness by calling for a focus on achieving results and managing performance. MAB was adamant that 'these changes do not imply any retreat from traditional values. Rather, the new and the old should reinforce each other'.[54]

The system in practice

Notwithstanding MAB's expectations, experience has shown that the system is not seamless and its elements are not all internally consistent. In fact, while the traditional Westminster values do tend to reinforce each other, subsequent studies suggest that their intersection with NPM values is less than mutually reinforcing.[55] According to *The APS Values and Code of Conduct in Practice*, public servants are likely to encounter, in addition to any complementarity between different values, a need to balance the distinct pulls of the old and the new. Under the heading 'Balancing the APS Values' it advises that:

> While the APS Values complement each other, there may be tensions between them. No Value should be pursued to the point of direct conflict with another. For example, being apolitical does not remove an employee's obligation to be responsive to the Government and to implement its policies and programs, nor does responsiveness permit partisan decisions or decisions that are not impartial. Compliance with the law always takes precedence over a public servant's obligations to achieve results and be responsive.[56]

In Australia as elsewhere,[57] conflicts between market-oriented and more traditional public values appear at all operational levels.[58] At a system-wide level, treating agencies as distinct businesses has the potential to constrain effective whole-of-government management. Agency-specific operating procedures and systems can undermine collaborative practices, just as agency-specific values can undermine the concept of a broader public service. At an agency level, the market model can increase exposure of public servants to values conflicts in areas such as recordkeeping, fraud prevention and outsourcing, as reported in the *2001–02 State of the Service Report*. For example, efficiency agendas encouraging agencies to cut red tape or streamline processes may increase the scope for fraud or compromise probity checks. A focus on benchmarking and performance indicators may encourage practices that actually compromise aspects of service delivery. For individual public servants, common tensions that have been identified include:

- divided loyalties between ministers, public service managers and the public;
- incompatibility between private ethics and impartial exercise of duties;
- private benefits derived from public decisions;
- observance of instructions or actions which might compromise due process; and
- administration of actions which are outside statutory responsibility, or compromise good financial management of a public sector agency.[59]

While these kinds of conflicts are certainly not new, many of the old rule-bound procedures for managing them in practice are gone, leaving the new system dependent on a set of APS Values whose application is often subjective and can drive behaviour in conflicting directions—a good example of what Stewart calls hybridisation:

> … the APS Values-mixture that constitutes new public management, as a result of which public servants are meant simultaneously to be professional, efficient, neutral, responsive. The market-oriented values have been overlaid on top of the more traditional public service ethos, to form a hybridized result. Hybrids such as this satisfy the need for an all-embracing rhetoric, although at the practical level, they give little real guidance for dealing with conflict.[60]

In a hybridised decision-making framework not all values are equal. Take the case of the APS Values. The Public Service Act was not designed to embed traditional Westminster values in public service behaviour; the old rule-based system did that just as well. It was designed to insert the Westminster values into a framework that was fundamentally focused on encouraging responsiveness to government priorities and managing for results.[61] Responsiveness and managing for results are not just APS Values, they are also the rationale behind the decision-making framework itself. In practice this framework has been further reinforced by a number of systems changes characteristic of NPM—such as devolved management structures, contestable policy advice and service delivery, and program budgeting and performance management—that are also about being responsive and delivering results.

As a consequence, values-based decision making in the APS is not simply a matter of individual public servants balancing different APS Values; the supporting systems that are in place situate and orient both reflective and routine behaviours. The idea of striking a balance between different Values suggests that bad decision making occurs when individual public servants make individual mistakes in weighing up issues or fail to recognise that a decision point has been reached. The approach is silent about the institutional framework in which these decisions are made, and how it organises the relations between the administrative and political arms of government. That is why, when taken on their own, the APS Values do not take us far when looking for the causes of systems failures such as those associated with the Departments of the Prime Minister and Cabinet and DIMIA in the case of Children Overboard, or those found by the Palmer and Comrie reports, or the role of DFAT in relation to AWB when overpayments were being made to Iraq.

This focus on individual choice—rather than on the systems and culture within which decision making occurs—is characteristic of public service commentary. The public service tends to shy away from institutional self-analysis unless it is upbeat or can be articulated in such a way as to quarantine the government from criticism. Instead, it offers 'do it yourself' advice targeted to individuals or human-resource areas. In the case of the APS Values, public service commissioners have released *Directions* (1999), *Guidelines on Conduct* (2003), *Embedding the APS Values* (2003), *Being Professional in the APS—Values Resources for Facilitators* (2005), and, with particular reference to interactions between public servants and ministers and their advisers, *Supporting Ministers, Upholding the Values*.[62] These aids operate at the level of principle and convention and advise on how to apply both to situations considered in the abstract. For example, *Supporting Ministers* talks of how to handle requests from ministerial advisers to amend ministerial briefs before those briefs are formally presented as departmental advice. Undoubtedly such situations arise and need to be addressed. And guidance is useful in making it clear that these things happen and that particular responses are appropriate when they do. But, generally speaking, the guidance is silent about how situations such as this are embedded in the institutional context: how do performance assessment and pay, contestability and outsourcing, devolution and technological change, and the new workplace relations arrangements construct the environment in which such situations arise and are understood, and in which decisions are defined and taken?

Individual agency heads and their senior executive can undoubtedly make a great difference in reducing the negative impact of any agency systems on employee decision making, but the *State of the Service* data cited throughout the discussion suggest that their doing so cannot be assumed. How, then, do the arrangements that have been used to embed these NPM systems in agencies intersect with the APS Values that are intended to characterise the public service? How does this intersection position the people 'down the line' including those at a remove from the offices of their ministers? How does it influence the thousands of decisions that they make, either actively or passively, on a day-to-day basis? More broadly, how do we distinguish a politically aware APS from a politically exposed APS?

The chapters that follow address these questions. They focus on separate NPM reforms but in so doing try to evince the way in which particular systems relate to and reinforce one another. Chapter 2 considers the impact of contestable policy advising and service delivery on public servants' understanding of what it means to be apolitical. How do agencies set about making themselves competitive with ministers' favoured lobby groups in the delivery of policy advice and how are individual public servants expected to add value to this process?

Chapter 3 sets out the role of performance management and assessment systems in further focusing public servants on the implicit and explicit expectations of their ministers, ministerial advisers and senior managers, and how due process can be affected when the implicit and explicit messages they receive are not the same. It raises the scope for a performance focus to cause public servants to be 'looking the wrong way' in cases of systems failure. It also raises the matter of how individual performance agreements can structure information sharing between individual public servants, depending on their position in the food chain and the agencies in which they work. Many public servants are sceptical of the contribution of performance assessment and pay to an agency culture in which the APS Values are upheld and in which individuals work together effectively.

Individual agency systems and cultures have grown in influence as centralised, service-wide controls and protocols have been replaced by agency-specific arrangements. This issue is addressed in Chapter 4. When the process of devolution was first being contemplated it was realised that 'to achieve greater flexibility it was probably going to be necessary to sacrifice many of the aspects of the public service which had provided the 'connective tissue',[63] and this is what happened. As 'connective tissue' has weakened, public servants have been increasingly exposed to the disciplines of results-oriented systems. Guidance on appropriate and inappropriate behaviour is the responsibility of agency heads and their senior managers, as are processes for raising concerns about breaches of public service values. Surveys suggest that in some agencies public servants are in some doubt as to whether agency heads and senior managers (themselves under the discipline of performance contracts) behave in accordance with the APS Values. In the event, both policy advising and due process have been put at risk, and in some cases, compromised.

Chapter 5 examines in particular the workplace relations systems at work in departments and agencies, including individual employment contracts (AWAs) intended to align employee values to those of the agency and its 'ultimate employer', the minister. It also examines other changes to the 'psychological contract' between employees and their agency heads following in the introduction of 'hard' HRM practices. As in the cases of contestability, performance management and devolution when considered separately, these industrial arrangements have the effect of reinforcing responsiveness to short-term demands and drivers, and reducing second thoughts.

Chapter 6 raises more broadly the question of what it is that distinguishes a public servant from other providers of services to government. Since the mid-1990s, NPM has taken contracting organisations into areas of government activity characterised by increasing risk, sensitivity and complexity. In the process it has turned a significant number of public servants—already on performance contracts themselves and increasingly being moved on to individual employment contracts—into contract managers. While public sector providers have been exhorted to behave more like those in the private and community sectors, the latter have been drawn into alignment with government through contracting arrangements emphasising partnership and a community of values. In a devolved environment with tasks specified in contracts, what, if anything, continues to distinguish the work and ethos of public servants from those of the community and private sectors?

These questions are of concern because, although NPM has undoubtedly increased the capacity of public servants to achieve results, it has exposed decision making to new drivers and disciplines that interact in ways that increase their exposure to political direction. This was, after all, the purpose of the exercise. Nevertheless, 'the shift in the last 25 years has been substantial, … steadily increasing political oversight and expectations of responsiveness by the bureaucracy to the elected government'.[64] Survey material cited in the course of the discussion that follows suggests that many public servants are disturbed by the extent of this exposure. Some have made bad decisions, either actively or passively, and as a result people outside the public service have been damaged. There is also an impact on Australians more generally. Public accountability goes missing where there is what Bartos (2006) calls 'a systematic lack of capacity to identify problems, keep accurate records, and draw these uncomfortable problems to the attention of Ministers'.

ENDNOTES

1 See, for example, P. P. McGuinness, 'A Politicised Public Service?' *Quadrant* editorial, no 93, Apr. 2007, at http://www.henrythornton.com/article.asp?article_id=4647, viewed 28 Feb. 2008; Robert Manne, 'The Nation Reviewed', *The Monthly*, no. 12, May 2006.

2 The Department of Immigration and Multicultural and Indigenous Affairs (DIMIA) has since become the Department of Immigration and Multicultural Affairs (DIMA) and subsequently the Department of Immigration and Citizenship. The earlier acronym is preserved through this study, as it is consistent with references to the agency in the Palmer and other reports.

3 See Parliament of Australia, 'Executive Summary,' *Senate Report on A Certain Maritime Incident*, 23 Oct. 2002, at http://www.aph.gov.au/senate/committee/maritime_incident_ctte/report/a06.htm viewed 20 Apr. 2006; M. J. Palmer, *Inquiry into the Circumstances of the Immigration Detention of Cornelia Rau: Report* (July 2005), 168, http://www.minister.immi.gov.au, viewed 13 Feb. 2006; Inquiry into certain Australian companies in relation to the UN Oil-For-Food Programme http://www.offi.gov.au/ viewed 15 Feb. 2008; and 'Haneef Inquiry to Go Ahead: Rudd', *Sydney Morning Herald*, 6 Dec. 2007, http://www.smh.com.au/news/National/Haneef-inquiry-to-go-ahead-Rudd/2007/12/06/1196812904358.htm, viewed 15 Feb. 2008.

4 The current legal definitions of these principles are set out later in this chapter.

5 Andrew Podger, 'Looking Upwards and Downwards: Key Issues and Suggestions for Managing Board/Minister/Departmental Relations', paper presented to the University of Canberra Conference on Governance, Mar. 1996, p 14.

6 Peter Shergold, 'Pride in Public Service', speech to National Press Club, Canberra, 15 Feb. 2006, at http://www.pmc.gov.au/speeches/index.cfm, viewed 15 Mar. 2006.

7 Stephen Bartos, 'The AWB Affair—Matters of Governance', National Institute for Governance, 1 May 2006, p. 19.

8 See, for example, Glyn Davis and R. A. W. Rhodes, 'From Hierarchy to Contracts and Back Again: Reforming the Australian Public Service', in M. Keating, J. Wanna and P. Weller (eds), *Institutions on the Edge? Capacity for Governance* (Allen & Unwin: Sydney, 2000), 74–98.

9 Paul Keating, 'Performance and Accountability in the Public Service: A Statement by the Prime Minister', Parliament House, 1 July 1993.

10 For a more substantial discussion, see John Wanna, 'Public Service, Public Values: The Implementation of a Charter of Values in the Australian Public Service', Australasian Political Studies Association Conference, Dunedin, 2005; John Nethercote, 'New Public Service Legislation: The *Public Service Bill 1997*', Parliamentary Library Background Paper 2 1997–8, 22 Sept. 1997, at http://www.aph.gov.au/Library/pubs/bp/1997-98/98bp02.htm, viewed 8 Jan. 2008.

11 Australian Public Service Commission, *APS Values and Code of Conduct in Practice: Guide to Official Conduct for APS Employees and Agency Heads* (revised) (Canberra, 2005), Ch. 1. http://www.apsc.gov.au/values/conductguidelines4.htm, viewed 22 June 2007.

12 See, for example, Peter Shergold, 'Goodbye to All that Power', *Public Sector Informant*, Apr. 2005, p. 2; and Patrick Weller, *Australia's Mandarins: The Frank and the Fearless?* (Allen & Unwin: Sydney, 2001). A number of political, public service and academic commentators addressed the issue for the ABC production *Corridors of Power: From Mandarins to Managers*, 26 July–30 Aug. 2002, at http://www.abc.net.au/rn/learning/lifelong/features/corridors/, viewed 15 Feb. 2008.

13 As asked of me in a performance assessment session.

14 Richard Mulgan, 'Truth in Government and the Politicisation of Public Service Advice', *Public Administration* 85(3) (2007), 570.

15 Australian Public Service Commission, *APS Values and Code of Conduct in Practice*, Ch. 2.

16 Mulgan, 'Truth in Government', 571.

17 See, for example, Peter Shergold, '"The Need to Wield a Crowbar": Political Will and Public Service: A Short Historical Discourse on Attempts to Overcome the Perceived Ossification and Inertia of Buttoned-up Public Servants (and Why They're Now the Better for It)', Dunstan Oration, Adelaide, 7 Apr. 2005 http://www.dpmc.gov.au/speeches/shergold/political_will_2005-04-07.cfm, viewed 23 Nov. 2005.

[18] Mulgan, 'Truth in Government', 578.

[19] Maria Maley, 'Australian Ministerial Advisers and the Royal Commission on Government Administration', *Australian Journal of Public Administration* 61(1) (Mar. 2002), 104.

[20] Royal Commission on Australian Government Administration, *Report* (AGPS: Canberra, 1976), 105.

[21] See Weller, *Australia's Mandarins*, 103.

[22] Maley, 'Australian Ministerial Advisers', 105.

[23] See Weller, *Australia's Mandarins*, 103.

[24] See Maley, 'Australian Ministerial Advisers', 106.

[25] Peter Shergold, 'Once was Camelot in Canberra? Reflections on Public Service Leadership', Sir Roland Wilson Lecture, Canberra, 23 June 2004, p. 7, www.pmc.gov.au/speeches/shergold/public_service_leadership_2004-06-23.cfm, viewed 19 June 2006.

[26] Public Service Commissioner, *2003–04 State of the Service Report* (Canberra, 2004), 40.

[27] According to the Public Service Commissioner's 2004–05 *State of the Service* report, 33% of the relevant population said they had faced such a challenge in the last 12 months, and 6% were not sure (*2004–05 State of the Service Report* (Canberra, 2005), 42). The 2002–03 *State of the Service* Report data is also comparable: about 1/3 of those employees who reported having had contact with their ministers or ministerial advisers in the last two years reported having faced a challenge in that relationship (*2002–03 State of the Service Report* (Canberra, 2003), 42) but the question establishing the relevant population was slightly different in that year: http://www.apsc.gov.au/stateoftheservice/0203/chapter4.pdf, viewed 19 June 2006.

[28] Public Service Commissioner, *2003–04 State of the Service Report*, 34.

[29] 'Direct contact' was defined (p.35) as 'contact in person, by telephone or email'. Employees reported the types of matters on which they came into direct contact with ministers or their advisers (Table 3.1), but because they were able to choose a number of options it is not possible to isolate which classifications addressed which matters.

[30] According to the Public Service Commissioner's *2004–05 State of the Service Report*, SES =1.6% of ongoing employees by classification; El =22.5%; and APS staff, trainees and graduates = 75.9% (p.16).

[31] Public Service Commissioner, *2004–05 State of the Service Report*, 41.

[32] Public Service Commissioner, *2003–04 State of the Service Report*, 40; Public Service Commissioner, *2004–05 State of the Service Report*, 42.

[33] Data on employee awareness of other protocols is set out at Table 3.2 at p.39 of the 2004–5 report.

[34] See *2004–05 State of the Service Report*, 42. The number of large agencies involved was 15: see Methodology, pp. 324-5.

[35] According to the Australian Public Service Commission, *State of the Service Employee Survey Results 2004–05* (Canberra, 2005), 26, 22, in 2004–05, 83% of employees reported being familiar with the APS Code of Conduct; 17% reported being partly familiar with it; and in percentageage terms none reported not having heard of it prior to the survey. Comparable figures for the APS Values were 85%, 14%, and 1%.

[36] Public Service Commissioner, *2002–03 State of the Service Report*, 28.

[37] Palmer, *Inquiry*, 164-5.

[38] Andrew Podger, 'The Australian Public Service: A values-based Service', presentation to 2002 IIPE Biennial Conference on 'Reconstructing "The Public Interest" in a Globalising World: Business, the Professions and the Public Sector, Brisbane, 5 Oct. 2002, at www.apsc.gov.au/media/podger051002.htm, viewed 16 Feb. 2008.

[39] Lynelle Briggs, 'APS Governance', keynote address to DEWR Governance Workshop, 22 Feb. 2005, at http://www.apsc.gov.au/media/briggs220205a.htm, viewed 16 Feb. 2008; and see Podger, 'Australian Public Service'; Pat Barrett, 'Results Based Management and Performance Reporting—an Australian Perspective', 5 Oct. 2004, at http://www.anao.gov.au/uploads/documents/Results_Based_Management_and_Performance_Reporting1.pdf, viewed 16 Feb. 2008; Peter Shergold, 'Administrative Law and Public Service', Australian Institute of Administrative Law Opening Address, 3 July 2003, at www.pmc.gov.au/speeches/shergold/administrative_law_2003-07-03.cfm, viewed 27 June 2006; and Australian Public Service Commission, *The Australian Experience of Public Sector Reform* (Canberra, 2003), 45.

[40] See, for example, Richard Mulgan's account of the VIP Affair of the late 1960s as 'a healthy antidote to any nostalgia for a supposedly golden age of public service integrity': 'Truth in Government', 585.

In his book on 'Nugget' Coombs, Tim Rowse notes: 'In 1984, journalist Tom Fitzgerald asked Coombs if the 1940s had been a "golden age' of government that could never be repeated. Coombs agreed': 'The "Responsive" Public Servant: Coombs the Man, Coombs the Report', *Australian Journal of Public Administration* 61(1) (Mar. 2002), 102.

[41] Rose Verspaandonk (revised by Ian Holland), 'Changes in the Australian Public Service 1975–2003', Parliamentary Library Chronology no. 1, 2002–3, 2 June 2003, at http://www.aph.gov.au/library/pubs/chron/2002-03/03chr01.htm. Reprinted with the kind permission of the Parliamentary Library.

[42] For the purposes of the Act, Australian public servants are those employed at the Commonwealth level; states and territories have their own, often similar, arrangements.

[43] 'Paper Prepared by the Royal Commission Staff Outlining Major Themes of the Report', in Cameron Hazelhurst and John Nethercote (eds), *Reforming Australian Government: The Coombs Report and Beyond* (Canberra, 1977), 175.

[44] Royal Commission on Australian Government Administration, *Report,* vol. 1 (AGPS: Canberra, 1976), 33, 34, 36.

[45] Geoffrey Allen, 'A Different Agenda: The Changing Meaning of Public Service Efficiency and Responsiveness in Australia's Public Services', Doctoral Dissertation, Griffith University, 2005, p. 129.

[46] See Peter Reith, *Towards a Best Practice Australian Public Service*, Discussion Paper issued by the Minister for Industrial Relations and the Minister Assisting the Prime Minister for the Public Service (Canberra, 1996), 11: 'Their role as Chief Executive Officers, responsible to the Minister for their agency's performance, needs to be explicitly recognised.'

[47] The Public Service Commissioner's Directions (Ch. 2, 2.12), at http://scaleplus.law.gov.au/html/instruments/0/26/top.htm.

[48] House of Representatives, Debates, 9 May 1984, p. 2152, quoted in Max Spry, 'Executive and High Court Appointments', Parliamentary Library Research Paper 7, 2000–1, Oct. 2000, at http://www.aph.gov.au/library/pubs/rp/2000-01/01RP07.htm#appointments, viewed 17 Feb. 2008.

[49] See John Halligan, 'Labor, the Keating Term and the Senior Public Service', in Gwynneth Singleton (ed.), *The Second Keating Government: Australian Commonwealth Administration 1993–1996* (Canberra, 1997), 55.

[50] See Organisation for Economic Cooperation and Development, 'Governance in Transition: Public Management Reforms in OECD Countries', OECD/PUMA (Paris, 1995); and World Bank, *Governance and Development* (Washington, D.C., 1992).

[51] Organisation for Economic Cooperation and Development, 'In Search of Results: Perfomance Management Practices', Feb. 1997, p. 10.

[52] Management Advisory Board, *Building a Better Public Service*, no. 12 (AGPS: Canberra, 1993), 4.

[53] Australian Public Service Commission, *Embedding the APS Values* (Canberra, 2003), 13: 'The values also reflect the role of the APS as an institution in Australia's democratic system of government. Various values within each of the groups reflect the core principles of public administration that have applied in Westminster systems of government for over a hundred years ... Each of these values is critical to the role and responsibilities of the APS. They complement each other in defining the professional behaviour expected of public servants. They are also supported by the provisions in the Code of Conduct', at http://www.apsc.gov.au/values/values3.htm, viewed 16 Apr. 2006.

[54] Management Advisory Board, *Building a Better Public Service*, 4.

[55] See, in particular, interactions with employment values considered in Ch. 5, p. 99.

[56] Public Service Commission, *APS Values and Code of Conduct in Practice*, Ch. 1, at http://www.apsc.gov.au/values/conductguidelines3.htm, viewed 22 June 2007.

[57] See, for example, John W. Langford, 'Acting on values: An Ethical Dead End for Public Servants', *Canadian Public Administration* 47(4) (2004), 429–50; Isabelle Fortier, 'From Skepticism to Cynicism: Paradoxes of Administrative Reform', *Choices: Journal of the Institute for Research on Public Policy* 9(6) (Aug. 2003),13ff.

[58] See Karen Legge, *Human Resource Management: Rhetorics and Realities* (Macmillan, London 1995), 200.

[59] Carolynne James, 'Economic Rationalism and Public Sector Ethics—Conflicts and Catalysts', *Australian Journal of Public Administration* 62(1) (2003), 95–108.

[60] Jenny Stewart, 'Value Conflict and Policy Change', *Review of Policy Research* 23(1) (2006), 188.

[61] The values also incorporate provisions that were added during the process of reaching bipartisan support for the legislation. The latter (sections 10(1) (l) (m) (n) (o)) deal with employment equity, reasonable community access to APS employment, affirmation of a career-based service and the assertion of a fair system of review of employment decisions.

[62] *APS Values: Extract from Public Service Commissioner's Directions* 1999, at http://www.apsc.gov.au/values/directions.htm; Public Service Commission, *APS Values and Code of Conduct in Practice*; Australian Public Service Commission, *Embedding the APS Values*; *Being Professional in the APS—Values Resources for Facilitators* (2005); *Supporting Ministers, Upholding the Values* (2006), all available on http://www.apsc.gov.au/values/index.html, viewed 19 June 2006.

[63] Tony Blunn, 'Public Service values in the New Millennium', *Canberra Bulletin of Public Administration* 107 (Mar. 2003), 29–30.

[64] Andrew Podger, 'What Really Happens: Department Secretary Appointments, Contracts and Performance Pay in the Australian Public Service',143.

Chapter 2. The regime of contestability

Almost immediately following the 1996 election, the new Government made it clear that it was now up to public servants to prove that they could offer the services it required as efficiently and effectively as the private sector.[1] At the same time, the Government reduced the size of the public service by around 10,000 people in each of the years 1997, 1998 and 1999.[2] The Government argued that the disciplines of contestability would mean increased cost-effectiveness for the public. For the public service, as one secretary argued, it meant:

> Just generally greater insecurity—not just for you but for your department. Really knowing that you're in a contestable, competitive environment ... knowing that you've always got ministers asking if you can do it better elsewhere, doing it outside the public service. So it's insecurity, not for myself but the insecurity of the public service environment, I think that's a profound change.[3]

The new onus of proof for public service delivery raised a notoriously difficult question of which services were core public sector activities and which were not. According to the Auditor-General, the answer was that 'any definition of core government seems to be constantly changing ... including even those that would be considered to be traditional public services, such as policy, including legal advising, corporate management and the delivery of welfare services.'[4] How, in practice, does the requirement that public servants contest their role in delivering policy advice for government intersect with the APS Values that are meant to characterise the public service? In particular, how can the public service compete with organisations that say (because it suits their constituency or because they, too, are competing) what a government prefers to hear? How can they compete with ministerial advisers, who will also have the minister's personal political interests at heart? What does responsiveness mean in such a context? Does apolitical professionalism really represent a competitive edge in getting the attention of government under such circumstances? Is competition a useful model for the delivery and receipt of policy advice? How do these questions affect the decisions made by public servants on a day-to-day basis? These are the questions that are considered below.

Contestability in theory

The answer, according to the former head of the Department of the Prime Minister and Cabinet, is that competition is honing the skills of public servants who have entered the new marketplace and are now 'vying' for ministerial attention:

> The administrative reforms that have marked generational change in the APS, often characterised as the 'new public management', have been

extolled, debated and criticised. But, beneath, something far more profound has happened almost unnoticed. Governance has been democratised … [and] the making of public policy has become increasingly democratic. There is more competition in ideas than ever before. Think-tanks, research institutes, consultancy companies, private sector lobbyists and community advocates each pursue their particular interests with increasing professionalism, vying with public servants for the ear of ministers and their political advisers. To my mind that's beneficial. Why would one want public servants to have exclusive access to a minister? Why would public servants not themselves want to listen to the views of those who share an interest in the outcomes of public policy?[5]

Vying for ministerial attention is not just about being interesting or novel, or even open and contestable. Increased competition for ministerial favour may not have the effect of broadening debate any more than increased competition in the fast food sector broadens the menu. In fact the market for ministerial attention is no simpler than other markets, and the competition of ideas is not a simple contest on an even ground, where the best idea wins. In practice it takes place in a highly landscaped playing field in which interests and interdependencies create gently rolling hills, pitfalls, wind tunnels and extensive deserts—and where the goalposts are moved constantly.

Contestability in practice

Take the very simple case of gathering data, which is an everyday reality for public servants in both policy and program-delivery departments. Let me offer a scenario that is, I suggest, not entirely unrealistic. The government wants a survey done that will enable it to claim support for a particular policy decision that it has already agreed to implement in exchange for the support of a particular interest group. It wants to be able to say that the research is wholly independent, so it asks the public service to commission an outside organisation to do the research. Once it is clear that the government wants data gathered outside the public service, the default public service approach is to try to ensure that it receives good quality evidence, and an academic consultancy is considered. The public service knows that there are individual academics and particular institutions with views that have not been supportive of government policy in the past and is aware that the government (not unnaturally) does not wish to commission those groups. For this reason, the public service has established, in agreement with the minister, research panels that include academics who are supportive of the government's policies, and it proposes to commission one of these without going through the rigors of a public tender process.

At the same time the government wants (also not unnaturally) to control the questions that will be used to gather the data, and it also wants to include among them some that are not consistent with the usual academic standards for setting survey questions, but are consistent with the government's reasons for wanting the data collected (push-polling). The favoured academics decline to proceed with the questions concerned, and the government then decides to commission a private sector organisation that will conduct a survey that includes any question for which it is paid. In addition, the government wishes to support the interest group that supports the government's policy (and indeed lobbied for it in the first place) to undertake its own independent research among its own membership that will subsequently reinforce the government's position.

The government may also decide to engage an eminent person, who is supportive of a much more radical version of their policy, to undertake a study that advocates the more extreme view and, thereby, make the government's position look moderate. In this case, it is not the policy usefulness of the consultancy but the known policy position of the eminent person that is important. In the end, the survey company and the eminent person are commissioned by the public service and the interest group receives a small grant to survey its constituency; the evidence is duly found and the arguments are duly made. The government points to the independence of its sources and the moderation of its policy. The policy becomes draft legislation; and the quality of the data underpinning the legislation becomes a matter for sporadic debate in the Parliament.

There is nothing about this scenario that is dependent upon applying the principles of NPM: public servants have never had exclusive access to a minister or a monopoly on advice. There have always been lobby groups and think tanks and academics that are sympathetic to the government of the day and those that are not, and governments have always used the former strategically and the latter sparingly, or preferably not at all. The difference following NPM is partly a matter of degree. It is also, I suggest, the unquestioning legitimation—even celebration—of the proposition that competition for the ministerial ear, of necessity, increases the range of what ministers hear and thereby improves the democratic foundation of their decision making. This is only likely to happen if ministers actually want it to. If they don't want to hear from a range of competitors, they won't; or they will send in a public servant to do the listening for them. If the implicit argument here is that increased contestability will broaden public debate even if it does not affect government's policy predispositions, the jury is still out. But if the implicit argument is that government itself has become open to a wider range of opinion, then the evidence has not been forthcoming.

Take the case of the *WorkChoices* legislation. According to an insider—albeit one without sympathy for the legislation—'the detail of policy guidelines and drafting instructions … was supplied in the main by drawing upon submissions from the Business Council of Australia, one mining industry peak council, and several other national employer bodies'.[6] It is reasonable to assume that in this, as in other cases of significant Howard Government policy initiatives, any mooted 'growth in … alternative sources of policy advice'[7] did *not* occur independent of increased demand from Government. The interaction of supply and demand for non-APS organisations (considered below) has been evidently affected as much by the laws of politics as those of economics, strictly speaking. For the APS, any increased reliance by government on alternative sources of advice raises two questions: what is the role of an 'impartial and professional' APS in maintaining the uneven playing field for policy advice, and what is the impact of contestability on the apolitical or professional nature of the APS's own role in advising on policy?

For a comprehensive view of how interest groups stage their interactions with government, it is worth considering the chronology of business, community and government commentary on legislative change to the Australian workplace relations system produced by the Parliamentary Library in 2007.[8] The actions and interactions, pronouncements and campaigns of those involved suggest that there is considerable orchestration of the public release of contestable policy advice to government on these issues. It is not by any means clear, for example, what proportion of public lobbying of government is actually directed to government and what proportion is directed to building community support for (or opposition to) intended government policies, whether or not those policies have been publicly announced. Ambit claims are made of government in order to radicalise its position, and are cited by government in order to make its position appear moderate. There is no means of distinguishing between those who are vying for the ear of ministers and their political advisers and those who are being used, willingly or not, as stalking horses, unless they themselves are happy to say as much:

> The Institute of Public Affairs is Melbourne's most prominent think tank and regularly acts as a policy ambit setter for the Federal Government. Its head, John Roskam, says part of its role is to push the boundaries of debate so political parties can move in that direction. By not moving as far, politicians are seen as pragmatic and considered, he says.

> For example, the Institute wants a radical deregulation of the labour market, arguing the Government's new industrial relations laws don't go anywhere near far enough—a helpful point of view when the Government is trying to convince a sceptical public that its laws are moderate.[9]

In this case the democratic contest of ideas is not between the APS and other sources of policy advice, or among those sources with the APS abstaining, but between public relations strategists for control of public opinion. The Institute of Public Affairs may be fully committed to a radical deregulation of the labour market, but both it and the then Government knew, at least in broad outcome, what the short-term policy outcome would be.

It is not clear, either, whether the 'vastly increased alternative sources of policy advice' to government are offering different views from each other, or only different views from those offered by the previous government. The hypothetical increase in alternative sources of policy advice would surprise many academic commentators, who have argued that neither the supply of nor the demand for scholarly policy input is flourishing. On the supply side, Edwards has identified problems associated with available funding, data access, comprehension of the policy process and government timelines amongst researchers, and effective communication of academic research findings. On the demand side, she has identified:

- anti-intellectualism in government: the policy process is driven by an ethos that militates against the use of research in policy making—a fear of the critical power of ideas;
- government capacity to absorb research: policy-makers and leaders being dismissive, unresponsive or incapable of absorbing research; and
- politicisation of research: lack of objectivity of many policy-makers and researchers.[10]

Those demand factors have also influenced changes to institutional arrangements intended to increase central control over what can be said—for example, the CSIRO's instructions to its scientific experts not to comment on issues that have policy implications, and the replacement of the entire board of the Australian Research Council by an advisory committee with no decision-making power.

More broadly, academics are now required to make their contribution to the competition of ideas within a financial environment characterised by increasing reliance on industry research funding, fee-based courses and consulting services. These trends, in turn, involve closer attention to the needs of 'consumers' and 'markets'. While there is a case to be made for some industry funding to act as a lever to prioritise and increase relevance of research, 41 per cent of Australian social scientists responding to a 2001 survey of social scientists from 13 universities, 'reported that they had experienced discomfort with publishing contentious research results (13 per cent to a major extent) and almost half (49 per cent) reported they had experienced a reluctance to criticise institutions that provide large research grants or other forms of support (16 per cent to a major extent).'[11] The consequence of these developments is that some academics, at least, are finding it challenging to establish a direct line of sight from increased competition for the attention of ministers to increased democracy in the making of public policy.

The hypothetical 'vastly increased alternative sources of policy advice' might also come as a surprise to some community advocates, who have argued, conversely, that governments at both state and federal levels have deliberately reduced the size of the nonprofit sector by 'nationalising groups of nonprofit organisations, by ending their funding arrangements or by changing the rules by which nonprofits receive government funding to provide services; or by using their power as the main source of funds to force amalgamations of several nonprofits'.[12] Federal governments have generally been selective at best about involving the community sector in the democratisation of policy making. Shortly before the 1996 election, for example, the leader of the Opposition made a virtue of proposing to exclude 'interest groups' outside 'the one mainstream' from 'the ear of the government' if elected, on the ground that they had had too firm a hold on the ear of the previous government:

> The power of one mainstream has been diminished by this government's reactions to the force of a few interest groups. Many Australians in the mainstream feel completely powerless to compete with such groups, who seem to have the ear completely of the government on major issues.

> This bureaucracy of the new class is a world apart from the myriad spontaneous, community based organisations which have been part and parcel of the Australian mainstream for decades. These trends reflect a style of government which will change profoundly under the Liberal and National Parties.[13]

The reported experience of community advocates following the 1996 election—particularly those singled out in the new Prime Minister's pre-election lecture—supports the view that, with honourable exceptions, their contribution to the contest of ideas was not encouraged by the Government either as part of policy input or as part of the consultations that occur following decision making:

> Three quarters of [NGO] respondents (76%) disagreed with the statement that 'current Australian political culture encourages public debate', with one quarter disagreeing strongly. Similarly, three quarters (74%) believe that NGOs are being pressured to make their public statements conform with government policy. 92% of respondents said they disagree with the view that dissenting voices are valued by government as part of a robust democracy; 42% strongly disagree. Similarly, 90% of respondents believe that dissenting organisations risk having their funding cut.[14]

The capacity to award government grants enables governments to shape, in a broader way, the democratic competition for ideas by ceasing to provide funding for those non-government organisations that are dependent on support made available under previous governments, as happened following the 1996 election in the case of selected groups representing women and youth.[15] Conversely, governments can fund those organisations whose views they believe should be aired. This process is not unique to any specific government; many demonstrate their democratic credentials by funding those voices they want to hear, and ceasing to fund those whose views are likely to be less compatible with their own. NPM has, however, added contracting and competitive tendering to the resources available to government for these purposes. This new discipline is considered at greater length in Chapter 6. In the present context, it is enough to note that, in 2004, 'among those [NGOs] fully or partially funded by government, around 70% reported that, at times, their government funding restricted their ability to comment on government'.[16] A subset of this group was not explicitly constrained by funding agreements, but nevertheless saw a need for self-censorship, referring to the inadvisability of 'biting the hand that feeds them'. Even in the case of very high profile community organisations and those not contractually prohibited from speaking, government funding through grants or contracts can still have the effect of encouraging them to 'choose their battles'.

When individuals rather than organisations are considered, it is still not clear whether increased contestability of policy advice means more actors vying with public servants for the ear of ministers and their political advisers or fewer actors doing it more frequently and possibly in different hats. Take Peter Hendy, until recently the Chief Executive of the Australian Chamber of Commerce and Industry (ACCI). He was an adviser to Peter Reith, the Minister for Industrial Relations during the waterfront dispute and later, during the initial work on what became the *WorkChoices* legislation.[17] Subsequently he became ACCI's spokesperson on the same legislation; undertook a benchmarking study for the Treasurer that covered, *inter alia*, business tax; and then, following the 2007 election, left ACCI to become Chief of Staff to the new Leader of the Opposition. He is like many other people who meet themselves coming and going in ministers' offices, shuffling the hats of ministerial adviser, interest group representative and consultant.

This recycling of ministerial advisers is far from a recent development. From 1972 to 1974 Dr Peter Wilenski was principal private secretary to Prime Minister Gough Whitlam and in later years he revolved through a number of positions inside and outside the public service that enabled him to both advise on and shape public administration, including the *Members of Parliament (Staff) Act 1984*, which provided authority for Ministers to employ their own staff and to engage consultants. Of course it is not to be expected that ministerial advisers will cease to seek and to find employment once they have left the minister's office. It would be hard to argue that people with an understanding of particular issues should not be able to take that understanding across sectors, or even that such movement might not broaden their policy perspective. Broadening your perspective is one thing, being able to respect the distinctive roles of a lobbyist and a public servant is another (which is considered below). A third issue is whether the recycling of lobbyists and advisers can properly be said to contribute to the increasing contestability of policy, or the process of 'making of public policy ... increasingly democratic':

> Grains Council people go on AWB board, Grains Council people go on WEA, the gun-totin' Trevor Flugge steps down from AWB but is hired by government to undertake a mission to Iraq: and the Ministers concerned (especially Vaile as Trade Minister and a senior National Party Minister) all know these people and interact with them continually. Grains Council, NFF, National Party, senior Trade officials, senior Agriculture Department officials – see each other regularly, form part of the same club ... One of the key players in affected agencies at the time, Peter Langhorne, went from a senior position in DPIE to a senior position in Austrade to heading up John Andersen's [sic] office in 2001 as Chief of Staff; and as revealed in Andersen's press release of 13 March 2001, had also been an office bearer of the National Party while in senior public service policy advising positions. These are frequently highly competent people – some of them, like Peter Langhorne, I have worked with closely and have utmost respect for. What I am suggesting is that it is hard for any of us – whether a Minister or departmental official – to ask difficult and confronting questions to someone who is part of your own intimate circle.[18]

The kind of access to ministers being described here is qualitatively different from simply taking a role in the public debate. Certainly journalists, academics and policy advocates of all persuasions can go to the media and through the media can get a hearing from government. Nevertheless, particular benefits flow from more direct access to ministers and, therefore, it is worth asking whether increased contestability means that government is listening to more people or just more often to the same or even fewer people? Is the contest for the ear of ministers and their political advisers a continuing one, or is government listening more often to those people who already are, or are prepared to become, willing to say what it wants to hear?

Role of the APS in facilitating advice from outside the public service

What is the role of the APS in a contestable environment? Setting aside for the moment its own role in policy advising, the public service is not an impartial third party refereeing a contest for the ear of the minister and ministerial advisers. Fairness would involve the re-engineering of the entire playing field. And although the resulting 'competition in ideas' might be of academic interest to public servants, experience suggests it is not likely to interest government. The APS may be required to be impartial, but governments are not; naturally they have favoured friends, policy interests and stalking horses. And just as the public service knows the government's policy interests, it also quickly learns to know those who share them.

The APS is often more useful to government in managing those who do not have its ear than in facilitating the access of those who do. It has relatively little to do with ensuring ministers get access to informal advice—the sort that arrives from spouses, cronies, party think tanks, those who donate to political campaigns, favoured lobby groups, and people seated next to the minister at dinner or on a plane. For these informal advisers, the APS is at best a secondhand gatekeeper, providing detailed briefing and commentary on what is sought by those who are favoured, and talking points in rebuttal on the commentary of government critics.

Nevertheless, it is probably fair to say that the APS has a broader consultation brief with respect to policy development than most if not all corporate research, advocacy organisations, consultancy firms, public policy think-tanks and academic departments. Agencies responding to the *2005–06 State of the Service* agency survey were offered a list of groups that could have been consulted, namely: the public, local government agencies, state/territory government agencies, tertiary education and research groups, unions, industry and NGOs. 62 per cent of all agencies reported that they usually or sometimes consulted one or more of these groups about the development of government policy, and 45 per cent reported consulting five or more.[19] However, it is not clear—cannot be clear—what contribution the 'formal' consultation recorded in the *State of the Service* data makes to contestable policy development or program design. Formal consultation, particularly when conducted by the administrative rather than the political arm of government, may be of the variety that takes place after a decision, whatever it is, has been taken. It may legitimately influence the fine-tuning of a policy, or its implementation arrangements, but 'consult is also a code word ... for having in mind a particular outcome that you want rather than just asking people what they think—sometimes yes and sometimes no—but in the end, you want to have a document that says, 'we spoke to 10,000 people about this'.[20]

What we know from public servants themselves about the nature of their public involvement is that they tend to see themselves as bearers of messages from the public to government or bearers of administrative directives from government to the public:

> ... involvement was highest in traditional areas of contact such as attending meetings with stakeholders to hear their views, or managing

contracts, projects and/or programmes. Involvement in areas of active participation such as negotiating with stakeholders to develop mutually agreed policy positions tended to be lower.[21]

Indeed, of the 76 per cent of employees who had dealt directly with interest groups or with people from other levels of government over the preceding 12 months, 25 per cent reported simply attending meetings with stakeholders to hear their views, and half as many (12 per cent) reported actually negotiating with stakeholders to develop mutually agreed policy positions.[22] At least some of those who may have attended meetings but did not actually negotiate then or at any other stage, may have fallen into that subgroup for whom 'consult' is a code word. This may include, for example, some of the 32 per cent of NGOs that report finding the federal government sometimes uninterested in what they have to say, the 50 per cent that find them often uninterested, and the 11 per cent that find them always uninterested—just as state public servants may find themselves closeted with the 52 per cent of NGOs that report finding the state government sometimes uninterested, the 28 per cent that find them often uninterested, and the 6 per cent that find them always uninterested.[23]

It cannot be assumed, then, that the consultations conducted by public servants and referred to in the *State of the Service* data are genuinely indicative of who is or is not making an effective contribution to the contest of ideas in the minds of ministers. According to one public servant, 'people from within government understand each other, but it's so hard to deal with people externally (e.g. NGOs), who don't understand why/that you can't be more helpful when faced with a perfectly reasonable position'.[24] This observation may offer some insight into the finding that 35 per cent of employees who had dealt directly with stakeholders or with people from other levels of government over the preceding 12 months had faced a challenge in balancing the need to be fair and effective, impartial and courteous in delivering services to the Australian public, and responsive to the government (as per the APS Values).[25]

In addition to managing consultations, the APS, as the administrative arm of government, also manages the funding, by means of grants or consultancies, for those 'think-tanks, research institutes, consultancy companies, private sector lobbyists and community advocates' mentioned by Dr Shergold from whom the government wishes to hear or wishes the public to hear. Once it has learned who these people are, the APS can anticipate the government's wishes. There is little point in not doing so: in the first place it would represent a breach of responsiveness; in the second place, it would bring down the wrath—or at least the outspoken dissatisfaction—of ministers and their advisers; and in the third place, putting up briefs that do not favour the government's preferred contestants would have no effect on the outcome of a given selection process. The selection process itself is often hedged in with guidelines that incorporate 'impartial and professional' features of public administration, including due process, transparency and accountability. But as the Public Service Commission's good practice guide on *Supporting Ministers* makes clear, 'guidelines are simply that—guidelines for APS employees'[26] and not for ministers. As long as the law is not broken, and regardless of any baggage of short lists and credentials, 'decisions about spending Government money are made by portfolio ministers'.[27] The worst of it is that the uneven playing field is also a training ground for public servants: after years of watching how the game is played, it is remarkable that so many public servants continue to see themselves as operating outside it.

With respect to the contestable advice that has been received, public servants label, digest, zip, unzip, order, categorise, integrate, compare and contrast it and turn some of it into options and speaking points for ministers. They know whose contestable advice triggers the big brief on implementation feasibility and whose triggers the short brief on fundamental flaws. And if they do not, the process of seeking performance ratings from ministers and their offices on ministerial briefs, considered in the next chapter, will provide an opportunity to be 'informed and improved by ongoing discussions with political advisers: [who] on occasions ... will have a keener sense of the range of issues that need to be addressed'.[28]

Impact of contestability on the APS's policy-advising role

Policy advising is an area in which the APS has a greater capacity for institutional creativity than would be available to it while acting simply as groundskeeper and referee during the contest for the ministerial ear. It is also an area in which the public service has been regarded as having what the Public Service Commissioner has described as a 'natural advantage' related to its 'impartiality and focus on the national interest',[29] as well as its grasp of the history of Commonwealth institutions and its understanding of the connections between them:

> By definition we have no barrow to push, no interest group to serve and no profit to make from the policy advice we provide ... We have an institutional memory that goes back to Federation and that can assist the Government to keep history from repeating itself. We are uniquely placed to weigh up the advice that the Government receives from other players, which, as Andrew Podger [the previous Public Service Commissioner] asserts, almost always reflects some sectoral interest or political view.[30]

Like the government, the APS is meant to consider a broad public interest, and for this reason the former is assumed to see particular value in the advice of the latter. This is probably an optimistic assumption, given that 'just how small the core public sector can become without jeopardising the public interest is still open to debate.'[31] And in any case, although the APS may rise above sectoral interests in providing government with impartial advice, it would be deliberately naive to argue that impartiality, even in the presentation of factual material, necessarily constitutes a reliable advantage in the view of all ministers and their advisers in a contestable environment. This is because, as in the case of the weapons of mass destruction:

> While the factual elements of advice are assumed to be distinguishable from the broader political context within which they sit, in practice they are closely related. Normative policy positions typically depend on certain factual assumptions and can be weakened by the falsification of these assumptions.[32]

If the numbers provided by the relevant public service agency do not support the government's preferred position, a public servant can be directed by the minister to buy in a new data collection. If the minister is dissatisfied with a departmental legal opinion, a public servant can be directed to commission a legal opinion from a nominated lawyer in a private sector firm. Where necessary, the minister can also use the reputation of the public service for apolitical professionalism to establish the independence of those alternative inputs ('research commissioned by my department has found …'). This is not a problem for the government: a government is entitled to look for other opinions and there are many cases where it does so. It is, however, a problem for the contestability of the public service if it is repeated too often. What the public servant may gain from insisting on the integrity of departmental data and the reliability of departmental legal advice is an irritated minister and an increased likelihood of being bypassed in future when advice is required. If, conversely, the department sees its way clear to editing its factual or legal advice to government to support the government's anticipated preferences, then it has effectively compromised its longer-term natural advantage to enhance its short-term contestability. A good minister would quickly get over any irritation with advice that has that has obvious integrity, and would appreciate the pitfalls of relying on 'advice' designed only to support a possibly poorly informed decision. But not all ministers have such appreciation; nor do all their advisers.

Take the further case of the marketing of government policy decisions. Formerly a political responsibility, media management has moved in recent times to a more central position on the responsiveness agenda. According to the former Prime Minister John Howard: '[t]he public service is a lot more conscious now of the need to explain, the need to justify, the need to defend.'[33] According to advice prepared for the public service and drawing on interviews with ministers, secretaries and advisers, the 'willingness to market Government policies' is a key value creating factor for good policy advising.[34] 'Marketing' here may mean anything from to explaining the decisions of government in public forums; to social marketing, as with anti-smoking campaigns; to making public relations 'part of the wider strategic management decision-making process'.[35] In all of these cases, 'there is a fine line between explaining government policy and selling it, and between using marketing to achieve program objectives and implement policy initiatives, and becoming partisan'.[36]

Clearly, it is not always a straightforward exercise to draw the line between explanation and selling, particularly when one is 'a lot more conscious now ... of the need to justify, the need to defend'. In particular it is not straightforward when the final speech or media material is ministerial (and not public service) and raising concerns where it is understood that material has been shaped to suit the government's purposes may, in some cases, do little more than revive old and unwelcome debates long since laid to rest. Public servants ought to ensure that whatever facts are presented in the media are accurate, but can generally be expected to remain silent when countervailing facts are omitted. It is improper—a breach of the Code of Conduct—to seek to do otherwise in public, and there is an 'understandable reluctance of public servants to risk penalties (including jail) for revealing how advice has been manipulated'.[37]

There are further gradations of media support. It is possible, for example, to provide the facts about a set of legislative provisions but remain silent about the systemic disadvantages of that legislation for particular groups of people, or keep one's own counsel concerning the legal underpinnings of reassuring phrases like 'prohibitions on duress'. Or, showing more responsiveness, public servants could prepare material for the minister that sets out the facts truthfully but misleadingly. For example, they could highlight increasing numbers of Australian Workplace Agreements (AWAs), overstating the rate by assuming that no affected workers resigned, were promoted or were dismissed.[38] Or they could proceed beyond factual material into the territory of explanation and from there slip into the region presided over by party political polemic.

These issues have most recently and specifically been debated in relation to the high-profile involvement of a public servant in the Government's *WorkChoices* media campaign. Barbara Bennett was appointed as head of the Workplace Authority in 2007, because, according to the relevant Minister, 'of the fact that I think Barbara has the capacity to be a very public face of the Workplace Authority'.[39] And indeed her face became public almost immediately, appearing in a prominent television media campaign, 'Know where you stand,' created by the advertising agency responsible for the 'Chains' advertising campaign introducing the GST. The 'Know where you stand' campaign responded to research into public perceptions of the Government's industrial legislation that reported "key emotions' in the community of fear, panic, insecurity, cynicism, distrust and disempowerment over Work Choices'.[40] In the televised segments, Ms Bennett was to be seen advising any such concerned citizens that there were many myths around about individual contracts, and that 'the biggest myth is that employees are alone and unprotected and that's just not true'. She went on to speak about the role of her Authority while footage showed her and other officials conferring and pointing at documents. This is believed to be the first time a public servant has been used in such a campaign—or, in the Minister's words, has been 'such an important component of the advertising'.[41]

While the agency head's behaviour in this case appears to exceed what *Supporting Ministers, Upholding the Values* calls 'assisting with media presentations on technical matters',[42] it was defended by her minister's office on the ground that she 'was merely fulfilling part of her role as a public servant: explaining policy, and giving important factual information about the workplace relations system'.[43] In the view of the last Public Service Commissioner, the 'Barbara Bennett advertisements', as they came to be known, reflected poor judgement about how much ministerial support is too much, for a number of reasons including the controversial nature of the policy area, the imminence of the election, the 'myth-busting' language used and the fact that the public servant concerned appeared 'more as an advocate than an explainer'.[44]

The present Public Service Commissioner took a more black letter approach to the Bennett advertisements, making a statement to *The Australian* that 'public communication by public servants explaining to stakeholders how new policy arrangements will work is not inconsistent with APS values'.[45] While this statement is open to interpretation—one suspects deliberately so—the Prime Minister was able to cite it in Parliament, where he noted that 'firstly, the "Barbara Bennett advertisements", as [Mr Rudd] calls them, are legitimate information campaigns; and, secondly—not only that—they are completely in accordance with the APS Values of the *Public Service Act*, as certified by none other than the Public Service Commissioner, Lynelle Briggs'.[46] These comments serve to focus analysis on the endlessly debatable question of where factual information leaves off and political advocacy begins. Is 'if you need help or advice just call us on the workplace info line' sufficient to constitute 'explaining policy, and giving important factual information about the workplace relations system'? Does what the Minister called 'the face behind the name Workplace Authority'[47] also represent important factual information?

To what extent does the increasing pressure to compete with other service providers to government push the envelope on what public servants are prepared to do? Should public servants be concerned when—as one public servant in the Department of Communication, Technology and the Arts is reported to have put it in 2007—they 'have one brief—shoot down Labor's plan and promote the Government's plan'?[48] The 'natural advantages' of the public service as set out by the Public Service Commissioner—its reputation for impartiality, institutional memory, grasp of whole of government intersections, and broad perspective on the public interest—should mean that public servants are comfortable with the presence of other players in the field. But interest groups, private sector think-tanks, academics, NGOs, and consultants have their natural advantages as well, particularly those who are on the high ground of the uneven playing field under a given government. They are not required to reveal who is paying for their research. They are not expected to remain silent if their research is manipulated. They are able to act as stalking horses for radical policies, access and use the media, encourage their constituencies to support the legislation of the government of the day and encourage political donations. They can work in concert with government when they like and point vigorously to their independence when it suits them. They are only required to be transparent if the government is paying them and wants them to be. Setting aside the academic institutions, most of them do not have to be accountable for the quality of their legal, scientific and financial advice. Take, for example, the reported case of advice to the Blair Government on the cost implications of a Private Finance Initiative (PFI) for infrastructure improvements to the London underground:

> Proposals for a PFI initiative to fund improvements to the London Underground have been shown to cost about twice as much as bond financing. Despite this, two of the big five accounting firms, hired by the Blair government, have signed off on the claim that the project represents 'value for money', relative to a public-sector comparator. (A third, Deloitte and Touche, hired by opponents of PFI, reached the opposite conclusion.)[49]

If such practices and scenarios reflect wider reality, or even pockets of reality, they make old-style policy advising—clarifying objectives, identifying the alternative means of achieving those objectives, considering the consequences of each alternative, and evaluating each set of consequences—look very clunky. They make old-style responsiveness—providing advice that is 'frank, honest, comprehensive, accurate and timely' according to s.10(f) of the *Public Service Act*—look lumbering. They can make the pursuit of a 'more traditional approach to public service'[50] an uphill battle.

Can public servants hold the line between being responsive to government policy directions and telling ministers whatever it is that they want to hear?

If there is market competition for the ears of ministers and their advisers, will the public service be drawn into competing in that market by increasingly telling ministers whatever it is that they want to hear? Some ministers will continue to be convinced of the long-term benefits of impartial advice but, like public servants, they will have to maintain that conviction in the face of Dr Shergold's 'think-tanks, research institutes, consultancy companies, private sector lobbyists and community advocates'—not to mention academics, employer associations and unions—'each pursu[ing] their particular interests with increasing professionalism, [and] vying with public servants for the ear of ministers and their political advisers'. The professionalism most pleasing to ministers may not always be of the apolitical persuasion, and the motivation to 'please' the minister, always a powerful driver, has been reinforced by institutional drivers intended to enhance the contestability of agencies. In a devolved environment, agency heads are now able to deploy performance assessment and pay (see Chapter 3), individual employment contracts, attraction and retention policies, and agency remuneration strategies (Chapter 5) to develop and reward staff who are comfortable with 'steadily increasing political oversight and expectations of responsiveness by the bureaucracy to the elected government'.[51]

These agency systems can be used to make particular organisations look and sound to the minister as if they were a lobby group in public service clothing, responsive to 'the belief on the part of governments—all governments—that they want not only support but *passion* from their public servants'.[52] The result is an increase in the numbers of 'hybrid' public servants, people who, as a job ad from one agency would have it, will be apolitical and yet 'like minded', impartial and yet 'passionate'.[53] From an agency perspective, this kind of competitive edge may only last as long as the government of the day retains power. However, once a government has become the Opposition, the reputation of a particular agency is not a matter of pressing concern for them anyway. Acceptable parachutes may even have been found for the relevant agency heads and senior managers. It is the work of the agency and the public service more generally that are damaged, and the trust of the new government and the public that is compromised.

ENDNOTES

[1] See Peter Reith, *Towards a Best Practice Australian Public Service: Discussion Paper issued by the Minister for Industrial Relations and the Minister assisting the Prime Minister for the Public Service* (Canberra, 1996), p. x; Pat Barrett, 'Corporate Governance in the Public Service Context', *Canberra Bulletin of Public Administration* 107 (Mar. 2003), 8.

[2] Australian Public Service Commission, *Australian Public Service Statistical Bulletin, 2004–05*, Table 1, p. 13.

[3] Patrick Weller, *Australia's Mandarins: The Frank and the Fearless?* (Sydney: Allen & Unwin, 2001), 104–5.

[4] Barrett, 'Corporate Governance', 8.

[5] Peter Shergold, 'Pride in Public Service', speech to National Press Club, Canberra, 15 Feb. 2006, at http://www.pmc.gov.au/speeches/index.cfm, viewed 15 Mar. 2006.

[6] Paul Munro, 'The *WorkChoices* Legislation: A Factor in the Rationale for Founding the Australian Institute for Employment Rights', 30 Nov. 2005, at http://www.buseco.monash.edu.au/mgt/research/aier/speeches.php, viewed 30 Aug. 2006.

[7] Peter Shergold, 'Two Cheers for the Bureaucracy: Public Service, Political Advice and Network Governance', Australian Public Service Commission Lunchtime Seminar, 13 June 2003, at http://www.pmc.gov.au/speeches/index.cfm, viewed 27 June 2006.

[8] Parliamentary Library, 'Workplace Relations Reforms: A Chronology of Business, Community and Government Responses', *Chronologies Online*, last updated 6 Dec. 2007, at

http://www.aph.gov.au/library/pubs/BN/2007-08/Workplace_Relations_chron.htm, viewed 17 Feb. 2008.

9 Ewin Hannan and Shaun Carney, 'Thinkers of Influence', *The Age*, 10 Dec. 2005, p. 6.

10 Meredith Edwards, 'Social Science Research and Public Policy: Narrowing the Divide', Academy of Social Sciences in Australia: Policy Paper No 2 (Canberra, 2004), 4.

11 Carole Kayrooz, Pamela Kinnear and Paul Preston, 'Academic Freedom and Commercialisation of Australian Universities: Perceptions and Experiences of Social Scientists', The Australia Institute Discussion Paper No 37, 2001, p. 8, at http://www.tai.org.au/documents/dp_fulltext/DP37.pdf., viewed 1 Mar. 2007. The survey had a 20% response rate (165 respondents).

12 Bernadine Van Gramberg and Penny Bassett, 'Neoliberalism and the Third Sector in Australia', Victoria University School of Management Working Paper Series, May 2005, p. 7, citing M. Cleary, 'The Role and Influence of the Nonprofit Sector in Australia', APPC Conference on Governance, Organisational Effectiveness and the Nonprofit Sector, 5–7 Sept 2003, p. 23.

13 John Howard, 'The Role of Government: A Modern Liberal Approach', The Menzies Research Centre, National Lecture Series, 1995, p. 4, at http://www.ozpolitics.info/election2004/1995-rolegovt.htm viewed 1 Mar. 2007.

14 Sarah Maddison, Richard Denniss and Clive Hamilton (eds), 'Silencing Dissent: Non-government Organisations and Australian Democracy', The Australia Institute Discussion Paper no. 65, June 2004, p. x (see also full table at p. 39).

15 Ibid. 2–4.

16 Ibid. 34.

17 Discussion papers outlining the proposal to simplify the industrial relations systems by using the corporations power began to be issued by Peter Reith during 2000, under the general heading 'Breaking the Gridlock'.

18 Stephen Bartos, 'The AWB Affair – Matters of Governance', National Institute for Governance, University of Canberra, 1 May 2006, pp. 16–17. For another example, see also Clive Hamilton, 'The Dirty Politics of Climate Change', speech to the Climate Change and Business Conference, Adelaide, 20 Feb. 2006, p. 2, at http://www.tai.org.au/, viewed 30 Aug. 2006.

19 Public Service Commissioner, *2005–06 State of the Service Report* (Canberra, 2006), 240.

20 National Institute for Governance, 'Engaging Stakeholders: Why, When and How?', transcript of the proceedings of a seminar presented by Professor David Zussman, President of the Canadian Public Policy Forum, University of Canberra, 22 Apr. 2003, p. 4.

21 Public Service Commissioner, *2005–06 State of the Service Report*, 244.

22 See Australian Public Service Commission, *2005–06 State of the Service Employee Survey Results* (Canberra, 2006), 33, questions 46 and 47.

23 Maddison et al., 'Silencing Dissent', 34.

24 Public Service Commissioner, *2005–06 State of the Service Report*, 243.

25 Ibid. 247. Note that while they were challenged, they were, overall, highly or very highly confident (72%) about their capacity to manage that challenge.

26 '... except where a grant creates a funding commitment of more than 12 months, which requires the prior approval of the Minister for Finance and Administration': Australian Public Service Commission, *Supporting Ministers*, 53.

27 Ibid.

28 Shergold, 'Once was Camelot in Canberra?', 8.

29 Lynelle Briggs, 'Public Service Reform', SES breakfast, 12 May 2005, at http://www.apsc.gov.au/media/briggs120505.htm, viewed 25 June 2007.

30 Lynelle Briggs, 'A Passion for Policy?', ANZSOG/ANU Public Lecture Series, 29 June 2005, at http://www.apsc.gov.au/media/briggs290605.htm, viewed 30 Aug. 2006.

31 Barrett, 'Corporate Governance', 8.

32 Richard Mulgan, 'Truth in Government and the Politicisation of Public Service Advice', *Public Administration* 85(3) (2007), 572.

33 John Howard, 'Ethical Standards and values in the Australian Public Service', *Canberra Bulletin of Public Administration* no 80 (Sept. 1996), 3.

[34] Allan Behm, Lynne Bennington and James Cummane, 'A Value-creating Model for Effective Policy Services', *Journal of Management Development* 19(3) (2000), 171.

[35] Public Sector Management Program Unit 2: Managing out: The Public Sector in the Community, p. 328.

[36] Andrew Podger, 'Citizen Involvement—The Australian Experience', presentation to the CAPAM Malaysia High Level Seminar Kuala Lumpur, 8 Oct. 2003, at http://www.apsc.gov.au/media/podger081003.htm, viewed 17 Feb. 2008; and see also his 'The Australian Public Service: A values-based Service', presentation to 2002 IIPE Biennial Conference on 'Reconstructing "The Public Interest" in a Globalising World', Brisbane, 5 Oct. 2002, at http://www.apsc.gov.au/media/podger051002.htm, viewed 22 Nov. 2007.

[37] Geoffrey Barker, 'The Public Service', in Clive Hamilton and Sarah Maddison (eds), *Silencing Dissent: How the Australian government is controlling public opinion and stifling debate* (Crows Nest: Allen and Unwin, 2007), 128.

[38] See the Department of Education, Employment and Workplace Relations, Submission to the Senate Inquiry into the *Workplace Relations Amendment (Transition to Forward with Fairness) Bill 2008*, 29 Feb. 2008, at http://www.aph.gov.au/Senate/committee/eet_ctte/wr_tff08/submissions/sub27.pdf, viewed 7 Mar. 2008.

[39] Joe Hockey, 'Appointment of Director and Deputy Director, Workplace Authority, and Workplace Ombudsman', press conference, 21 June 2007, at http://www.joehockey.com/mediahub/transcriptDetail.aspx?prID=383, viewed 17 Aug. 2007.

[40] Lara Sinclair, 'Voters Fearful of IR Laws', *The Australian*, 3 Aug. 2007, at http://www.theaustralian.news.com.au/story/0,25197,22180820-5013404,00.html, viewed 17 Aug. 2007.

[41] Joe Hockey, quoted by Mark Davis, 'Workplace Ad May Breach Public Service Code, Says Gillard', *Brisbane Times,* 17 July 2007, at http://www.brisbanetimes.com.au/news/national/workplace-ad-may-breach-public-service-code-says-gillard/2007/07/16/1184559705331.html, viewed 17 July 2007.

[42] Australian Public Service Commission, *Supporting Ministers*, 66.

[43] David Lawrence, 'Calls for Govt to Drop Latest Workplace Ads', *Lateline*, broadcast 1 Aug. 2007, at http://www.abc.net.au/lateline/content/2007/s1994498.htm, viewed 17 Aug. 2007.

[44] Andrew Podger, 'Pride and Prejudice: Ms Bennett as the New Face of a Very Public Service', *Public Sector Informant*, 7 Aug. 2007, p. 6.

[45] Lynelle Briggs, quoted in Matthew Franklin, 'Workplace Authority Boss in Clear over Ads', *The Australian*, 1 Aug. 2007, p. 2.

[46] Commonwealth of Australia House of Representatives, Hansard, 7 Aug. 2007, p. 21, at http://www.aph.gov.au/hansard/reps/dailys/dr070807.pdf, viewed 20 Aug. 2007.

[47] Joe Hockey, Address and Q&A to the QLD Media Club 27th Sept. 2007, at http://www.joehockey.com/mediahub/transcriptDetail.aspx?prID=541, viewed 17 Feb. 2008.

[48] Jason Koutsoukis, 'Dirt Unit to Fight Labor's Net Plan', *The Sunday Age*, 15 July 2007, p. 1.

[49] John Quiggin, 'The Enron Approach Masks Hidden Dangers', 15 Apr. 2002, Evatt Foundation, at http://evatt.org.au/news/23.html.

[50] Andrew Podger, 'What Really Happens: Department Secretary Appointments, Contracts and Performance Pay in the Australian Public Service', *Australian Journal of Public Administration* 66(2) (2007), 140.

[51] Ibid. 143.

[52] Patrick Weller, *Don't Tell the Prime Minister* (Scribe Publications: Melbourne, 2002), 67–8.

[53] From an advertisement placed by the Department of Employment and Workplace Relations in the *Weekend Australian*, 8–9 Apr. 2006, p. 29.

Chapter 3. Individual performance management and assessment and 'assumption cultures'

While addressing the National Press Club in 2006 about claims that public servants had been politicised, Peter Shergold did not dispute the nature of their behaviour, only the reasoning behind it:

> Public servants, it is suggested, now willingly do what governments require of them because they are politicised. In fact they do it because they remain steadfastly apolitical. They would do it for any government.[1]

The question is whether this is the good news or the bad news. For those who question whether public servants may be 'so concerned to serve the government of the day … that the urge to serve overpower[s] the need to be critical,'[2] the argument that they would do the same for any government on any day is hardly reassuring. It suggests that 'willingness to perform' is the default position of public servants regardless of what is asked of them.

Individual performance management, performance assessment and performance pay were eminent in the suite of private sector strategies introduced following RCAGA and subsequent public sector reviews as a means of fusing efficiency and responsiveness. The Management Advisory Committee urged the historical inevitability of these developments in its *Performance Management in the Australian Public Service* with the hindsight of 2001:

> Through the 1980s a wave of reform in public administration engaged the APS with trends in management thinking, including from the private sector. Significant among these trends was an increasing focus on managing by outcomes and accountability of agencies for improving management and performance. This coincided with a renewed interest in performance management.[3]

In order to ensure that efficiency gains were diligently pursued, management for improved agency performance was to be reinforced by a second focus on managing individual performance. Between 1992 and 1996 the Labor Government oversaw a highly standardised and centralised approach to performance-based pay, which was limited to the senior executive service and senior officers. Arrangements for merit pay under the Coalition Government elected in 1996 were introduced in conjunction with the first round of agency agreement making conducted under the Workplace Relations Act 1996. These provided for greater experimentation with performance management and compensation processes at the agency level, and included all APS employees.[4] This focus on individual performance was to be linked to agency performance by identifying individual performance goals with specified organisational performance outputs and outcomes endorsed by the minister. By the time of Dr Shergold's comment above, most public servants had been advised that their organisation either had or was growing a performance culture, and nearly all agencies had individual performance agreement and assessment systems to help hone the individual and collective willingness of their staff to focus on achieving results agreed with government.[5]

Nevertheless, while performance management itself has been critical to public sector reform, and while individual performance management, assessment and pay followed from it, experience suggests that the latter has not been successful. As will be seen, public servants who have improved their productivity do not rate it at all highly as a factor contributing to that improvement.[6] A 2004 Audit Report into its operation found that 'that staff do not see the performance management system as a valid tool to gauge their own performance.'[7] Rates of dissatisfaction with underperformance remain high despite performance management and assessment systems: only 11 per cent of staff responding to the ANAO's audit survey considered that under-performance was effectively managed in their agency; nearly 70 per cent considered that this was not the case.[8] More importantly, its impact on the agency culture is questionable: the ANAO reported employees' perceptions of 'a substantial gap between the rhetoric and the reality'[9] in agency systems. The *State of the Service Employee Surveys*, as will be seen, raise issues about the impact of performance assessment and pay regimes on a culture in which employees are able to work together effectively. Most importantly, they also raise questions about their contribution to a culture that upholds the APS Values. In 2005–06, only 37 per cent of staff agreed that, in their experience, the performance pay system in their agency contributed to a workplace culture that upholds the APS Values—and this was the highest percentage ever found by the *Employee Survey*.[10]

Individual performance management and assessment in theory

Section 10(1)(k) of the Public Service Act includes a focus on 'achieving results and managing performance' among the APS Values. This is one of the NPM-inspired values. Its purpose is to ensure that, to the extent that this is not already the case, public servants lift their eyes above purely process issues and in so doing find ways of increasing their capacity to deliver on the government's policy objectives. Increases in efficiency and effectiveness are anticipated as a result of operating in a more flexible and less rules-based environment, and as a result of the encouragement to think creatively about changes that might be made to processes in order to deliver agreed outputs more quickly or more comprehensively. Public servants are to set less store by the means and greater store by the ends. In so doing, agencies are to bear in mind the broader ethical framework established by other APS Values in which they are to operate, and to strike what the then Auditor-General called the 'appropriate balance between conformance and performance.'[11]

It is important to the overall functioning of the service that when public servants lift their eyes above process issues they see how their work fits into the objectives of the organisation as a whole. In the course of preparing its 2001 guidance on *Performance Management in the Australian Public Service,* the Management Advisory Committee had undertaken interviews with a number of private sector executives '(mostly CEOs)' about their experience with and reflections on performance management. These interviews reinforced its own views, firstly, that private sector CEOs often faced 'the same challenges that their public sector peers face', and secondly, that these challenges included the means of establishing 'a clear "line of sight" between the business plans and corporate strategies and staff performance contracts'.[12] For both private and public sector performance management to work, it was felt that performance management plans should be seen to 'cascade down' from organisational to individual goals in order to establish the link between managing for results and managing individual performance. Experience in the private sector also suggested that individual performance management and assessment would increase efficiency and effectiveness in two ways: firstly, by giving individual public servants a sense of how their work fit in with the whole and, secondly, by giving managers the carrot of performance pay and the stick of under-performance proceedings.[13]

Individual performance management and assessment in practice

Inevitably, performance management through individual performance agreements and assessment became a bureaucratic process. The Minister for Industrial Relations, Peter Reith, had made it clear that the broad role of performance agreements would be to 'strengthen the commitment to achieving the outcomes set by government,' and specified that they were to be mandatory, but not prescriptive.[14] Agencies were permitted to develop their own systems, but these had to operate within both the *Public Service Commissioner's Directions* and the *Policy Parameters for Agreement-making* published by what became the Department of Employment and Workplace Relations (DEWR).[15] The Public Service Commissioner's Directions (Chapter 2.12) require agencies to put in place a fair and open performance management and assessment system that covers all employees; guides salary movement; is linked to organisational and business goals and the maintenance of the APS Values; and provides employees with a clear statement of performance expectations and an opportunity to comment on those expectations. Furthermore, this is to be done in a way that is consistent with 'the APS Value about achieving results and managing performance'. The

DEWR *Policy Parameters* required that salary advancement be guided by performance, and should only occur where an employee's performance had been assessed as effective or better.[16]

Linking dollars to performance required the establishment of a rating scale that enabled employees to be graded—usually from 1–4 or 1–5—with each number corresponding to fixed verbal descriptors along the lines of 'unsatisfactory', 'satisfactory', 'fully competent', 'exceeds expectations', and 'outstanding'. Once ratings had been introduced a number of agencies found it desirable to record and adjust their distribution across a normal curve in order to address concerns that those subject to 'hard markers' would be treated fairly *vis à vis* those subject to 'easy markers'. Ratings distributions in their turn highlighted the need in some agencies for a system of review and moderation to change ratings where necessary. 'Because of lack of trust and acceptance and concerns about the rating and moderation processes being used',[17] the Management Advisory Committee recognised the further need for a system of appeals.

The insertion of performance assessment and pay mechanisms into performance management processes affected the relationship between employee and employer. This is considered at greater length in chapter 5, where the psychological contract between employer and employee is discussed in the context of workplace relations. In brief, so far as the carrot element of individual performance management was concerned, the traditional system for rewarding Commonwealth public servants for superior performance lay within a comprehensive system of promotion through the classification system. From the perspective of the individual employee, performance assessment and pay mechanisms meant that what had been a long-term relationship in which employee commitment was exchanged for skills development and career progression—usually over a number of years—was refocused as a short-term, annualised relationship, in which certain behaviours and outputs were to be evaluated, converted into a single number, and exchanged for additional remuneration ('a "tit for tat" mentality').[18] The expectations of the parties and the nature of the underlying relationship were changed as a consequence. Of course individual performance management did not depend on the introduction of performance pay, but the discipline of performance pay did affect the nature of performance management, as the Secretary of the Department of Defence, who supported one but not the other, pointed out:

> In general terms, the purpose of pay is to provide fair recompense for work done, and to recruit and retain people. Schemes involving performance bonuses, tying people's pay to individual performance and increasing the proportion of 'pay at risk' are in place or being introduced elsewhere in the public sector. I do not support these sorts of schemes. I believe that 'performance appraisals' linked to pay can lead to distorted

results and raise issues of equity, ratings moderation and forced distributions. I see little evidence of positive effects on motivation or organisational performance. Rather, I believe that performance pay is divisive and undermines relationships between staff. My approach with civilians in Defence is based on building performance through feedback and a developmental focus without scores and ratings.[19]

So far as the system of performance pay was concerned, individuals' judgement of their own conduct, and of the public's interest in their conduct, was secondary to the formal judgement of their supervisors translated into a single summary rating. Where those individuals were on individual workplace agreements (AWAs), 'a greater proportion of pay [was] generally based on performance and therefore at risk'.[20] Around 95 per cent of formal performance feedback was delivered from direct supervisors[21] —a trail that led directly back through a Senior Executive Service almost wholly on AWAs to agency heads who were themselves subject to performance assessment by ministers and termination at any time. Reflecting on the implications of these arrangements for the behaviour of secretaries, Andrew Podger has noted that:

> My experience as both assessee and adviser to the assessor is that a single measure of performance translated into a bonus will inevitably focus primarily on responsiveness to the government, and be coloured by immediate, media-fuelled issues at the expense of possibly more important factors such as building organisational capacity and developing and implementing reforms of longer term public interest.[22]

It lay with secretaries and their senior managers to ensure that if there was an excessive or improper focus by ministers on the services they were to receive from public servants, this was not passed down the line through senior managers to staff. Surveys have established a direct correlation between the confidence of public servants in senior managers and their confidence in their own ability to balance the legislated values of responsiveness, apolitical professionalism, and impartiality.[23] That is at least in part because these senior managers were the people who would determine whether, in their daily conduct, the individual public servants next down the line had been sufficiently responsive to ministers or efficient in managing for results. Some senior managers may have protected their staff; some certainly did not, or did not do so effectively. In 2005, just over half of the respondents to the *State of the Service Employee Survey* (51 per cent) said that their senior managers led by example in ethical behaviour.[24] In 2006, the number was 55 per cent.[25] These figures are the average across both 'happy' and 'unhappy' agencies, meaning that, in a number of agencies, more than half of all employees surveyed may not have felt that they experienced ethical leadership from senior managers.

As these systems of individual performance assessment and pay were being bedded down, other measures of responsiveness began to be directly included in the agency's measures of its own performance. In addition to instituting internal peer review, a number of secretaries also invited Ministers and their advisers to rate briefs that had been prepared for them by public servants.[26] Ratings scales were similar to those developed for performance assessment and pay systems (i.e. a 1–4 or 1–5 scale). By 2004–5, 44 per cent of the 59 agencies providing regular services and advice to ministers reported having a formal rating system to collect ministerial feedback; 22 per cent reported having had a formal requirement that oral feedback be collected from ministers; 27 per cent had a formal requirement that oral feedback be collected from ministerial staff. The *2004–05 State of the Service Report* indicates that, of the 26 agencies that used some sort of formal ratings system to seek formal ministerial feedback, the criteria most likely to be in use were 'quality of material' (used by 88 per cent of agencies) and 'timeliness' (used by 81 per cent).[27] Agencies then 'use[d] ratings provided against briefs from their minister's offices to provide an indication of policy-advice performance.'[28]

According to the *2004–05 State of the Service Report*, most agencies providing regular services to ministers also included target measures of the level and quality of those services in their portfolio budget statements and then reported against them in their annual reports. Examples drawn from agency annual reports in 2002–03 and cited in *Supporting Ministers* include:

- Department of Transport and Regional Services: 98 per cent satisfaction with briefing and Ministerial correspondence relating to outcome 1, and 96 per cent for outcome 2;
- Department of Education, Science and Training: at least 96 per cent of policy advice rated satisfactory or higher on three criteria: presentation, timeliness and quality;
- Department of Agriculture, Fisheries and Forestry: 'the Ministers and Parliamentary Secretary, and their staff, have expressed formally and informally to the Department's Executive their satisfaction with the quality and timeliness of policy advice and programme administration'; and
- Department of Finance and Administration: 98 per cent of Budget advice, Ministerial and briefing documents that were rated were rated satisfactory or above.[29]

Other agencies disaggregated the data for internal reporting purposes. In every case, it is clear that once formal systems were in place for collecting such data, agencies had a capacity to attribute poor performance to identifiable organisational units where managers would be able to make the connection to returned briefs prepared by individuals within the unit. Briefs prepared by public servants were 'graded' by the minister or the minister's adviser with feedback provided to officers on the quality of the brief and their briefing performance generally. Some managers ensured the rating system for ministerial briefs became an indicator in their own performance plans.[30] Everyone concerned would then be on notice that services to ministers would be scrutinised in individual performance assessment processes.

Both the Public Service Commissioner and the Australian National Audit Office have, in the course of their evaluation work, identified formal ministerial ratings systems as an 'essential element of any strategy to improve service,'[31] useful for honing quality in terms of analytical rigour and accuracy, timeliness, relevance and usefulness, as well as responsiveness to set policy directions. Nevertheless, there are risks in the system to APS policy advising and implementation at an operational level. If even in the case of departmental secretaries 'it was evident that the criterion concerning responsiveness to the government dominated in the final assessment'[32] of overall individual performance, how could that assumption not surface further down the line? And if it does, will those further down the line pursue responsiveness to the point where it 'permit[s] partisan decisions or decisions that are not impartial'?[33] Indeed, to some extent public servants are intended to say what ministers are believed to want to hear, if only on the assumption that ministers want advice that is 'responsive to the directions set by government and committed to the effective delivery of policy positions taken by government'.[34] From one perspective this is perfectly sensible. The government is the executive of the day and public servants should not waste ministers' time and invite poor ratings with advice that is not government policy or percieved to be more closely aligned with the policies of the Opposition. On the contrary, public servants should school themselves to provide advice that is framed within policy positions already taken by government, and within the language it prefers to use to characterise those positions.

Take the case of the change of government in 1996. When the Howard Government came to power, the public service knew that the new government would not want briefs couched in the language used by the former Keating Government, which the new Prime Minister, John Howard, had identified, repeatedly, as 'political correctness'.[35] It was understood that the new government did not want to hear political correctness in any form, including anything that related to uneven playing fields with particular reference to the 'few interest groups' that had, in the Prime Minister's view, diminished 'the power of one mainstream'.[36] Indeed, the Howard Government wished to restore the use of 'relevant' descriptors that had been displaced by the politically correct discourse of the Labor Party, which had been characterised as 'the noisy, self-interested clamour of powerful vested interests with scant regard for the national interest'.[37] The Labor Party had, generally speaking, believed the reverse, and its preferred discourse reflected that fact.

From the perspective of the public service, what was clear was that the dominant advisory paradigm had changed; the kinds of things that could be said and the way they could be said had also changed. When, for example, briefings considered the interactions of the parties when establishing terms and conditions of employment, the Government expected the words 'bargaining' and 'negotiation'—which assumed an 'adversarial' relationship and a role for unions—would be replaced with the term 'agreement making', which smoothed over any little differences between the interests of the parties and reinforced the direct relation between employer and employee. In fact, the language of policy and the policy options necessarily 'made sense' of each other. Stewart argues that the use of such exclusive language 'eliminates alternatives even before they are considered … by forcing policy discourse into a particular frame, which privileges some values over others, and forces participants to 'speak the same language'.[38] This is arguably consistent with the Westminster system, which presumes that the policy alternatives and mandates have already been established through the election.

It is also consistent with the Westminster system for ministerial advisers to advise public servants on what to put into briefs. 'It is true,' Dr Shergold advised in 2004, 'that the development of policy advice will be informed and improved by ongoing discussions with political advisers: on occasions they will have a keener sense of the range of issues that need to be addressed.'[39] Not only do they have a keen sense of the range of issues that need to be addressed, they also have a keen sense of what the minister may want to hear and/or what they themselves may want the minister to hear. And although advisers are not entitled to instruct public servants as to what policy positions should go into briefs, they can make it uncomfortable for those who do not treat their advice as if it were instruction. Formal ratings systems give advisers the capacity to punish and reward public servants, either directly on the minister's behalf or by advising the minister about the rating deserved by the advice provided. In more extreme cases, such ratings may disguise and reinforce bullying or discrimination by advisers. This is not meant to occur, but that does not mean that it does not.[40]

It is also important to understand that these interactions are ongoing: public servants can expect to have their policy advice 'improved by ongoing discussions with political advisers' time and again, over a period of years. In addition, since much advising work is broken up by subject-matter areas, particular advisers will work repeatedly or continuously with the same public servants (in ways that can over time naturalise party political positions as objective best policy). The same sorts of ongoing relations are also established between public servants. Policy advising involves more than advising government; it also involves collaboration with other people engaged in the same line of work. Under such circumstances, pressure to behave improperly can be gradually ratcheted up. The Public Service Commissioner has offered a number of examples of how this occurs:

> What do you do when another public servant is so gung ho about what they perceive to be the Government's interests and policies that they suggest that you might do something that is quite inappropriate? How do you handle a situation where a colleague goes beyond their apolitical role and doesn't provide Ministers with the advice that they should? What do you do when others are behaving in a way that is inappropriate because they perceive that to be Government policy, even although it isn't?[41]

What do you do when those who are doing this are your managers and are responsible for the assessment of your performance? *Supporting Ministers, Upholding the Values* proposes strategies for public servants who find themselves at the wrong end of inappropriate requests from ministers and their advisers, but that advice tends to assume that managers are not themselves part of the problem. Responses to *State of the Service Employee Survey*s noted above suggest that such is not always the case.[42] This is not to argue that policy advising in the public service as a whole has been forcibly politicised, just that the system itself does not, in its operation, support a balance between managing for results and managing for apolitical professionalism, while public servants are nevertheless required to find one.

Like their policy-advising colleagues, public servants administering programs and delivering services may also experience 'challenges' in handling briefing on the administration of particular grants and the management of particular appointments processes:

> What do you do when a ministerial staffer is screaming at you down the phone to recommend a particular project, or when they are adamant that you should recommend funding a project because the Minister 'really wants' to fund it? How do you manage yourself in situations where a staffer insists that the name of someone in particular should be on the list of possibilities for appointment to a board or should be the preferred tenderer in a procurement process? What do you do when they tell you what your advice to the Minister should be and what your advice shouldn't include? And what about being asked to include political material in a departmental submission to a Parliamentary inquiry?[43]

Characteristically, the advice provided to public servants in response to these questions goes to the quality of individual decision making, rather than to the decision-making framework. The challenges outlined by the Commissioner, however, tend to arise at relatively senior executive levels in agencies whose main work is not policy advising. For the vast majority of public servants exercising regulatory responsibilities or administering programs, responsiveness is not directly linked to interactions with Parliamentarians—especially once the Government put in place a network of Local Liaison Officers to 'provide faster and more coordinated support for Senators and MPs when constituents raise issues with them concerning any DHS [Department of Human Services] agency'.[44] Instead, responsiveness is built in through formal performance agreements which establish 'a clear line of sight' between the individual public servant and the agency's goals, as agreed with the portfolio minister, and the payment of employees according to pre-established indicators of efficiency and effectiveness for their contribution to delivering on those goals.

Following the line of sight

There have always been three critical issues to be addressed in establishing working performance agreement, assessment and pay systems for public servants undertaking day-to-day activities associated with regulatory programs or service delivery. The first is identifying useful performance indicators. The second is applying those indicators in ways that encourage rather than discourage flexibility and initiative. The third and more fundamental problem is establishing a 'clear line of sight' between the government's goals, the agency's goals, the line area's goals and the individual's personal performance agreement and indicators. As Figure 2 suggests, these are meant to cascade, with 'a focus on managing performance to meet the Government's required outcomes'.[45]

Maintaining a clear line of sight to 'government's required outcomes' as agreed between the secretary and the minister should in fact have the effect of clarifying those ministerial policy goals that should concern public servants and those political goals that should fall outside individual performance criteria (always assuming the ministers in question are among those who can 'distinguish between their own political aspirations and the duties of a Secretary'[46]). Staff were to be assisted in making these distinctions by corporate planning and governance statements (set to the side in the Figure 2 but meant to help shape the flow) articulating the APS Values and behaviours desired of them in meeting their performance requirements. Take two such statements from agencies responsible for driving performance as the system was evolving: the Departments of Finance in 2001–02 and Employment and Workplace Relations in 2002–03. (*New Finance Valued Behaviours*, it should be noted, were announced on 1 July 2003 some time after a change of Departmental Secretary following the 2001 election. The *New Finance Valued Behaviours* (Figure 3) were said in the annual report of that year to 'more closely align Finance values with APS values'. The fact that the APS Values changed following the departure of the secretary—who then moved on to DEWR—is an indication of the importance an agency's senior management can have in the conduct of performance management as plans cascade down to agency employees.)

Figure 2

A Generalised Performance Management Framework

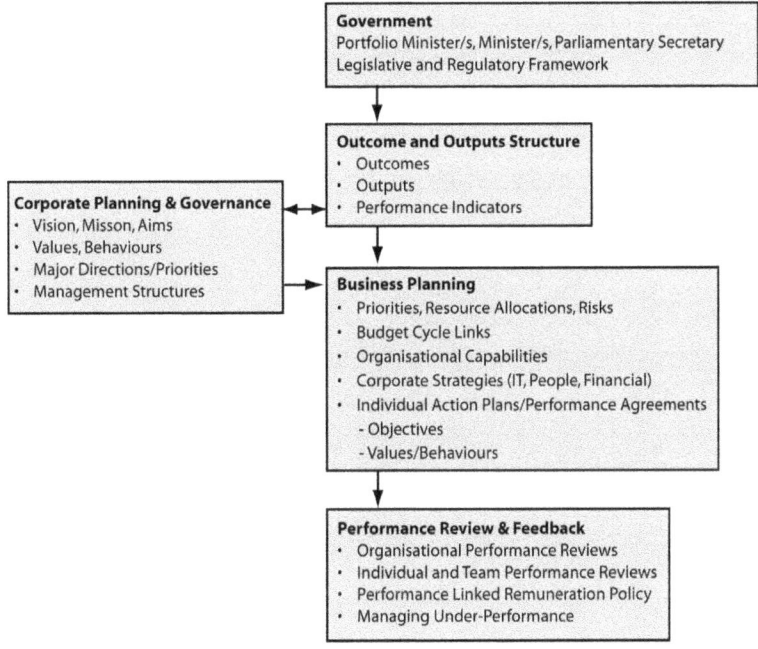

Source: Management Advisory Committee 2001, Performance Management in the Australian Public Service: A Strategic Framework. p. 8.

Figure 3

Vision and values (Finance)

Finance is a forward-looking department that aims for continuous improvement. We are committed to being agile in our approach, open to new learning experiences and willing and prepared to accept challenges. Our vision and our work are underpinned by the Australian Public Service (APS) values contained in the *Public Service Act 1999*, and our four core organisational values:

- **our Ministers are our customers** – they are always our first priority and we aim to exceed their expectations in the services that we provide;
- **performance driven** – we are motivated by a desire to excel; we aim to be the best in our field of providing advice and services to Ministers;
- **responsive, adaptable and open to change** – we are prepared to innovate, create and challenge the status quo;
- **absolute integrity and the highest ethical standards** – we are open and honest in our dealings with one another. We do not cut corners on ethics nor do we compromise our integrity.[47]

DEPARTMENTAL VALUES (DEWR)

The department is committed to building a high performing organisation and places importance on:

- our Ministers as key customers
- serving our key clients on behalf of our Ministers:
  - job seekers
  - Indigenous communities
  - employers and employees
  - high standards of performance and accountability
  - effective people management
  - learning
  - striving to make a difference.

The department's key behaviours stem directly from these values:

Responsiveness

Ethics and integrity

Service to Ministers and clients

Professionalism

Enthusiasm

Creativity

Teamwork.[48]

Even setting aside elements of 'advertising-speak' in the Finance vision statement, it is certainly made clear that, as the Management Advisory Committee advised, 'ministers are the key client'.[49] Whatever public servants do, it is in the service of the minister-as-client or minister-as-customer—a metaphor that does little to clarify the special relationship between the administrative and political arms of government that is part of the Westminster tradition.[50] Ethics and integrity appear to have a role in the conduct of public servants, certainly, but their particular application to ministerial relations is not evident from the documentation provided, apart from what can be inferred from the allusion to the Public Service Act. The overall 'takeaway message' from early corporate guidance of this sort was ambiguous at best, and could prove more likely to encourage than discourage a very broad view of client responsiveness, particularly when supported by individual performance agreements incorporating key performance indicators requiring officers to 'meet their minister's requirements'.

For public servants involved in delivering programs, then, particularly those working outside Canberra (the majority of all public servants), the line of sight was more likely to be directly to those outcome statements directly relevant to their program than to the minister's direct requirements. This also applies to many public servants exercising regulatory oversight, where decision making can involve the exercise of a discretion, as the Public Service Commissioner has argued:

> The exercise of regulatory authority has to balance the burdens regulation imposes (taxation, censorship, the denial of liberty, opportunity costs) and the policy outcome sought, and it has to do this within the broader framework of our national institutions. It is one thing to give officials the authority to make decisions that affect peoples' lives—in Centrelink, ATO and DIMIA, to name a few—but those officials also have to understand the nature of their authority: the broad legislative and constitutional framework from which it derives, its limits, the scope of any discretion and how to exercise it.[51]

Agency outcome statements advise on the 'policy outcome sought' through program administration or through any discretion to be exercised by the regulatory decision-maker. Take, for example, the outcome statements of DMIA for the period 2001–02. Outcome 1 is specified as 'Contributing to Australia's society and its economic advancement through the lawful and orderly entry and stay of people' and output component 1.2.2 (*Protection Visas (Onshore)*) is 'To ensure that Australia efficiently and effectively fulfils its international obligation not to return, directly or indirectly, refugees to their place of persecution'.[52] Now take the Prime Minister's broad vision of the same function, also in 2001:

> Well, Kerri-Anne, our position, my position is very simply that we and *we alone will decide who comes to this country and the circumstances in which they come.* That is a fundamental and absolute right of any Government … But it is certainly terrorists against the rest and we're certainly very strongly of that view and naturally we will continue to

strongly assert our right as a sovereign nation to protect our borders and to decide who comes to this country. That is what is at stake, it's not our tolerance or our openness, we will decide who comes, we won't be required by others to accept them irrespective of their entitlement.[53]

In the political space between the Prime Minister's statement—which set the tone for the 2001 election—and formal agency output indicators a whole series of silent assumptions might be made by public servants. The Prime Minister's words were not an authoritative statement of Government election policy, but they were 'the [2001 election] campaign slogan, the television message for the last weeks, the full page ads being prepared for the newspapers, the posters being printed for distribution from one end of Australian to the other'.[54] No doubt many DIMIA staff, particularly at more junior levels, would be considerably more familiar with these very widely circulated statements than they would be with their departmental outcome statement. In fact their subsequent behaviour suggests that not only was this the case, but that agency senior staff also took no steps to remind them of the difference between the two. According to the report of the *Inquiry into the Circumstances of the Vivian Alvarez Matter* (*Comrie Report*),

> It is difficult to form any conclusion other than that the culture of DIMIA was so motivated by imperatives associated with the removal of unlawful non-citizens that officers failed to take into account the basic human rights obligations that characterise a democratic society.

> For some DIMIA officers, removing suspected unlawful non-citizens had become a dehumanised, mechanical process. The Inquiry is particularly worried by the fact that some DIMIA officers it interviewed said they thought they would be criticised for pursuing welfare-related matters instead of focusing on the key performance indicators for removal.[55]

Without formal confirmation, what a minister says in a media interview, or even in an election advertisement, should not, of itself, carry authority. On the contrary, departmental outcome statements, which have been agreed with the minister, should provide the policy guidance. But to the extent that there was no clear connection between the emphases being adopted in ministerial public commentary and in agency documentation, what public servants may be expected to do can only be a matter for conjecture. In the absence of guidance from senior management to the contrary, this will generally involve assuming that either the prime ministerial media commentary or the agency outcome statement or both involve considerable spin for the consumption of particular audiences, but that on the whole it is better to mouth the agency's words (on the assumption that this is what they are there for) and obey the Prime Minister's signals (on the assumption that this is what both the Prime Minister and the organisation want). In the end, the exercise of regulatory oversight was considered by Comrie 'unreasonable and therefore, by implication, unlawful'.[56]

The report of the Palmer Inquiry, which also looked at the conduct of regulatory decision making at DMIA, argued that ongoing reliance on implicit rather than explicit direction fosters the development of an 'assumption culture' in which, because some things are assumed to be right, others must be assumed to be wrong:

> Within the DIMIA immigration detention function there is clear evidence of an 'assumption culture'—sometimes bordering on denial—that generally allows matters to go unquestioned when, on any examination, a number of the assumptions are flawed. For example, [it] is assumed … [that c]riticism of the processes or systems is generally voiced by people who do not understand the complexity of the system or have their own agendas and therefore do not need to be considered seriously.[57]

Such a culture is defensive because in fact it cannot articulate a fully formed defence. The rationale for its behaviour is somewhere in the difference between the Prime Minister's construction of the prerogatives of government and the organisation's understanding of its international responsibilities. Defensive behaviour is simply a means of turning the attack away from those inside the agency ramparts and towards those outside them: either those outsiders who are still numbered among the politically correct (which links the agency's behaviour with generalised responsiveness to government) or those who are uninformed regarding process issues (which covers practically everyone outside the agency itself).

When public servants are caught between implicit political direction and explicit organisational directives, and when agency leadership does not extricate them by saying something unambiguous, they will tend to put their heads down and focus only on their own individual performance indicators. The result in DIMIA's case was diagnosed as an 'environment in which people are unwilling to accept ownership of matters beyond their immediate responsibilities, regardless of the importance of the matter and the obvious need for continuity in its management'.[58] Even in more benign environments than DIMIA, individual performance indicators can distort the clear line of sight to organisational objectives given the tendency of the measurable to drive out the important. Thus, for example, team leaders at the Australian Taxation Office (ATO) reported that 'part of our message to our staff is, do our work, do it well and pass back to the other business lines what is theirs, because we're not funded for it and all it does is make our performance look bad'.[59] While this practice is clearly consistent with their low-level performance indicators, it is not consistent with 'the overall ATO value of providing a responsive and integrated service'.[60] In the case of DIMIA, immigration policing and detention were in separate areas of the department, and for the public servants concerned they were in separate performance agreements. Had those individuals felt their first duty was to contribute to 'the lawful and orderly entry and stay of people' consistent with outcome 1, they may have identified some process issues, but in fact according to Palmer, 'the predominant, and often sole, emphasis [was] on the achievement of quantitative yardsticks rather than qualitative measures'.[61] Due process lapsed into simple processes, applied against a background of high profile media commentary from the Government on 'terrorists against the rest'.

The capacity of low-level performance indicators to re-introduce a process-driven approach to implementation and break the line of sight to the high-level agency outcomes they are notionally intended to deliver was also identified by the 'Independent Committee of Review of Breaches and Penalties in the Social Security System' in relation to service delivery at Centrelink (considered in more detail in Chapter 6). On the face of it, the problem lay with the low-level performance indicators themselves. In this case indicators of timeliness in handling reports on jobseeker activity appeared to have undermined other service delivery criteria, like attention to the regulatory environment and the application of procedural fairness:

> Numerical indicators and targets can be of great value in monitoring, managing and improving performance. But they must be developed and used with great care. They must not be allowed to effectively override or subvert legislation, policy instructions, or other standards and goals that, although not expressed numerically, should be given due attention. It is especially dangerous when a particular indicator is singled out and excessively promoted for narrow or short-term goals as a key basis for assessment and competition, at the expense of assessing and encouraging longer-term, balanced and effective performance.[62]

This extract from the findings of the Independent Review would appear to report a commonplace conflict between efficiency and effectiveness (or efficiency and equity), or the cost and quality of service. But the decisions in question relate to the reduction or termination of welfare benefits for failing to meet certain work activity tests (referred to as 'breaching' in reference to the 'breaching provisions' of the Act). For welfare recipients, and for the integrity of the welfare system as a whole, breaching is a sensitive matter, and the Committee of Review was concerned that corners might be being cut in this area because of the existence of a quota of breaches to be identified and upheld. Even had sufficient resources been provided to deliver a fair process (a matter at issue), it was felt that the quota established a bias towards the finding of a breach. In this case, the assumption-based culture arose because of the displacement of agency standards by performance-criteria goals set through contractual arrangements with another agency for the delivery of welfare services.

The impact of contestability and outsourcing on relations between the administrative and political arms of government is considered in more depth in Chapters 2 and 6. The point to be considered here in connection with individual performance management is that, for the public servants making decisions about the breaching of welfare recipients, contractual quotas on breaching were clearly consistent with public statements of the minister responsible for the portfolio administering the contract:

> But we can't abolish poverty because poverty in part is a function of individual behaviour.
>
> We can't stop people drinking.
>
> We can't stop people gambling.
>
> We can't stop people having substance problems.
>
> We can't stop people from making mistakes that cause them to be less well-off than they might otherwise be.[63]

Given the public profile of statements of this nature,[64] it is not surprising that public servants at Centrelink were focused on quotas for breaches, regardless of the fact that such quotas encouraged them, in the words of the Independent Committee of Review, 'to effectively override or subvert legislation, policy instructions, or other standards and goals'. The agencies concerned subsequently pointed out that their employees had misunderstood the intention and nature of the contractual quotas. If it was a misunderstanding, it was certainly a pervasive one, and found by the Independent Committee of Review to be so. Were public servants listening to a dogwhistle that was not really there? If so, how did it become a performance indicator?

'Assumption cultures' are by their nature entrenched over time, and an agency's leadership has a considerable capacity to either reinforce selected assumptions or to let them develop in default of any public guidance or, conversely, to provide such guidance and to ensure the system takes proper account of values, relationships, and behaviours as well as results. Take, for example, the case of a briefing note circulated to Centrelink staff that pursued 'broad principles' supported by the minister but remained altogether unknown to the minister until after an 'internal briefing note' was made available to the ABC:

> MARK WILLACY: ... Terms like 'job snobs' and 'work shy' resonate with the electorate. Keeping in this vein, the Government's welfare agency, Centrelink, is instructing its staff to give job-seekers a stark message. In a briefing note titled 'Now or Never,' staff are instructed to tell their clients, 'that if you can't get a job in Sydney this year, you never will, and you're not serious about work.'

TONY ABBOTT: Well, I'm not sure that there has been any document approved by the Government to that effect.

MARK WILLACY: Employment Services Minister, Tony Abbott, has drawn intense criticism from the Opposition for his approach to the jobless. Another critic has been the union movement. Mark Jepp is the Secretary of the Community and Public Sector Union which represents Centrelink workers. He scoffs at Tony Abbott's claim that he was unaware of the 'Now or Never' briefing paper.

MARK JEPP: Those policy directions are made directly by the Government and then they are handed to Centrelink. Centrelink do not have any discretion in these sorts of matters. They are directives that they receive either from Minister Abbott or Minister Reith's Departments.

MARK WILLACY: The briefing notes also instruct Centrelink staff to place clients in breach if they're [sic] job-seeking excuses are deemed to be unacceptable. Minister Abbott, while denying knowledge of the document, says he agrees with its broad principles.[65]

Whatever the resonance of the 'briefing note' with the electorate, it is difficult to reconcile the instruction to tell clients 'if you can't get a job in Sydney this year, you never will, and you're not serious about work' with the requirement under the Section 10(1)(g) of the Public Service that 'the APS delivers services fairly, effectively, impartially and courteously to the Australian public, and is sensitive to the diversity of the Australian public'. Nevertheless, although the actual author of the document is not known and its consistency with formal agency directives is ambiguous, it was evidently believed by some staff to have senior management support and was therefore accorded formal status as accepted operating policy.

Finally, take the more recent case of the Workplace Authority, an agency whose strategic objectives are to ensure that:

- More employers and employees are informed and confident about making an appropriate workplace agreement; [and]
- Parliament and the Australian Government have confidence in the Workplace Authority as a trusted and responsive authority on workplace agreements.[66]

In this case the line of sight from employees to the agency's strategic objectives lies through the behaviour modelled by the agency head. This behaviour is considered in Chapter 2. Its tendency to support the agency's formal strategic objectives is patchy. While the Howard Government may be assumed to have had confidence in the Authority as a consequence of the director's becoming 'such an important component of the advertising'[67] this was not the case with the Parliament more generally.[68] And the controversy generated by the advertising was also unlikely to have made a positive contribution to widespread 'confidence about making an agreement'. Nor did it produce confidence more generally in the professionalism of the APS; on the contrary, it 'reinforce[d] the perception of a service giving too much weight to responsiveness over apolitical professionalism, and undermine[d] the confidence of the Opposition in the capacity of the service to support its policies and programs should it become the Government in the coming election'.[69]

How are the employees of the Workplace Authority to understand their obligation to 'provide straightforward information in response to … questions on all aspects of workplace relations?'[70] How can they expect to be judged on whether their performance meets agency's core standard of 'professionalism'?[71] No wonder there is some confusion (or cynicism) among public servants about the 'line of sight' from high-level agency strategic objectives to their own understanding of what is actually required of them by their senior managers and ministers. No wonder that, while public servants from both policy and service delivery agencies place a high value on *regular* performance feedback,[72] they are overwhelmingly negative about the system of annual performance agreements complete with personal targets and indicators and, in the great majority of cases, with numerical rating scales associated with pay outcomes. Importantly, they seem to detect a gap between the theory and practice of system, between what it calls for and what it actually expects—a problem, according to the Australian National Audit Office (ANAO), that boils down to credibility:

> Significant issues remain in establishing credible performance management systems in the APS. The perception of APS employees, reflected in survey responses obtained as part of the audit, is that there remains a substantial gap between the rhetoric and the reality. While staff generally could be expected to be less sanguine about achievements, there is a degree of uniformity in survey views across agencies with differing performance. Many staff considered that the distribution of performance pay in their agency was unfair; that there was bias and favouritism exhibited in performance reward decisions; that the rewards offered were not worth the extra effort involved; and that there was a lack of clarity for them on what constitutes good performance. Staff also did not see the performance management systems as effective in assisting them to evaluate, or to improve, their own performance. At the very least, the ANAO considers that there is an issue of staff perceptions that needs to be addressed.[73]

In 2005–06, half of all APS employees responding to the *State of the Service Employee Survey* did not agree that the performance pay system in their agency operated fairly and consistently; and less than a quarter believed that the pay outcomes of performance assessments accurately reflected differences in individual performance (Table 1). These responses follow 2004 survey findings from the ANAO that many public servants were calling for more quantifiable performance indicators, as if that would simplify and bridge the gap between the theory of the system and their experience of its operation.[74]

Table 1. Responses from *State of the Service Employee Survey*

Question 70. Please rate your level of agreement with the following statements on the performance pay system in your agency:		strongly agree	agree	neither agree nor disagree	disagree	strongly disagree	not sure
		%	%	%	%	%	%
a. Provides appropriate rewards for top performers.	2003	4	36	26	24	7	3
	2004	5	42	24	19	7	3
	2005	4	36	25	25	7	4
	2006	6	44	22	19	5	4
b. Contributes to a workplace culture in which individuals work together effectively.	2003	4	37	27	22	8	2
	2004	4	34	27	25	8	2
	2005	4	33	28	25	9	1
	2006	6	37	25	24	6	2
c. Contributes to a workplace culture which upholds the APS Values.	2003	5	46	23	19	5	2
	2004	5	46	23	19	6	2
	2005	4	43	22	21	7	2
	2006	5	49	21	17	5	3
d. Accurately reflects differences in individuals' performance.	2003	2	20	26	37	11	4
	2004	2	20	28	33	13	4
	2005	2	18	26	37	14	4
	2006	3	21	26	34	11	5
e. Operates fairly and consistently.	2003	2	23	24	32	15	4
	2004	3	22	24	31	17	4
	2005	3	18	21	36	19	4
	2006	2	21	20	37	14	6
f. Acts as an incentive to perform well.	2003	2	22	35	28	11	3
	2004	2	24	35	25	12	2
	2005	2	18	37	28	12	3
	2006	3	25	35	24	8	5
g. Ensures performance assessment is managed systematically and regularly.	2003	2	32	38	17	7	3
	2004	4	31	36	16	9	4
	2005	3	28	35	20	9	5
	2006	4	33	34	17	5	6

Note: Respondents who answered 'No' or 'Not sure' to question 68 were not asked this question. The percentage of relevant respondents who did not answer this question in 2003 was: a − 0.2%, b − 0.3%, c − 0.3%, d − 1.2%, e − 1.2%, f − 1.6%, g − 1.0%. The percentage of relevant respondents who did not answer this question in 2004 was: a − 1.2%, b − 1.0%, c − 1.2%, d − 1.6%, e − 1.2%, f − 1.3%, g − 1.2%. The percentage of relevant respondents who did not answer this question in 2005 was: a − 1.0%, b − 1.1%, c − 1.1%, d − 1.1%, e − 1.0%, f − 0.7%, g − 1.2%. The percentage of relevant respondents who did not answer this question in 2006 was: a − 0.7%, b − 0.8%, c − 1.5%, d − 1.0%, e − 1.1%, f − 1.0%, g − 1.1%.

More broadly, public servants responding to both the ANAO and the *State of the Service Employee Survey*s did not see access to performance-related pay as a significant factor in improving their productivity as promised by NPM theorists.[75] In fact, when those who felt their productivity had improved over the year were asked by the Australian Public Service Commission to rate the contribution of performance-related pay to that improvement they ranked it at the bottom of the 16 factors from which they were asked to choose.[76]

There are no consistent trends in how different classifications of employees respond to having their performance broken down into indicators and assessed, although the *2005–06 State of the Service Report* found that overall employees in executive level classifications were most negative.[77] This is consistent with evidence that longer-serving, experienced public servants find the system more distasteful than new public servants.[78] There is, however, considerable variation between agencies in employees' views on the operation of individual performance assessment systems. This suggests that the credibility gap may be more evident in some agencies than others and is consistent with the scope for variation between agencies in what people believe themselves to be explicitly and implicitly expected to do to win performance pay; how transparently assessment processes are considered to work; and the extent to which assessment is linked to financial outcomes through rating scales. Among large agencies (for which statistically reliable employee responses are available), employee assessments of agency assessment arrangements varied markedly against a range of criteria. *State of the Service* reports indicate that:

- employee views that their agency performance assessment system 'operates fairly and consistently' were in the ranges 19–69 per cent in 2003–4, 20–54 per cent in 2004–05, and 24–66 per cent in 2005–06;
- employee views that their agency performance assessment system 'acts as an incentive to perform well' were in the ranges 16–56 per cent in 2003–04, 24–49 per cent in 2004–05, and 26–63 per cent in 2005–06.
- employee views that their agency performance assessment system 'ensures performance system is managed systematically and regularly' were in the ranges 24–70 per cent in 2003–04, 34–64 per cent in 2004–05, and 38–68 per cent in 2005–06;
- employee views that their agency performance assessment system 'provides appropriate rewards for top performers' were in the ranges 6–51 per cent in 2003–04, 9–48 per cent in 2004–05, and 14–45 per cent in 2005–6;
- employee views that their agency performance assessment system 'contributes to a workplace culture where individuals work together effectively' were in the ranges 11–51 per cent in 2003–04, 9–39 per cent in 2004–05, and 12–49 per cent in 2005–06; and
- the smallest ranges in opinion were for 'accurately reflects differences in individual performance' (the range in 2003–04 was between 11 per cent and 38 per cent and in 2004–05 was between 9 per cent and 26 per cent).[79]

It is not possible to push the analysis further and identify those agencies whose employees exhibit high levels of scepticism in relation to their performance assessment systems; neither does the *State of the Service Report* provide data which can be used to establish whether there are correlations between employee views of performance assessment systems and challenges they have experienced in dealing with their own portfolio ministers and their ministerial advisers.

It is, however, possible to look generally at whether employees of large agencies experienced performance assessment and pay systems as supportive of the range of values they are legally required to uphold under the Public Service Act. In 2006, between 23 and 55 per cent of employees in large agencies agreed that the performance pay system in their agency contributed to a workplace that upholds the APS Values.[80] Conversely, 62 per cent of all employees surveyed did not agree and 22 per cent actively disagreed. This is at least indicative of a view that no matter how clearly the ethical framework calls for balance between the APS Values, the performance system itself does not generally appear to reinforce it. Of course these may not always be the APS Values relating to direct interaction with ministers and their advisers, but in a system of 'managing for results' the views of ministers and advisers will often work in the background. For some policy advisers, performance criteria may have been assumed to call not only for an understanding of the government's policy priorities and the use of its preferred discourse but also for the anticipation of its unspoken preferences. For some public servants who deliver services and administer regulations, performance criteria may be assumed to call not only for a focus on low-level indicators but also for a rule-bound and punitive approach to groups that fall outside 'mainstream Australia'.

So, there is much ambivalence among public servants over the credibility of performance pay regimes. Some believe that they are there to signal an over-zealous approach to 'Meet[ing my] Minister's requirements for my area's Ministerial and Parliamentary Business'; at the other end, some believe that they are simply a means of offering retention bonuses in disguise. No doubt agency systems and practices are equally variable. What employees do know is that in 2005 the Council of the Order of Australia saw no inconsistency in awarding an Australian honour—an Officer in the Order of Australia—to the Secretary who presided for seven years over 'practices [that] have been in operation for a long time and seem to have given rise to an immigration detention culture that, in the opinion of the Inquiry, constrains thinking, flexibility and initiative and concentrates on functions, process and quantitative measurement to the detriment of the achievement of policy outcomes'.[81] The appointment was for 'service to the community through contributions to Australia's international relations and to major public policy development including domestic security, border systems, immigration, multicultural affairs and Indigenous service delivery'.[82] At the same time, the Government appointed Mr Farmer to one of Australia's most important diplomatic posts (Indonesia) as ambassador; shortly after, it ushered in 'a major organisational change process' led by a new secretary.[83]

Such an obvious disjunction helps explain public servants' concerns about the credibility of decision making in performance assessment, at least in some agencies, and that in those cases informal messages can be more important than formal ones when performance is being assessed and rewards (and punishments) are being handed around. Ministerial appeals to the electorate constitute an important source of such informal messages, and being 'informed and improved by ongoing discussions with political advisers'[84] constitutes another. How these messages shape the behaviour of individual public servants will depend on the agencies in which they work—including the leadership in the agency and the quality of its performance management arrangements—as well as their own position in the food chain and their own susceptibility. The public service has been devolved, and agency-specific systems have grown considerably in their capacity to influence individual behaviour. This is the issue that is addressed in Chapter 4.

ENDNOTES

[1] Peter Shergold, 'Pride in Public Service', speech to National Press Club, Canberra, 15 Feb. 2006, at http://www.pmc.gov.au/speeches/index, viewed 15 Mar. 2006.

[2] Patrick Weller, *Don't Tell the Prime Minister* (Scribe Publications: Melbourne, 2002), 69.

[3] Management Advisory Committee, *Performance Management in the Australian Public Service: A Strategic Framework* (Canberra, 2001), 17.

[4] See Michael O'Donnell and John O'Brien, 'Performance-based Pay in the Australian Public Service: Employee Perspectives', *Review of Public Personnel Administration* 20 (2000).

[5] 'In 92% of agencies it is mandatory for all employees to have a formal performance agreement': Public Service Commissioner, *2005–06 State of the Service Report* (Canberra, 2006), 162.

[6] Australian Public Service Commission, *State of the Service Employee Survey Results 2004–05* (Canberra, 2005), 42, question 64b. Employees who did not report having improved productivity were included the following year, with only marginally improved results. See Australian Public Service Commission, *2005-06 State of the Service Employee Survey Results* (Canberra, 2006), 46 question 62b.

[7] Australian National Audit Office, *Performance Management in the Australian Public Service*, ANAO Audit Report No 6, 2004–05 (Canberra, 2004), 84, para 6.36, at http://www.anao.gov.au/uploads/documents/2004-05_Audit_Report_6.pdf, viewed 23 July 2007.

[8] Ibid. 64, para 4.56.

[9] Ibid.14, para 9.

[10] Australian Public Service Commission, *2005-06 State of the Service Employee Survey Results,* 50, question 70.

[11] Pat Barrett, 'Auditing in a Changing Government Environment', paper based on a lecture presented in the Department of the Senate Occasional Lecture Series, 21 June 2002, p. 84, at http://www.aph.gov.au/Senate/pubs/pops/pop39/c05.pdf, viewed 4 July 2007.

[12] Management Advisory Committee, *Performance Management*, 18.

[13] Ibid.14.

[14] Peter Reith, *Towards a Best Practice Australian Public Service: Discussion Paper issued by the Minister for Industrial Relations and the Minister assisting the Prime Minister for the Public Service* (Canberra, 1996), 19.

[15] While this portfolio has undergone a number of administrative changes, the acronym DEWR is generally applied throughout this study for clarity's sake and because workplace relations and employment are the portfolio responsibilities relevant to the discussion.

[16] Department of Employment and Workplace Relations, 'APS — Supporting Guidance for the Policy Parameters for agreement-making in the Australian Public Service', June 2004, p. 25.

[17] Management Advisory Committee, *Performance Management*, 26.

[18] See Jane Loring, 'Changing Employment Contracts, Changing Psychological Contracts, and the Effects on Organisational Commitmen', Master of Science dissertation, Curtin University of Technology, July 2003, p. 12.

[19] Department of Defence Online media room, 'People Power', based on an address to the International Seminar of the Royal United Services Institute of Australia by Allan Hawke, Secretary of the Department of Defence, 17 Nov. 2000, at http://www.defence.gov.au/media/SpeechTpl.cfm?CurrentId=444, viewed 23 July 2007.

[20] Management Advisory Committee, *Performance Management*, 42.

[21] Australian Public Service Commission, *State of the Service Employee Survey Results 2004–05*, 43, question 66.

[22] Andrew Podger, 'What Really Happens: Department Secretary Appointments, Contracts and Performance Pay in the Australian Public Service', *Australian Journal of Public Administration* 66(2) (2007), 143. Comments by other secretaries are included in John Halligan, 'Labor, the Keating Term and the Senior Public Service', in Gwynneth Singleton (ed.), *The Second Keating Government: Australian Commonwealth Administration 1993–1996* (Canberra, 1997).

[23] Public Service Commissioner, *2004–05 State of the Service Report* (Canberra, 2004), 41.

[24] Public Service Commissioner, *2004–05 State of the Service Report*, 179.

[25] Public Service Commissioner, *2005–06 State of the Service Report*, 58.

[26] See, for example, ibid. 34; and Australian National Audit Office, *Developing Policy Advice*, Audit Report No 21, 2001–2 (Canberra, 2001), 52: 'DEWRSB uses a system to monitor against the quality performance indicator whereby all briefs are ranked by its ministers. This approach was agreed with the minister and uses a five point scale …'.

[27] Public Service Commissioner, *2004–05 State of the Service Report*, 32–3.

[28] Management Advisory Committee, *Performance Management*, 37.

[29] Public Service Commissioner, *2004–05 State of the Service Report*, 32–3; and *Supporting Ministers, Upholding the Values* (Canberra, 2006), 6.

[30] Management Advisory Committee, *Performance Management*, 37.

[31] See, for example, Public Service Commissioner, *2004–05 State of the Service Report*, 34; and Australian National Audit Office, *Developing Policy Advice*, 21.

[32] Podger, 'What Really Happens', 142.

[33] Public Service Commission, *APS Values and Code of Conduct in Practice: Guide to Official Conduct for APS Employees and Agency Heads* (revised 2005), Ch. 1, at http://www.apsc.gov.au/values/conductguidelines3.htm, viewed 22 June 2007.

[34] Peter Shergold, 'Once was Camelot in Canberra? Reflections of Public Service Leadership', Sir Roland Wilson Lecture, Canberra, 23 June 2004, 10, at www.pmc.gov.au/speeches/shergold/public_service_leadership_2004-06-23.cfm, viewed 19 June 2006.

[35] See Sean Brawley, 'A Comfortable and Relaxed Past: John Howard and the "Battle of History": The First Phase—February 1992 to March 1996', *Electronic Journal of Australian and New Zealand History* (27 Apr. 1997), at http://www.jcu.edu.au/aff/history/articles/brawley.htm, viewed 31 Aug. 2006.

[36] John Howard, 'The Role of Government: A Modern Liberal Approach', Menzies Research Centre 1995 National Lecture Series, at http://www.ozpolitics.info/election2004/1995-rolegovt.htm, viewed 1 Mar. 2007.

[37] Ibid.

[38] Jenny Stewart, 'Value Conflict and Policy Change', *Review of Policy Research* 23(1) (2006), 191.

[39] Shergold, 'Once was Camelot in Canberra?', 8.

[40] According to the 2003–04 *State of the Service Employee Survey* Results (response to question 54c), 1% of the 15% of all employees who had experienced discrimination in the workplace during the previous 12 months identified their 'minister or ministerial adviser' as responsible for the discrimination. According to question 55c, 1% of the 15 % of employees who experienced bullying in the workplace over the previous 12 months identified their 'minister or ministerial adviser' as responsible for the bullying. The question was not quarantined to the 20% of employees who had been in direct contact

with ministers or their advisers over the same timespan, suggesting that the proportion in those cases would have been notably higher.

[41] Lynelle Briggs, 'Supporting Ministers, Upholding the Values: A Good Practice Guide, Public Service Commissioner's Launch', Canberra, 9 Mar. 2006, at http://www.apsc.gov.au/media/briggs090306.htm, viewed 20 June 2006.

[42] See data on agency leadership and the APS Values, and ethical agency leadership, in Ch. 4 and the Employee Survey observation in the same chapter.

[43] Briggs, 'Supporting Ministers … Launch'.

[44] Public Service Commissioner, 2004–05 State of the Service Report (Canberra, 2005), 35.

[45] Management Advisory Committee, Performance Management in the Australian Public Service, 37.

[46] Podger, 'What Really Happens', 142.

[47] Department of Finance, Annual Report 2001 (Canberra, 2001–2), at http://www.finance.gov.au/pubs/annualreport00%2D01/fin%5Fannual%5Freport/ch2/chp2%5Ftxt2.htm, viewed 23 July 2007.

[48] Department of Employment and Workplace Relations, Annual Report 2002–3, at http://www.dewr.gov.au/dewr/Publications/AnnualReports/2002-03/, viewed 23 July 2007.

[49] Management Advisory Committee, Performance Management in the Australian Public Service, 37.

[50] See Haig Patapan, John Wanna and Patrick Weller (eds), Westminster Legacies (University of New South Wales Press: Sydney, 2005), 6.

[51] Public Service Commissioner, 2004–05 State of the Service Report (Canberra, 2005), 7.

[52] Department of Immigration and Multicultural and Indigenous Affairs, 2001–2 Annual Report, at http://www.immi.gov.au/annual_report/annrep03/report03.htm, viewed 21 Feb. 2006.

[53] Transcript of the Prime Minister the Hon. John Howard MP interview with Kerri-Anne Kennerley, Radio 2GB, 1 Nov. 2001, at http://www.pm.gov.au/news/interviews/2001/interview1434.htm, viewed 31 Aug. 2006.

[54] David Marr and Miriam Wilkinson, Dark Victory (Allen & Unwin: Sydney, 2003), 245–6.

[55] Neil Comrie, Report of the Inquiry into the Circumstances of the Vivian Alvarez Matter (Sept. 2005), p. 31.

[56] Ibid. p. xi, para 11.

[57] M. J. Palmer, Inquiry into the Circumstances of the Immigration Detention of Cornelia Rau: Report (July 2005), 168, at http://www.minister.immi.gov.au, viewed 13 Feb. 2006.

[58] Ibid.165.

[59] Eve Anderson, Gerard Griffin and Julien Teicher, 'From Industrial Relations to Workplace Relations in the Australian Tax Office: An Incomplete but Strategic Transition', Journal of Industrial Relations 47 (3) (Sept. 2005), 345 (focus group 4 June 2002).

[60] Anderson et al., 'From Industrial Relations to Workplace Relations', 345.

[61] Palmer, Inquiry, 171.

[62] Dennis Pearce, Julian Disney and Heather Ridout, 'The Report of the Independent Review of Breaches and Penalties in the Social Security System' (2002), para 8.17, at http://eprints.anu.edu.au/archive/00001515/01/index-8.html viewed 31 Aug. 2006. The Independent Review of Breaches and Penalties in the Social Security System was established by a number of organisations interested in issues relating to support for unemployed persons. The organisations are listed in appendix 1 of the report.

[63] Tony Abbott, transcript, Four Corners, 'Going Backwards', ABC, 2001, at http://www.abc.net.au/4corners/stories/s326017.htm, viewed 31 Aug. 2006.

[64] Kavita Ayer, 'Poor Choices: Cicero, Tony Abbott and the Agency of Poverty', Monash University, School of Historical Studies (2004), at http://www.arts.monash.edu.au/eras/edition_6/ayerarticle.htm provides a clear indication of the high-profile nature of these comments at note 7: 'Other examples of criticism include: Senator Natasha Stott-Despoja claimed the government should accept that poverty is also, in part, "a function of the Government's failing to give people enough money to live on", in a speech to the National Press Club — http://www.democrats.org.au/campaigns/natpressclub; Michael Raper, the president of the Australian Council of Social Service (ACOSS), called Abbott's comments "a cop-out" — www.abc.net.au/public/news/2001/07/item200107101015081.htm.' See also P. Mendes, 'Bullying the Poor: Tony Abbott on the Welfare State', Australian Quarterly, July–August 2002, pp.33–5, and 'Welfare Groups Lash out at Abbott's Comments', broadcast on ABC local radio on July 10th, 2001

– transcript available at www.abc.net.au/pm/s326684.htm, pp.1–3. The Prime Minister John Howard defended Abbott and denied that Abbott was becoming a 'liability' on television, for example on Channel Nine's Today program on the 11 July, 2001 — transcript available at www.pm.gov.au/interviews/2001/interview1120.htm.'

[65] Mark Willacy, 'Govt Says Even "Job Snobs" Can Find Work in Olympic Year', *The World Today* Archive, 28 June 2000, at http://www.abc.net.au/worldtoday/stories/s146078.htm, viewed 31 Aug. 2006.

[66] Workplace Authority Strategic Plan 2006–2009, at http://www.oea.gov.au/graphics.asp?showdoc=/aboutus/strategicPlan.asp, viewed 20 Aug. 2007.

[67] Joe Hockey quoted by Mark Davis, 'Workplace Ad May Breach Public Service Code, Says Gillard', *Brisbane Times*, 17 July 2007, at http://www.brisbanetimes.com.au/news/national/workplace-ad-may-breach-public-service-code-says-gillard/2007/07/16/1184559705331.html, viewed 17 July 2007.

[68] Julia Gillard Portfolio News website, Transcript Radio Interview with Leon Delaney, 2SM, 17 July 2007, at http://www.juliagillard.alp.org.au/news/0707/mediaportfolionews17-01.php, viewed 20 Aug. 2007.

[69] Andrew Podger, 'Pride and Prejudice: Ms Bennett as the New Face of a Very Public Service', *Public Sector Informant*, 7 Aug. 2007, p. 6.

[70] Workplace Authority, 'Current Vacancies, Level 2 Position Profile, Key Responsibilities', at http://workplaceauthority.nga.net.au/mjs_customer_data/workplaceauthority/job_files/237/PP%20-%20CC%20APS%204.pdf, viewed 20 Aug. 2007.

[71] Workplace Authority, 'Working for the Workplace Authority', at http://www.workplaceauthority.gov.au/graphics.asp?showdoc=/aboutus/workingHere.asp, viewed 20 Aug.2007.

[72] Public Service Commissioner, *2004–05 State of the Service Report*, 170.

[73] Australian National Audit Office, *Performance Management in the Australian Public Service*, ANAO Audit Report no 6, 2004–5 (Canberra, 2004), 14, at http://www.anao.gov.au/uploads/documents/2004-05_Audit_Report_6.pdf, viewed 23 July 2007.

[74] Ibid. 83.

[75] See, for example, David Osbourne and Ted Gabler, *Reinventing Government: How the Entrepreneurial Spirit Is Transforming the Public Sector* (Addison-Wesley Publishing: Reading, Mass, 1992); David Osbourne and Peter Plastrik, *Banishing Bureaucracy: The Five Strategies for Reinventing Government* (Addison-Wesley Publishing: Reading, Mass, 1997).

[76] Australian Public Service Commission, *State of the Service Employee Survey Results 2004–05* (Canberra, 2005), 42, question 64b. Employees who did not report having improved productivity were included the following year, with only marginally improved results. See Australian Public Service Commission, *2005-06 State of the Service Employee Survey Results* (Canberra, 2006), 46, question 62b.

[77] Public Service Commissioner, *2004–05 State of the Service Report*, 164 and *2005–06 State of the Service Report*, 165.

[78] Public Service Commissioner, *2004–05 State of the Service Report*, 164.

[79] Ibid. 162–3 and *2005–06 State of the Service Report*, 164–5.

[80] Public Service Commissioner, *2005–06 State of the Service Report*, 165.

[81] Palmer, *Inquiry*, 171.

[82] Australian Government Site, 'It's an Honour–Australia Celebrating Australians', at http://www.itsanhonour.gov.au/honours/honour_roll/search.cfm?breif=true&page=1&search_type=quick, viewed 31 Aug. 2006.

[83] Abdul Rizvi, 'Organisational Alignment: How Project Management Helps', in John Wanna (ed.), *Improving Implementation: Organisational Change and Project Management* (ANU E Press), 71–8, at http://epress.anu.edu.au/anzsog/imp/pdf/ch06.pdf, viewed 23 July 2007.

[84] Shergold, 'Once was Camelot in Canberra?', 8.

Chapter 4. Devolution

As the performance assessment and pay data indicate, the impact of broader systems changes introduced under the rubric of NPM is best understood in the context of agency-specific systems and culture. While the 'single, distinctive ethos of public service'[1] underpinned by the legislated APS Values and Code of Conduct was meant to sustain a service-wide link between APS employees, agency systems shape their daily experience. These systems implement the direct controls that agency heads and their executive are able to exercise over individuals; they 'hardwire' service-wide performance assessment requirements and other human resource practices into the daily experience of public servants. These in turn condition agency culture, including unwritten protocols around internal communications, record-keeping practices, and interactions with ministers and their advisers. The Comrie report pointed to the intersection of agency systems and culture when it referred to:

> … inadequate training programs, database and operating systems failures, poor case management, and a flawed organisational culture all [of which] contributed to the approach taken in Vivian's case. The convergence of these systemic problems provided the platform for failure.[2]

On the face of it, it would appear that the transfer of managerial power from central agencies to agency heads would mean a corresponding reduction in the power of the centre to affect the conduct of agency businesses. This was the experience with the implementation of NPM in the UK public sector, where it reinforced the relatively greater autonomy already in place and resulted in an increased diminution of control, referred to as the 'minimalist state'.[3] In Australia, however, the institutional and practical implications of devolution have been quite different. Service-wide procedures and conventions were displaced by vertical controls.[4] Devolution increased the managerial and operational power exercised by departmental heads over public servants, but it also increased the power over departmental heads exercised by ministers and by the Prime Minister in particular: control over appointment and termination as well as performance assessment and pay. Within agencies, this has left employees increasingly exposed to the direction of senior managers, ministerial advisers and the ministers whom they serve.

Devolution in theory

Devolving the public service was critical to the implementation of NPM.[5] The process was slow and progressive, consistent with the desire to change cultures as well as systems. The aim was a public service reoriented along market lines, in which 'the responsibilities of departmental secretaries and agency heads were

… similar to those wielded by CEOs in the private sector.'[6] The analogy between the agency head in the public sector and the CEO in the private sector may be less than comprehensive, but it was clearly important to Minister Reith to pursue it:

> The Government is considering the introduction of formal performance agreements for all Agency Heads. This acknowledges the important strategic leadership role of Agency Heads. Their role as Chief Executive Officers, responsible to the Minister for their agency's performance, needs to be explicitly recognised. The exercise of their wide-ranging managerial powers needs to be set in an accountability framework which articulates criteria for the measurement of performance. For these reasons, it is proposed that Agency Heads/Secretaries would be re-classified commonly as Chief Executive Officers.[7]

In addition to the reasons given, one further possible appeal of the term 'CEO' to Minister Reith was that it would reinforce on a daily basis how far agency heads had come from being 'permanent heads' since 1984, when the Hawke Government had amended s. 25(2) of the Public Service Act 1922 to make it clear they were no longer 'permanent heads' but departmental secretaries appointed to particular positions for a term of five years. In 1994 the Keating Government had introduced letters of appointment (commonly referred to as 'contracts') for secretaries that enabled the government of the day to terminate the appointment 'at any time for any reason'.[8] The term 'CEO' reaffirms this arrangement rhetorically, setting departmental heads at an even further remove from permanent heads and closer to a model in which they can be terminated on 'lack of confidence of a minister, whether or not lack of confidence was well founded'.[9] Importantly, Reith identified the expression CEO as explicitly recognising departmental heads' responsibilities *to* the minister and *for* agency performance. It was his intention to free these CEOs from the 'unnecessary restrictions and arcane details'[10] generally associated with the public sector, so that they could harness their 'strategic leadership' to their 'wide-ranging managerial powers' in the interests of more effectively 'achieving the outcomes set by government'.[11] Using performance pay 'as a tool for motivating people,' and assisted by more flexible practices, they would enable the public service to 'to operate efficiently and competitively within a dynamic environment that has made improved performance imperative for all sectors of the economy'.[12]

In institutional terms, devolution began with the progressive transfer to agency heads of responsibility for 'running costs' and proceeded to the dismantling of the centralised staffing controls of the then Public Service Board over fixing pay, establishing employment conditions, appraising staff and overseeing industrial relations. Between them, the *Financial Management and Accountability Act 1997* and Public Service Act formalised the control of agency heads over staff management, workplace relations, agency finances, assets, resources and technology. By the time these pieces of legislation were passed, they were mostly confirming actual arrangements that had already been put in place administratively, some of which had been operating for some years.[13] By 2000, agency heads experienced relatively little regulatory interference from central agencies in staffing matters (with the exception of Public Service Commission controls over Senior Executive Service appointments and promotions and the strict controls maintained by DEWR on what agency heads could *not* do through their workplace agreements). As for other matters, the impact of NPM on the role of central agencies was for a time 'resounding'. Progressive changes had:

> … reduced the old Public Service Board to a shadow of its former self (Campbell and Halligan 1993). Finance moved through several stages during the reform era, eventually adopting a 'strategic' role (Wanna and Bartos 2003), but was so heavily purged in the second wave of market reform (in the second half of the 1990s) that debate came to centre on whether it would survive organisationally (one option being to re-integrate it with Treasury from whence it was originally derived). Finance's experienced a loss of 'policy' competence (Campbell 2001) as its role was diminished by this pursuit of a minimalist agenda. The Department of Prime Minister and Cabinet had withdrawn from active intervention except where required and was no longer providing leadership for the public service.[14]

There appears to be widespread agreement at the top of the public service that the efficiency impact of devolution 'has been largely beneficial', that '[p]roductivity has risen progressively' and that '[p]ublic servants now do more, better, with less'.[15] The former Secretary of the Department of the Prime Minister and Cabinet and the former Public Service Commissioner agree on this point[16] and there has been research broadly supporting their views—although no research can precisely quantify the productivity impact of developments in information and communications technology. The Management Improvement Advisory Committee of the Management Advisory Board (forerunner of the Management Advisory Committee) undertook the review of how best to achieve cost-effective personnel services in selected agencies and reported early gains in November 1995;[17] in 2001–02 and 2002–03, the ANAO undertook a benchmarking study of nine 'people management practice areas' in selected agencies and reported further improvements;[18] the DEWR bargaining guidelines have consistently required that 'improvements in pay and conditions are to be linked to improvements in organisational productivity and performance'[19] in agencies. Despite the absence of measures of productivity growth in the APS (the Australian Bureau of Statistics does not produce measures of productivity growth in public administration[20]) the government demonstrated its belief in agency productivity growth by further increasing the efficiency dividend that it reaps annually from agency resources.[21]

However, devolved systems have also been in operation during many of those 'failures of public administration'[22] considered by Dr Shergold to be the consequence of:

> … inadequate managerial control, weak direction and poor organisational communication exacerbated by an unacceptable tardiness in acknowledging and correcting the mistakes that had been made. In the first matter [children overboard] there was a failure to balance carefully the twin demands of timeliness and accuracy—information was passed from public servants to ministers before it had been adequately corroborated. In the second instance [mistreatment of Cornelia Rau and Vivian Solon] relatively junior officers were not adequately trained or supervised to exercise appropriately the considerable powers that they wielded. Worst by far, failures in both instances were compounded by organisational silos, poor record-keeping, a reluctance to clarify the record and, in a few instances it would seem, attempts to cover up the initial mistakes.[23]

Were these failures simply isolated instances of bureaucratic inefficiency— 'inadequate managerial control, weak direction and poor organisational communication'—compounded by failures of individual integrity? If so, undoubtedly they are of the type that could occur in any management framework. But the problem in the case of Children Overboard was not simply a 'failure to balance carefully the twin demands of timeliness and accuracy'; it was the fact that 'within three days of the initial statements, the story was known to be untrue',[24] but no correction was made until after the election, a month later. The problem in the cases of Cornelia Rau and Vivian Solon was not simply lack of training, organisational silos, and poor record-keeping. In the case of Cornelia Rau it was also that 'through its actions and approach, executive management has sent staff a clear message that process is paramount and should not be questioned'.[25] In the case of Vivian Solon, it was also, as DIMIA staff told the Comrie inquiry:

> … that in some situations they deliberately left their actions unrecorded. They said they did this because of perceptions that they would be in breach of departmental policy if they tried to help suspected unlawful non-citizens with welfare-related matters.[26]

These are more than simple administrative lapses; they go to staff understanding of agency and ministerial expectations, and they resulted in broader systems failures. Could they have happened under old service-wide procedures and arrangements? In the case of DIMIA, Palmer referred to arrangements that were 'process-rich' and 'outcomes poor'—the same criticisms that had been levelled at public service throughout the period under consideration; but he also found that this conduct was not the result of outmoded practices but of a 'clear message' from management. The question, then, is not whether process-rich systems would have performed better; it is whether having, as we now do, a devolved system, there is scope for systems failure which is a consequence of devolution itself. How much does due process rely on systems themselves and how much on 'strategic leadership' and the agency culture in which the systems are embedded? To what extent do agency cultures interact with the service-wide culture that remains after systems are devolved? How has devolution worked in practice?

Devolution in practice

Devolution has meant substantial change in the day-to-day operations of agencies. Agencies run their own recruitment campaigns; they have their own human-resource management strategies and industrial agreements. This means they have their own classification structures, job titles and pay scales. These changes overlay other agency-specific arrangements that reinforce the daily experience of public servants that they are agency employees: agencies have their own intranets featuring management billboards and staff billboards and agency newsletters. Employees have passes to get into their agency that do not work for other agencies—an arrangement that may not be directly traceable to devolution but certainly reinforces it every time an employee walks in the door. Even where service-wide administrative arrangements have been introduced they have to be 'tailored' to agency differences, as in the case of performance-assessment schemes. All this difference is intended to support the variation in the type of work done in diverse agencies, and their need to go about it differently in order to be effective. For this reason, agencies have their own CEOs, as Minister Reith wished them to be known, and those CEOs issue their own Chief Executive Instructions. These market-based operational models were intended to remove many of the long-standing protocols that agencies had in common while at the same time strengthening vertical connections running between agency employees and agency heads and through them to ministers, who were, in turn, intended to reap the benefits of the new arrangements in the form of increased productivity and responsiveness.

At the time it was recognised that 'to achieve greater flexibility it was probably going to be necessary to sacrifice many of the aspects of the public service which had provided the "connective tissue"'[27] —and these sacrifices were duly made. Certainly some of the 'connective tissue' of the public service was largely symbolic to begin with, but it was no less important for all that: organisational cultures often draw on symbols. When, for example, it was decided that agencies should move from service-wide to agency-specific logos, the change was regarded as symbolic of the new emphasis on a service-delivery culture and on building direct relations between agencies with the public. When the Government later decided—for reasons considered below—that it wanted 'the removal of individual agency logos and establishment of a single distinctive "brand", the Australian government, represented by the Australian coat of arms', the change was met with 'territorialism' and 'unexpected and sustained resistance'[28] from agencies. Why was the resistance to abolishing agency-specific logos unexpected? The devolved model was never intended to support a 'single distinctive "brand", the Australian government'; indeed, the introduction of logos was part of a deliberate strategy of cultural change intended to align the hearts and minds of public servants—as well as those of the Australian public—to the agency's particular business focus.

As the logo episode suggests, the alignment process appears to have been effective: by 2005, 60 per cent of APS employees saw themselves as primarily employees of their agency rather than of the APS.[29] And so they were: their employer was their agency head; their workplace and performance agreements were with that agency head and with their line managers; they were bound by the agency head's Chief Executive Instructions; they were accountable through the agency head to the minister. It was a 'highly devolved public management model, [in which] the individual agency was the focus, individualisation provided the basis for public servant employment, and a disaggregated public service was the result'.[30] The remaining service-wide cultural link between APS employees was described in 2003 by the Secretary of the Department of the Prime Minister and Cabinet (who had been the Public Service Commissioner between 1996 and 1998) as 'a single, distinctive ethos of public service'[31] sustained by the statutory APS Values and Code of Conduct. And even these were expected to be adapted to agency operations/priorities/activities through agency systems and then supplemented by agency-specific values if the agency head wished.[32]

Many agency heads did wish to have business-specific values: by 2004–05, 78 per cent of agencies had their own values in addition to those that were in legislation and meant to apply service-wide. The annual *State of the Service Report* gives an indication of how effective the resulting combination of APS-wide and agency-specific values was in sustaining a common service-wide ethos in 2004–05. Responses to the *Employee Survey* showed that the proportions of employees in the 21 large agencies who reported that they were familiar with the actual legislated APS Values varied quite widely, as in previous years, ranging from 65 per cent in some agencies to 93 per cent in others.[33] In addition, employees were often confused about which were the legislated values and which were specific to their own agency: the proportion of employees from large agencies which had their own agency-specific values, principles or behaviours and believed this to be the case varied from 25 to 81 per cent in 2004–05. In large agencies that had not developed their own values, between 33 per cent and 63 per cent of employees thought that they had.[34]

Under the provisions of the Public Service Act (s.12), departmental secretaries and agency heads are not only responsible for arrangements that uphold and promote the APS Values, but also for supporting their employees in applying them. These are the individuals, as public servants in their agencies well know, who are operating on contracts (or letters of appointment) and under performance assessment and pay systems that to a greater or lesser extent have shaped their own application of the APS Values:

> All secretaries are affected, and they are being dishonest or fooling themselves if they deny it. They will hedge their bets on occasions, limit the number of issues on which to take a strong stand, be less strident, constrain public comments, limit or craft more carefully public documents and accept a muddying of their role and that of political advisers. To some extent, there has always been an incentive to please; and public servants have a tradition of caution and anonymity, relating to their role to protect the public interest and to defer to politicians particularly in the public arena. But the political messages to secretaries today are more explicit, and secretaries are, I believe, more cautious in avoiding disputes with ministers and in ensuring any public image of themselves is aligned with the government's position. This is not to suggest a significant lack of courage, but to acknowledge the reality of the incentive framework that has purposely been put into place.[35]

Not only has the incentive framework for secretaries purposely been put in place, but so too have secretaries themselves. Staff know whether they have a history as ministerial advisers, or as members of interest groups favoured by the government of the day. If they are long-standing public servants, they know their history and reputation, and whether or not they have been known to pull their punches. They know what the secretary said (or did not say) when the new minister announced that the department would be regarded as an extension of his/her ministerial office. They know which senior executives refer to government policy as 'our policy' and which obligingly revise draft responses to parliamentary questions to insert the usual political gibes. They know which do not. They hear (in person or on the net) the responses to Senate Estimates questions and compare them to their own experience of what occurred. Word gets around very quickly. When asked, 38 per cent of employees responding to the 2005–06 State of the Service Employee Survey agreed that the leadership in their agency was of the highest quality. 62 per cent did not.[36]

These are the agency leaders who control how much employees hear about service-wide values. They control what the APS Values mean in practice by interpreting them through Chief Executive Instructions and agency systems and processes.[37] They control the seriousness with which the APS Values are taken by the seriousness with which they themselves are seen to take them. As the *State of the Service Report* data suggests, there is considerable agency-to-agency variation in all of these matters, and a corresponding variation in agency employees' own confidence in their capacity to apply the APS Values in their daily work for ministers and their advisers. Surveys have established a direct correlation between employees' confidence in their ability to balance being responsive, apolitical, impartial and professional, and their views on whether senior managers in their agency act in accordance with the APS Values.[38] In 2004–05, in 18 large agencies (from which statistically significant responses are available), between 63 and 76 per cent of employees were confident that their most senior agency managers did act in accordance with the APS Values; in one large agency fewer than 50 per cent were confident.[39] In 2005–06, large-agency confidence varied from a low of 61 per cent to a high of 86 per cent.[40]

As was noted earlier, agency protocols to guide interactions with ministerial offices constitute another factor that is correlated with employee confidence in their ability to balance being responsive, apolitical, impartial and professional. Whether or not agency heads have sanctioned and promoted particular protocols in their agencies to support the APS Values in interactions with ministers and their advisers is also subject to considerable variation. Table 2 sets out the number of large agencies (those employing more than one thousand people) with such protocols. It also sets out, for all large agencies with a given protocol in place, the variability in the proportion of employees who were aware of such a protocol.

The Table provides scope for speculation on the impact of agency systems and culture on individual decision making. Take the data relating to the availability of a written protocol for resolving staff concerns that may arise about the nature of requests from ministerial offices. In the best-case scenario, an employee who is concerned about something they have been asked to do by a minister or a ministerial adviser would be in one of the two large agencies (call them A and B) that has a protocol to assist them. If they are in agency A, they may be one of the 8 per cent of agency employees who are aware that their agency has such a protocol. If this is also an agency in which the agency head and senior managers are known to take a robust and supportive approach to the APS Values, many of the remaining 92 per cent of employees in agency A (or 68 per cent in agency B) would be able to turn confidently to their senior managers for advice. Some of those senior leaders may be able to refer them back to the relevant agency protocols. Others may even give them the same advice as that contained in the protocol—although in a devolved environment they may still be carrying baggage from another portfolio.

Table 2. Relevant employees' awareness of protocols to guide interactions with ministerial offices – employees in large agencies that reported the protocol(s) in place, 2003–04 and 2004–05

Agency Protocol	Year	Number of large agencies with protocol in place	Employee Survey results (% range)		
			Aware of protocol (%)	Not aware of protocol (%)	Not sure (%)
Requirement for a minimum classification level for signing off ministerial briefs	2004–05	15	52–96	0–8	4–48
	2003–04	12	69–99	0–7	1–27
Requirement for a minimum classification level for phone contact with ministerial office advisers	2004–05	3	13–26	28–35	46–52
	2003–04	2	23–32	28–33	41–44
Requirement that oral briefing to Ministers or Ministers' staff on key issues is confirmed in writing (including emails or follow-up minutes)	2004–05	9	24–63	0–20	37–66
	2003–04	3	27–39	16–23	44–55
Requirement that file notes are routinely made after significant phone calls or oral discussions with Ministers and ministerial advisers	2004–05	10	30–65	6–20	28–61
	2003–04	6	31–62	9–26	25–45
Requirement that significant email communications with ministerial advisers be retained	2004–05	13	47–75	1–12	19–48
	2003–04	8	43–87	5–21	8–49
Agreed unwritten processes for resolving staff concerns that may arise about the nature of requests from ministerial offices	2004–05	9	16–29	6–24	53–71
	2003–04	10	21–33	0–20	48–78
Agreed written processes for resolving staff concerns that may arise about the nature of requests from ministerial offices	2004–05	2	8–32	6–32	61
	2003–04	0	NA	NA	NA

Note: The ranges provided are derived from agency-specific *Employee Survey* results of up to 15 large agencies in 2004–5 (and 12 large agencies in 2003–4) that reported the protocol(s) in place. They do not include the APS-wide results. Source: *2004–05 State of Service Report*, Table 3.2.

In the worst case, agency employees who are feeling both under pressure and concerned about what they may regard as implicit and explicit political directions from the office of the minister will have no agency protocol, no reliance on agency senior leadership, and no trust in the ethical behaviour of their managers. There may be no real senior leadership to speak of, or they may experience their leadership as so focused on delivering outcomes for the government of the day that the end will always be assumed to justify the means. They may also feel that the systems of performance management in their agency and/or the culture in which they operate are weighted in favour of responsiveness and against due process (see Chapter 3). They may feel that this weighting is deliberate.

The Palmer Report into the conduct of affairs at DIMIA recommended that, in such circumstances 'where an officer or a lower level manager believes that particular arrangements or performance measures are producing bad or negative outcomes, commonsense should prevail and the matter should be raised with executive management'.[41] Common sense may prevail on many occasions. The data available suggests that in the particular subset of occasions when APS employees witness a serious breach of the Code of Conduct, around half do not report it.[42] The main reasons for their silence are that the breach had already been reported or had been reported in the past and nothing had been done about it; concern about retribution or victimisation that would result from reporting; and concern about the negative effect reporting would have on their career.[43] If they do report it and executive management takes no corrective action, employees have no recourse short of resigning or bringing a code of conduct complaint against their own agency's senior leadership—a complaint turning on a question of balance in a matter subject to interpretation. And since confidence that discrimination or harassment would not result from reporting a suspected breach of the code of conduct by a manager or senior manager is correlated with overall confidence in the operation of the APS Values in the agency, the problem in poorly performing agencies could be assumed to be much more significant. An employee with ethical concerns about the behaviour of those up the line may have no recourse but to do nothing at the time and then to approach those affected 'afterwards to say that he was deeply unhappy … and wanted to distance himself from the actions of his superiors'.[44]

The cultural changes associated with devolution—the emphasis on vertical accountabilities and responsiveness, on one hand, and the loss of 'connective tissue', on the other—are accelerated by turnover. There were 10,482 separations of ongoing employees during 2004–05, an increase of 44.2 per cent on the previous year.[45] Over time, these numbers will only rise. In June 2005, APS employees in the 45 and over age group, who would be eligible for retirement in 2014–15, accounted for 40.4 per cent of ongoing employees.[46] In 1996, this group accounted for only 30.5 per cent of ongoing employees. The 'old guard' is leaving the public service and taking with them one source of informal advice and mentoring about the operation of service-wide conventions. If the staff replacing them believe that particular arrangements or performance measures are producing bad or negative outcomes, they will be increasingly dependent on going 'up the line' with their concerns—which may leave them more inclined to settle quietly into the default agency custom.

In particular, the 'new guard' may have a reduced capacity to pass on the service-wide conventions associated with the Westminster tradition. New employees may not even be aware that there are any lines to be drawn in delivering services to the agency's 'key customers'. An increasing proportion of APS vacancies are being filled from outside the APS, from 33.7 per cent in 1995–96 to 47.6 per cent in 2004–5.[47] Whatever the undoubted skills and qualifications of these employees, they are unlikely to include an understanding of the application of the caretaker convention, or cabinet confidentiality, or mandated standards for record-keeping. At the same time, as noted in Chapter

1, the numbers of ministerial advisers are growing and with them the number of public servants at the other end of the telephone. In a devolved environment, and in an output-focused ('can do') culture, these employees will find themselves increasingly isolated when it comes to taking anything but the default agency standard of responsiveness to requests from ministers and their advisers. As has been noted, the Public Service Commissioner issued broad *Guidelines on Conduct* in 2003 and more comprehensive general protocols under the heading *Supporting Ministers Upholding the Values* in 2006. But the Public Service Commissioner is also operating in a devolved environment. As one employee reported to the 2004–05 *Employee Survey*:

> You can have all the protocols you want, but if the Minister's office wants something you give it to them … In previous jobs I had been told by my SES to NOT put things on email so there was NO record of it.[48]

Individual isolation is compounded by current technology and is likely to be reinforced by future technology. Email and mobile phones can be used to contact individuals at all levels of the bureaucracy, making employees accessible at all times, virtually anywhere. Technology enables ministers and their advisers to bypass layers of senior management and leave lower-level employees directly exposed to requests and directions that are personal, urgent, and possibly inappropriate. Ministers and their advisers also generally demand speed as part of overall public service responsiveness, often because the media demand it of them, but the overall effect of the demand for urgent turn-around of advice is to require public servants to choose between being responsive and meeting agency's own clearance protocols.

Devolution has also given agency heads the power to reinforce vertical lines of control and to break down collective culture in their own agencies by putting into their hands the power of settling the agency's industrial arrangements, the hiring and firing of employees and the setting of remuneration and terms and conditions of employment. The new industrial framework encourages responsiveness by encouraging competition in relation to performance ratings, access to accelerated advancement, and gaining the attention and regard of those well positioned to deliver either or both. People have always sought to behave in ways that would earn them promotion, but this is promotion compressed in time and raised in visibility. It has little to do with long-term mentoring relationships or skills development, and much to do with senior managers-as-audience. Direct supervisors may award ratings, but senior managers oversee ratings distributions and moderation. As a consequence, 'People strive for visibility. They're looking for opportunities in which they can achieve things, tangible results, quickly.'[49] The system relies on short-term incentives and—as Allan Hawke predicted and both the *State of the Service* and Audit Office survey findings confirm—is 'divisive and undermines relationships between staff'.[50]

(It is worth recalling in this context that employees in large agencies were unlikely to agree that their agency performance assessment system 'contributes to a workplace culture where individuals work together effectively'; in fact, agreement was as low as 11 per cent in 2003–04 and 9 per cent in 2004–05). It is a model that, in the absence of active and judicious agency leadership, fosters isolation but not independence and nurtures a 'control-motivated culture'.[51]

In a control-motivated culture—where senior managers have sent a 'clear message that process is paramount and should not be questioned'—devolved management can foster the fixation on rules it was meant to replace. When such an agency culture settles into place, 'due process' can become degraded to 'mere process', regardless of the formal guidance that has been put in place. In 2005–06, 62 per cent of respondents to the *State of the Service Employee Survey* agreed that their agency had procedures and systems that ensured objectivity in decision making. 12 per cent actively disagreed and 22 per cent neither agreed nor disagreed.[52] This is a very mixed result, not least because 'ensures objectivity' may be difficult to interpret in this context. The level of systems documentation is not, of itself, the deciding factor. According to the Palmer Report, DIMIA was 'process rich' but uninterested in how its processes interacted with people.

In the case of the scrutiny conducted by the Department of Foreign Affairs and Trade (DFAT) of the Australian Wheat Board's (AWB) contracts with Saddam Hussein's regime, the problem was, conversely, a lack of process ('the exporter was not required to certify to the Commonwealth the accuracy or completeness of the contractual documents said to constitute the agreement with the foreign entity'[53]). Process issues were also identified in the Senate report on *A Certain Maritime Incident* ('The Committee is not questioning the integrity of the individual participants on the Taskforce, but finds substantial weaknesses in its basic administrative operations, including record keeping, risk management and reporting back'[54]). In fact, it has been argued in the cases of DIMIA and *A Certain Maritime Incident* that the presence or absence of particular processes is not so much the point as the intersection of agency activities with an assumption culture, with the default set to responsiveness:

> The *Palmer Report* is a refreshingly blunt document that rightly highlights the legal responsibilities of public servants, and calls for leadership and careful management to ensure that the enforcement and application of policies are justified and equitable. Yet I feel it downplayed the possible impact of the culture of political responsiveness on exercising legal responsibility, and perhaps inadvertently confused the issue. Palmer says the DIMIA management approach appeared to be 'process-rich' and 'outcomes poor'; maybe the problem also was that it was too 'can-do' and not enough 'due process'. To my mind, that was one of the lessons from the Tampa case and subsequent intercepts with unauthorised

arrivals when the pressure was on officials and defence service personnel to avoid circumstances where their legal authority was transparent and their legal responsibility might have led to an increase in the number of arrivals of asylum seekers ... [H]ighlighting of the 'process rich and outcomes poor' line allows too much of the blame to be placed on the public service, and too little emphasis to be given to the political context and how public servants should handle that context.[55]

Once the political context is used to frame the administrative failures surrounding 'Children Overboard' and Cornelia Rau (and AWB), it appears that in each case 'can-do' outweighed 'due process'. In each case 'can-do' was consistent with political if not departmental rhetoric, and in each case, we are assured, the Government did not explicitly ask for it to be done:

The government did not direct public servants to provide false information or fail to correct the record or act outside the law. Nor did it intimate that such behaviour was acceptable. Nor did Ministers put impenetrable barriers around themselves.[56]

This may be true, but in a system that fosters and rewards responsiveness to ministerial expectations as well as ministerial requests, it is not a sufficient defence.

Recent adjustments to the devolved model

In his 1996 discussion paper on best practice in the Australian public service, Minister Reith had argued that, in making devolution work,

One inhibitor is the centre. It survives still. Central agencies must learn to 'let go' in practice as well as theory. Standards must be maintained, service-wide policies implemented, advice provided and best practice promoted. But the culture must be one of facilitation not regulation.[57]

While departmental secretaries subsequently agreed that devolution had enabled them 'to align their staffing, administrative resources and assets to the objectives government has set them', they have also agreed that it has not always been good for the responsiveness of the system as a whole. 'There is some risk,' they have acknowledged, 'that devolution of authority to agency heads and a clear vertical accountability for agency outcomes may make collaboration across organisational boundaries more difficult.'[58] The problem at an operational level was succinctly put by a respondent to the *2004–05 State of the Service Employee Survey*, commenting on inter-agency communication:

Oral communication is just proving to be adequate but written is poor (as it appears staff do not want to be recorded as having provided information or advice to another agency). The motivation appears to be a growing concern that staff will be held accountable (i.e. punished) for having consulted/assisted on a matter that may result in an outcome that does not accord with what could be anticipated may be their own Minister's preferred position. This means misinformation is being provided (or poorly articulated positions are being put) to Government as part of the deliberative process.[59]

In terms of the implementation process, coordinated service delivery was recognised by secretaries to be an organisational boundary issue, together with Indigenous support, national security, environmental management and drug abuse issues. There was concern that public servants at all levels, motivated by what one agency celebrated as the 'will to win'[60], were acculturated to looking vertically up lines of accountability to their ministers but not horizontally across them to each other. The old central agencies in particular were *proposing*, but line agencies were not *disposing*, or at least not with sufficient gusto. 'Political control and performance issues'[61] were emerging within the highly devolved framework, and the Government was becoming 'concern[ed] that political priorities were not being sufficiently reflected in policy directions, and were not being followed through in program implementation and delivery'.[62]

Accordingly, while citing 'considerable evidence' of the positive impact of devolution on agency productivity,[63] secretaries identified the need to improve collaboration across organisational boundaries. They issued guidance for whole-of-government cooperation and put in place mechanisms for 'connecting government'.[64] But despite the rhetorical enthusiasm, the relevant guidance stipulated that horizontal collaboration was to occur 'while maintaining vertical accountability'.[65] The top-down drivers of bottom-up responsiveness were not to be substantially changed: '[m]arket testing, outsourcing, organisational devolution and performance management have become central parts of public service working life' and were to remain in place.[66] Instead, (re)centralisation was pursued in a way that had the effect of reinforcing rather than offsetting the vertical accountabilities put in place through devolution. One of the principal vehicles for this recentralising was the Government's response to the Uhrig Report:

> The report was undertaken after extensive lobbying by the business sector and was prepared by businessman John Uhrig who, at the time of the Inquiry, was chair of the mining giant Santos Ltd. After a largely internal review process, he handed down a report containing recommendations that, according to Wettenhall, 'were in line with, and helped give form to, the Howard Government's own thinking.' That thinking was based on the notion that ministers should have complete control over the activities of public agencies unless those agencies are engaged in a commercial operation or there is some other exceptional circumstance warranting independence.[67]

The structural changes undertaken following the Uhrig Report simply buttress top-down controls. Six delivery agencies were been brought together and put under departmental oversight, including Centrelink and the Health Insurance Commission, whose governance boards were abolished and replaced by an executive management structure 'to establish a more direct Ministerial role in their operation'.[68]   A further five agencies that were once statutorily independent—the Australian National Training Authority (ANTA), National Occupational Health and Safety Commission (NOHSC), National Oceans Office (NOO), Australian Greenhouse Office (AGO) and the Australian Government Information Management Office (AGIMO)—were moved back into departments. According to the then Secretary of the Department of the Prime Minister and Cabinet, it 'is a process designed to clarify the lines of authority, to establish responsibility for decision making and to enhance Ministerial (and Secretarial) accountability'.[69] It is also a process that reflects the Prime Minister's view, communicated to his ministers, that they should be 'conscious of the extent to which the establishment of these bodies limits the government's own sphere of control and constrains the options available to them'.[70]

Statutory authorities that were not moved back into departments were required to work through portfolio secretaries rather than directly to ministers. Other changes, now subject to reversal by the Rudd Government, included the selective shortening of contracts for heads of statutory authorities from five to two or three years (not a Uhrig proposal), and the vetting of all senior appointments to public agencies directly by the Prime Minister's Office.[71] Advisory boards and committees were streamlined, also with the effect of 'enhanc[ing] Ministerial (and Secretarial) accountability', most famously by the removal of the employee representative on the ABC Board and the replacement of the entire board of the Australian Research Council by an advisory committee with no decision-making power—also under the aegis of Uhrig:

> Replacing the board with a chief executive who reports directly to the minister will, Dr Nelson says, expedite funding and increase certainty. So why aren't the beneficiaries cheering? Universities see the minister's words as euphemisms for one word: control.
>
> The ARC shake-up is one of the first outcomes of a review of corporate governance of 170 statutory authorities by businessman John Uhrig. He offered another option, enabling the ARC board to finalise grants without ministerial approval, a move that would speed up the grants process. Only one option increased ministerial power.
>
> … If there is a conflict between political and academic agendas—between, say, research into renewable energy or the fossil fuel technology favoured by Government energy policy—it's not hard to guess which is now more likely to win funding.[72]

It would appear that the prediction that 'the devolved model is unlikely to survive faddish inclinations once active political executives become disabused of ideological fixations'[73] has been working itself out. Active political executives do not like giving away control, even in the interests of pursuing a market model. In the Coalition's Indigenous Coordination Centres, for example, those doing the coordinating of Indigenous health, housing and employment services remained responsible, respectively, to the heads of the health, housing, and employment agencies.

The response to the loss of connective tissue in the public service brought about by devolution has been to strengthen top-down policy controls over policy development and implementation by increasing the power of central agencies. Government 'concern that political priorities were not being sufficiently reflected in policy directions, and were not being followed through in program implementation and delivery' noted above, was addressed by new whole of government mechanisms noted above and by the creation of the Cabinet Implementation Unit in the Department of the Prime Minister and Cabinet. This body enables the Prime Minister to look over the shoulders of his portfolio ministers while they are looking over the shoulders of their agency heads while they drive agency performance. Both the new whole of government mechanisms and the Uhrig changes were part of the broader 'reinforcement of and significant extension to vertical relationships' brought to bear through a series of structural adjustments summarised by Halligan as:

1. resurrection of the central agency as a major actor and of control over departments;
2. whole-of-government as the current expression of a range of forms [of] coordination;
3. central monitoring of agency implementation and delivery; and
4. control of non-departmental bodies by departmentalisation (absorbing statutory authorities) and reclaiming control of agencies with hybrid boards to accord with corporate governance prescriptions.[74]

The result is 'more political instruments for securing and sustaining control and direction … a brace of instruments for working the system strategically and at several levels'.[75] Because of the form it has taken in the Australian political and institutional context, devolution has enabled the government to increase its control over increasingly isolated public servants in increasingly isolated agency-businesses to exact ever higher levels of responsiveness. This means that when it wants it can require agencies to work together to deliver centrally orchestrated policy making involving coordinated responses. It also means, conversely, that at all other times there may be a presumption in favour of their not interacting effectively when, as in the case of Children Overboard or DFAT's

oversight of AWB, it is necessary that 'mandarins and their masters manage …
to miss what is going on'.[76]

ENDNOTES

[1] Peter Shergold, 'Regeneration: New Structures, New Leaders, New Traditions', speech delivered at the Institute of Public Administration Australia National Conference, Canberra, 11 Nov. 2004, http://www.pmc.gov.au/speeches/shergold/regeneration_2004-11-11.cfm, viewed 26 June 2006.

[2] Neil Comrie, *Report of the Inquiry into the Circumstances of the Vivian Alvarez Matter* (Canberra, 2005), 77.

[3] See Glyn Davis and R. A. W. Rhodes, 'From Hierarchy to Contracts and Back Again: Reforming the Australian Public Service', in Michael Keating, John Wanna and Patrick Weller (eds), *Institutions on the Edge? Capacity for Governance* (Allen & Unwin: Sydney, 2000), 77.

[4] See John Halligan, 'The Integrated Performance Model in the Australian Public Sector and its Consequences for Public Sector Organisations', paper presented at Panel on Autonomy and Steering Models of Public Sector Organisations, 9th International Research Symposium on Public Management, SDA Bocconi, Milan, 6–8 Apr. 2005.

[5] The 1976 Report into government administration (Coombs Commission) recommended, among other reforms, devolution of responsibility, as well as greater flexibility and diversity in organisational styles; more efficient and economical use of human resources, and a more open public service. See Royal Commission on Australian Government Administration, *Report* (AGPS: Canberra, 1976).

[6] Peter Shergold, 'The Australian Public Service in 2035: Back to the Future', speech to CPA Annual Conference, Melbourne, 18 May 2005, at http://www.pmc.gov.au/speeches/shergold/aps_2035_back_to_the_future_2005-05-18.cfm, viewed 25 Apr. 2006.

[7] Peter Reith, *Towards a Best Practice Australian Public Service: Discussion Paper issued by the Minister for Industrial Relations and the Minister Assisting the Prime Minister for the Public Service* (Canberra, 1996), 11.

[8] Andrew Podger, 'What Really Happens: Department Secretary Appointments, Contracts and Performance Pay in the Australian Public Service', *Australian Journal of Public Administration*, 66(2) (2007), 136.

[9] Ibid.

[10] Reith, *Towards a Best Practice Australian Public Service*, p. v.

[11] Ibid. 19.

[12] Ibid. p. ix.

[13] In addition to administrative implementation of some financial management reforms, the Workplace Relations Act 1996 and the Workplace Relations Regulations 1996 allowed APS employers to override prescribed provisions of the Public Service Act 1922 (principally those relating to dismissal and retirement) in agency agreements. In 1998 a number of provisions of the Public Service Bill 1997 were implemented by administrative means.

[14] Halligan, 'Integrated Performance Model', 5.

[15] Shergold, 'Regeneration'.

[16] See, for example, Shergold, 'Australian Public Service in 2035'; Andrew Podger, 'Looking Upwards and Downwards: Key Issues and Suggestions for Managing Board/Minister/Departmental Relations', paper presented to the University of Canberra Conference on Governance, Mar. 1996, pp. 2–3.

[17] Management Improvement Advisory Committee of the Management Advisory Board, *Achieving Cost Effective Personnel Services* (1995) and *ACEPS Stage 2: Re-engineering People Management: From Good Intentions to Good Practice*, at http://www.apsc.gov.au/publications/archive.htm, viewed 21 Feb. 2008.

[18] Australian National Audit Office, *Managing People for Business Outcomes: Year Two*, ANAO Audit Report no. 50, 2002–3 (Canberra, 2003).

[19] Department of Employment and Workplace Relations 2003, 'APS—Workplace Relations Policy Parameters for Agreement Making in the Australian Public Service' (Dec. 2003).

[20] MFP measures are not presented for public administration because the volume estimates of gross value added are derived using a method in which input data are used as measures of output. As a result, the measure of real gross value added effectively assumes that there has been no change in productivity. Australian Bureau of Statistics, Cat. 5216.0, *Australian National Accounts: Concepts, Sources and Methods,*

2000, at http://www.abs.gov.au/AUSSTATS/abs@.nsf/66f306f503e529a5ca25697e0017661f/65a7a1b617 fd3461ca2569a70003feef!OpenDocument, viewed 21 Feb. 2008.

[21] Public Service Commissioner, *2003–04 State of the Service Report* (Canberra, 2004), 99.

[22] Peter Shergold, 'Pride in Public Service', speech to National Press Club, Canberra, 15 Feb. 2006, at http://www.pmc.gov.au/speeches/shergold/pride_in_public_service_2006-02-15.cfm, viewed 15 Mar. 2006.

[23] Ibid.

[24] Patrick Weller, *Don't Tell the Prime Minister* (Scribe Publications: Melbourne, 2002), 4.

[25] M. J. Palmer, *Inquiry into the Circumstances of the Immigration Detention of Cornelia Rau: Report* (July 2005), 169, at http://www.minister.immi.gov.au.

[26] Comrie, *Report*, 32–3.

[27] Tony Blunn, 'Public Service Values in the New Millennium', *Canberra Bulletin of Public Administration* no 107 (Mar. 2003), 29–30.

[28] Shergold, 'Regeneration'.

[29] Australian Public Service Commission, *State of the Service Employee Survey Results 2004–05* (Canberra, 2005), 16, question 20. The data refer to questionnaire responses for the year following the logo change, but that is the first year for which data are available.

[30] Halligan, 'Integrated Performance Model', 5.

[31] Shergold, 'Regeneration'.

[32] Australian Public Service Commission, *Embedding the APS Values* (Canberra, 2003), 13, at http://www.apsc.gov.au/values/values7.htm, viewed 26 June 2006.

[33] See Public Service Commissioner, *2004–05 State of the Service Report* (Canberra, 2005), 142.

[34] See ibid. 147.

[35] Podger, 'What Really Happens', 143–4.

[36] Australian Public Service Commission, *State of the Service Employee Survey Results 2005–06* (Canberra, 2006), 18, question 21a.

[37] See discussion of 'The Role of Leadership': Australian Public Service Commission, *Embedding the APS Values*, Ch. 6, at http://www.apsc.gov.au/values/values7.htm, viewed 26 June 2006.

[38] Public Service Commissioner, *2004–05 State of the Service Report*, 41; see also correlation for the previous year between employees' levels of confidence that their most senior managers act in accordance with the APS Values and their own confidence in their ability to balance being responsive, apolitical, impartial and professional in the *2003–04 State of the Service Report*, 40. The question on leading by example in ethical behaviour was not asked in 2003–4.

[39] Public Service Commissioner, *2004–05 State of the Service Report*, 144.

[40] Public Service Commissioner, *2005–06 State of the Service Report*, 58.

[41] Palmer, *Inquiry*, 170.

[42] Specifically, 50 % in 2004; 50 % in 2005; and 44 % in 2006. See Australian Public Service Commission, *State of the Service Employee Survey Results 2005–06*, 28, question 39b.

[43] See Public Service Commissioner, *2005–06 State of the Service Report*, 61. These responses were coded from an open-ended question.

[44] Ian Lowe, 'The Research Community', in Clive Hamilton and Sarah Maddison (eds), *Silencing Dissent: How the Australian government is controlling public opinion and stifling debate* (Crows Nest: Allen and Unwin, 2007), 68.

[45] Public Service Commissioner, *2004–05 State of the Service Report*, 25.

[46] Ibid. 19.

[47] Of that group, over half had never worked in the APS before. See ibid. 24–5.

[48] Ibid. 40.

[49] Michael O'Donnell and John Shields, 'Performance Management and the Psychological Contract in the Australian Federal Public Sector', *Journal of Industrial Relations* 44(3) (2002), 447.

[50] Department of Defence Online media room, 'People Power', based on an address to the International Seminar of the Royal United Services Institute of Australia by Allan Hawke, Secretary of the Department of Defence, 17 Nov. 2000, at http://www.defence.gov.au/media/SpeechTpl.cfm?CurrentId=444, viewed 23 July 2007.

[51] Palmer, *Inquiry*, 173.

[52] Australian Public Service Commission, *State of the Service Employee Survey Results 2005–06*, 18, question 22.

[53] Terence Cole, *Report of the Inquiry into Certain Australian Companies in Relation to the UN Oil-for-Food Programme*, vol. 1, Nov. 2006, Recommendations, p. lxxxiii.

[54] Report of the Senate Select Committee on *A Certain Maritime Incident*, 23 Oct. 2002, Executive Summary, at http://www.aph.gov.au/senate/committee/maritime_incident_ctte/report/a06.htm, viewed 20 Apr. 2006.

[55] Podger, 'Looking Upwards and Downwards', 15.

[56] Shergold, 'Pride in Public Service'.

[57] Reith, *Towards a Best Practice Australian Public Service*, 21.

[58] Management Advisory Committee, *Connecting Government: Whole of Government Responses to Australia's Priority Challenges* (Canberra, 2004), 6.

[59] Public Service Commissioner, *2004–05 State of the Service Report*, 283.

[60] Department of Finance and Administration, *Annual Report 1999–2000* (Canberra, 2000), 59, at http://www.finance.gov.au/pubs/AnnualReport99-00/pdfs_word/completereport/Annualreport.pdf, viewed 29 June 2007. See also O'Donnell and Shields, 'Performance Management', 449: 'Such competition for visibility and performance ratings can also lead to a form of dysfunctional individualism where employees refuse to share valuable information. In the case of DOFA [Finance], there were concerns that some employees were hoarding their knowledge.'

[61] Halligan, 'Integrated Performance Model', 1. See also Peter Shergold, 'Plan and Deliver: Avoiding Bureaucratic Hold-up', speech to the Australian Graduate School of Management/Harvard Club of Australia, 17 Nov. 2004, National Press Club, at http://www.dpmc.gov.au/speeches/shergold/plan_and_deliver_2004-11-17.cfm, viewed 27 June 2006.

[62] Halligan, 'Integrated Performance Model', 7.

[63] Management Advisory Committee, *Connecting Government*, 6.

[64] See *Management Advisory Committee, Connecting Government: Good Practice Guides*, at http://www.connected.gov.au/home, viewed 3 Sept. 2006.

[65] Management Advisory Committee, *Connecting Government*, 15.

[66] Shergold, 'Regeneration'.

[67] Andrew Macintosh, 'Statutory Authorities', in Hamilton and Maddison, *Silencing Dissent*, 152.

[68] Public Service Commissioner, *2004–05 State of the Service Report*, 274.

[69] Shergold, 'Regeneration'.

[70] Letter from the Prime Minister dated 29 Nov. 1996, leaked to the media in early 1997, and quoted by Macintosh, 'Statutory Authorities', 154.

[71] Ibid. 152.

[72] Editorial, *The Age*, 20 July 2005, at http://www.theage.com.au/news/editorial/nelson-calls-the-research-tune/2005/07/19/1121538971011.htm, viewed 3 Sept. 2006. A detailed account of this process is set out in Stuart Macintyre, 'Universities', in Hamilton and Maddison, *Silencing Dissent*, 41–8, 56.

[73] Halligan, 'Integrated Performance Model', 3.

[74] Ibid. 7–8.

[75] Ibid. 17.

[76] Editorial, 'Time to Account for AWB Scandal', *Weekend Australian*, 30 Sept.–1 Oct. 2006, p. 18.

Chapter 5. Aligning the service: the impact of workplace relations

While it has become almost a commonplace to point to the likely link between secretaries' contracts of employment and the politicisation of the public service,[1] this issue has arisen much less frequently in relation to ordinary public servants, probably because of the widespread association of public servants with secure employment. Nevertheless, the contract model has been increasingly extended into the usual activities of public servants. State governments make widespread use of fixed-term contracts for senior executives[2] while, at the Commonwealth level, relations are increasingly being structured along the lines of a contract. Under the outcomes and outputs structure, the budget has been changed, at least in language, from a funding mechanism into a contractual arrangement under which government purchases outputs from agencies. Agencies enter into contractual (or quasi-contractual) arrangements with each other for services, and then parts of agencies contract with other parts to provide, for example, legal or corporate services. Staff are required to enter into performance agreements with their senior managers. Until the change of Government in 2007, there was increasing pressure on individuals to enter into individual industrial agreements that set their terms and conditions of employment. According to DEWR data, by the end of June 2005, a total of 11,823 employees had done so: 1937 (virtually all) of the Senior Executive Service, 5966 executive level staff (21 per cent), and 3837 APS 1–6 staff (around 3 per cent).[3]

In short, the industrial arrangements governing the employment of public servants, introduced alongside the broader suite of NPM reforms, have increasingly mimicked and reproduced broader systemic change. They have introduced contestability, performance assessment and devolution into the terms under which individual staff are employed, changing not only the employment contract but also the 'psychological contract' between public servants and those who employ them. These industrial arrangements were structured to discourage the growth of service-wide 'connective tissue', to isolate employees industrially and to increase their sensitivity to managerial prerogative. As will be seen, they have a rhetoric of their own that does not necessarily represent workplace realities—a kind of industrial spin—and that can contribute to the development in agencies of an assumption culture. While individual contracts have contributed to the making individual public servants more 'results-oriented', they have also had the effect of encouraging a narrow and short-term interpretation of the requirement for 'responsiveness'.

Industrial relations in theory

In the early to mid-1980s, NPM was gathering momentum and so was a new model of employment relations. Like the broader changes to the public sector, Human Resource Management (HRM) drew its authority from globalisation and the drive to increase cost efficiency. Just as there were different models of NPM there were also different models of HRM, although they had a common policy goal: to create an adaptive workforce capable of maximum productivity through maximum utilisation. Employers had the capacity to take a high- or low-cost approach to establishing an adaptable workforce. The high-cost option was called 'functional flexibility' and relied on building employees' skills over time and using job security to encourage a long-term creative engagement with production issues. The low-cost option was called 'numerical flexibility' and relied on strengthening managerial capacity to employ, direct and dismiss individual staff as required. These alternatives, as they were embedded in organisations, were known as 'soft' and 'hard' HRM respectively and were characterised in the work of Karen Legge in 1995 along the following lines:

> The 'soft' normative model of HRM is depicted as individualistic with committed employees working flexibly and 'beyond contract' in pursuit of competitive advantage. The 'hard' model implies that employees are a resource to be used like any other, at management's discretion, in whatever way best achieves strategic objectives.[4]

The rhetoric of HRM as it was to apply in the Commonwealth was largely of the 'soft' or humanistic type. It was characterised by a preference for a committed rather than a merely compliant workforce—a preference that called for changes to both cultural and industrial arrangements.[5] In its early days, the rhetoric of 'soft' HRM had a brave new worldishness to it: it was about hearts and minds and how they could be made to internalise the organisation's goals.[6] It is the rhetoric used by the Minister Assisting the Prime Minister for the Public Service in introducing the Public Service Bill 1997, when he said that 'in place of the old adversarial system both the public and private sectors are now encouraged to place emphasis on direct workplace relationships and mutual interest'.[7]

In practice, this internalisation of mutual interests was believed to be best served by individual rather than collective bargaining. Unions and industrial tribunals, unlike employers and employees, did not have the interests of the organisation at heart. They were outsiders, and they tended to involve other outsiders. They favoured industry-based awards made by independent tribunals and inserted themselves into workplace collective bargaining. Individual agreement making would build closer, more mutually satisfying relations between employer and employee. These individually based arrangements were to be as flexible as possible, increasing individual adaptability as well as individual dependence on and trust in the organisation's managers and their application of its human resource policies. This would result in increased employee commitment and willingness to adapt in the interests of the firm (or in the case of the APS, the agency), resulting in continuous productivity improvement in response to the global challenge.

In this narrative, 'soft' HRM appears to be the opposite of 'hard' HRM. Both call for an increase in management prerogative but for opposite reasons: 'soft' managers would use their prerogative to build employee commitment and 'hard' managers would use theirs to buy and sell skills as required by the interests of the organisation. Thus the implementation of 'hard' HRM leads in a different direction from 'soft' HRM: away from a reliance on employee commitment:

> In particular if flexibility takes the form of casualising labour and outsourcing, this may make it more difficult to encourage employee commitment to the enterprise. It does not seem plausible to expect that an employee who is not assured of job security will have much reason to show much loyalty, and where outsourcing takes place, the worker's primary loyalty will logically be to another organisation altogether.[8]

Despite the very considerable notional differences between the two versions of HRM, academic studies would suggest that the actual distinction was largely the one between theory and practice, that is, that 'even if the rhetoric of HRM is "soft", the reality is almost always "hard", with the interests of the organisation prevailing over those of the individual'.[9] It would appear that as management prerogative becomes increasingly influential, the organisational focus shifts from eliciting the commitment of workers to gaining control over them, and 'soft' HRM practice hardens, although often more opportunistically than strategically. The rhetoric of 'soft' HRM, Legge argues, can change more slowly than actual workplace practice and so provide a rhetorical cover for the transition from a 'soft' to a 'hard' management approach to HRM.[10] Although her argument is based on the experience in the United Kingdom, it reflects similar developments in the public sector observed in Australia. In fact, she argues that in the UK public sector services were prominent among organisations in which 'hard' HRM practices were adopted.[11] Does the experience of the APS conform to the same pattern?

In 1995, in Australia, Kitay and Lansbury were commissioned by the Productivity Commission (then the Economic Planning Advisory Commission, or EPAC) to map workplace practices in Australia against developments in HRM overseas. As part of this exercise they developed a table setting out the key features of the old and new systems (see Table 3). In so doing they emphasised that the table represented 'a comparison between the practice of the old—typically a warts-and-all portrayal, with an emphasis on the warts—and the theory of the new, emphasising the positive aspects'[12] or 'soft' HRM approach, and that it could not therefore be relied on to predict how HRM would work itself out in practice. This, as shall be seen, proved to be the case. Nevertheless, the table offers a fair overview of the discourse and priorities of 'soft' HRM at a point in time when NPM was giving agency heads the capacity to shape public sector employment relations—or, in the terminology used in the table, to make the *locus of control* of employees 'internal' to the agency, breaking down its external links to service-wide industrial arrangements. Industrial relations would become workplace relations and then employee relations.

Table 3. Assumptions Underlying 'Old' and 'New' Models of Employment Relations

	Compliance	Commitment
Psychological contract	Fair day's work for a fair day's pay	Reciprocal commitment
Locus of control	External	Internal
Employment relations	Pluralist Collective Low trust	Unitarist Individual High trust
Organising Principles	Mechanistic Formal/defined roles Top-down Centralised	Organic Flexible Roles Bottom-up Decentralised
Policy goals	Administrative efficiency Standard performance Cost minimisation	Adaptive workforce Improving performance Maximum utilisation

Source: Guest 1991, from EPAC, Human Resource Management and Workplace Change (May 1995) p. 27

Now that we are in a better position to see how the 'soft' rhetoric of HRM has translated into practice, the EPAC table also presents a useful analytical framework within which to examine how agency heads have gone about settling their contracts with employees and aligning their human resources towards delivering the government's priority outcomes. We will leave the 'psychological contract' for last and begin with the 'locus of control'.

Locus of control

Devolution of the industrial framework for public service employment was meant to focus employees' attention on the government's goals for their agency and their own roles in enabling the agency to reach those goals. It localised power, making the agency head an employer and creating a direct line of sight between the manager and the managed. It was part of a broader system involving organisational performance targets and individual performance management and assessment that was intended to increase productivity and responsiveness.

In practice, however, APS agency heads have never had all of the powers of a private sector employer over their human resources. They are in fact 'responsible for ensuring that all of their agency agreements are consistent with the ... policy requirements' articulated by DEWR, requirements which in turn 'promote the Government's interests as the ultimate employer of APS employees'.[13] Before the *WorkChoices* amendments, DEWR's policy parameters for agreement making in the APS focused on the Government's interests in shifting the locus of control to exclude third parties from the workplace and in supporting individualised bargaining. They recommended:

- fostering more direct relations between agencies and their employees;
- protecting freedom of association;
- providing scope for comprehensive AWAs to be made with staff; and
- displacing existing agreements and, wherever possible, awards.[14]

DEWR would vet all agency agreements and where it identified deficiencies from the point of view of the Government's interests, agency heads were required to draw those concerns to the attention of their minister when seeking ministerial approval of any agreements they may have reached. As early as 1998 it had been observed that 'the current watchdog role of the Department of Workplace Relations and Small Business (DWR&SB) appears to be a highly interventionist one that is obviously attempting to ensure high degrees of procedural, if not substantive, uniformity across all federal government employment'.[15] In theory, the DEWR parameters call for a shift in the locus of control from outside to inside the workplace. In practice, they represent yet another of the 'brace of instruments for working the system strategically and at several levels' described in Chapter 4, which have the effect of asserting vertical political control over the operations of devolved agencies.

From an HRM perspective, this leaves the locus of control for human resources vexed. The model calls for control to be established by management and internalised by employees. In fact, employees are presented with a compliance-based framework based on 'the Government's interests as the ultimate employer' transmitted to them through the agency head in the shape of an individual or collective agreement. The agency head's interests (as the less-than-ultimate employer) are well down the pecking order, after the Minister for Employment and Workplace Relations (also, usually, the Minister Assisting the Prime Minister for the Public Service), the Secretary and relevant staff of DEWR, and the agency head's own minister. It would appear that some things just cannot be devolved, and that as a consequence '[t]o some extent a command and control process has been reinvented but in a very new guise, one in which employees are expected to take control of their work and achieve outcomes, but what is achieved and how it is achieved is centrally determined and structurally imposed'.[16] Employees are well aware of these arrangements and know also that when terms and conditions of employment are at issue the devolved framework applies only as long as it is consistent with a centralised locus of control.

Employment relations

While key vertical controls persist in the employment framework, much of the service-wide 'connective tissue' has been removed, including 'the concept of public office, common conditions of employment and the 'special' labour market arrangements that existed for the APS.'[17] Before devolution, the public service had been characterised by common job classifications and transferable terms and conditions of employment presided over by the old Public Service Board. These, in turn, were underpinned by a highly unionised environment, an industrial determination (later award) and some generally applied industrial legislation (such as that relating to superannuation and maternity leave). From an agency point of view, employment relations were pluralist, that is, they were based on the view that employer and employee interests would not always coincide and, therefore, there was a legitimate role for mechanisms such as the Public Service Arbitrator (later the Australian Industrial Relations Commission) and union consultative forums to prevent and resolve disputes.

In 1986, the Public Service Legislation—Streamlining Act 1986, as its title suggests, streamlined appointment, promotion and redundancy procedures, giving public service managers increased control over process issues associated with staffing matters by reducing or eliminating avenues of review. The legislation had been developed without union consultation (and with minimal departmental participation, other than through the Cabinet processes), and when consultation did occur, it was undertaken essentially on the basis that the reforms, which had then been approved by the Government, were not negotiable in relation to their general tenor and key content. The following year awards were restructured and classifications simplified from over 100 to 8, enabling employees to undertake a wider range of tasks at their classification level. It meant, among other things, that employees would be expected to undertake routine work such as photocopying, filing and keying in final drafts of documents in addition to their substantive tasks, and that, over time, a number of lower-level positions would no longer be required. This was a matter of industrial and not legislative reform, and accordingly the Labor Government proceeded along the lines it was recommending to other sectors undergoing award restructuring.[18] Departments were required to establish joint union/management committees which in turn were involved in examining improvements to work organisation made possible by the intersection of award restructuring, simplified classifications and information technology. The Management Advisory Board (MAB) reported that 'experience with a co-operative rather than an adversarial approach to industrial relations has paid off ... (and) ... union organisations can positively contribute to the outcome of any organisational change initiative'.[19]

In December 1992, the scope for workplace change in agencies was broadened when, following the introduction of the *Enterprise Bargaining Principle*, a framework agreement was reached that allowed for service-wide pay increases to be linked to service-wide productivity initiatives while at the same time providing for agency-based increases to be linked to agency-level initiatives. Again, the Government saw the necessity of using its own workforce as an exemplar of how productivity gains could be made, particularly in the service sector. Many public servants felt that because of their budget-dependency, all they had to trade off for wage increases under enterprise bargaining was, effectively, the jobs of other public servants. Nevertheless, enterprise bargaining was as much part of the broader union agenda as it was part of the broader Government agenda, and the public sector unions had little choice but to make the best of it, as the President of the ACT Branch of the Community and Public Sector Union (CPSU) during the period is reported to have admitted:

> The acceptance of agency bargaining was a pragmatic choice made by the union in the belief that the government would not be shifted from its determination to impose it on its employees. She noted that the framework agreement for the APS had only been accepted by the membership after 'very and [sic] strong and bitter debate'. There was a lingering 'dislike of agency bargaining from a theoretical and practical points of view'. Nevertheless, the system provided an opportunity for the union to promote its long standing policies on such issues as child care and part time work.[20]

Following the passage of the Industrial Relations Reform Act 1993, agency-specific agreement making accelerated. The 1994 *Enterprise Bargaining Report* found that 24 agreements covering 33 agencies had been certified under the APS framework agreement, covering 55 per cent of employees and bringing to 73 per cent the number of employees covered by agency agreements.[21]

With the change of Government in March 1996, and the introduction of the *Workplace Relations Bill*, bargaining was further decentralised. Framework agreements were no longer available. Agency heads were always able, subject to the DEWR parameters, to develop their own remuneration policies, negotiate their own rates of pay, broadband agency classifications, and to seek through negotiation to establish their preferred form of industrial instrument. These administrative changes were reinforced through the Public Service Act.[22] The APS award became a minimum rates award, increasing the dependence of public servants on agency agreements to maintain or improve their existing rates of pay.

Like the previous Labor Government, the new Coalition Government used its position as employer to position the APS as an operational model of its industrial policy.[23] Public servants were advised early on that 'this Government starts from a fundamental proposition: namely that the industrial and staffing arrangements for the public service should be essentially the same as those of the private sector'.[24] While these arrangements were nominally neutral about freedom of association, the Government as employer did not favour union involvement in any of its workplaces. Employees were advised by the minister that they had been 'victims of workplace structures, systems and cultures which seek to control through regulation rather than through trust'[25] and that accordingly they 'should have an opportunity to benefit from a more direct relationship with their employers rather than be managed through rules, regulations and third party relationships'.[26] People formerly known as union officials became union 'bosses'[27] and unions became 'third parties'. Public servants were instructed that in future the process of settling workplace agreements was to be called 'agreement making', rather than 'bargaining' or 'negotiating', in order to convey a community of interests between employer and employee.

At the same time, consistent with the DEWR parameters, support was being offered to those employees choosing to enter into more direct relationships with their employers. Employees were advised by the Minister Assisting the Prime Minister for the Public Service, Peter Reith, that (whether or not they were aware of it) 'in particular they want more direct relationships with their employers'.[28] Peter Reith's successor, David Kemp, translated:

> The *Workplace Relations Act* has been significant in recasting the role of unions in the public sector workplace. It has removed their privileged position and replaced it with one that better reflects members' preferences and ensures more responsible behaviour. Meanwhile, the Government is strongly pressing Agency Heads to actively pursue agency level agreements with their staff to advance the Government's reform agenda.[29]

Following the passage of the Workplace Relations Act 1996, agencies were advised of the Government's decision that the payroll deduction of union dues should be contingent on individual employees in Australian Government employment confirming each year that in fact they did not want more direct relations with their employers but rather wished to continue to have union dues deducted from their pay. Not surprisingly, some employees discontinued their union membership; others took union advice and had their dues deducted from their bank accounts rather than be obliged to signal their continued union membership to a less than enthusiastic employer. Kemp was clearly gratified:

> In the event almost 40% of staff using this payroll deduction facility opted to have the deduction cease. It is clear that very large numbers of public servants, dissatisfied with the representation provided by the CPSU and other public sector unions, voted with their feet. They left the unions.[30]

Agency heads and managers were put on notice that providing opportunities for more direct relations would 'be a key responsibility of agencies and a major test of leadership'.[31] By June 2004, the parameters were advising that consistent with the Government's legislation uninvited 'third parties' would find that their access to workplaces had been constrained.[32]

The Howard Government's clear preferences regarding the state of unionism in their workplaces had the effect of foregrounding the either/or argument at the more doctrinaire end of 'soft' HRM. The rhetoric assumed that, in the absence of third parties, employment relations would be unitarist rather than pluralist, meaning that there would be 'one set of objectives common to all members of an enterprise ... usually defined in terms of the goals of senior executives'. Organisational goals cascaded down from the top to employees, who were encouraged to enter into direct relations with their senior management consistent with the minister's vision for the APS of the future. For most employees, 'direct relations' meant being offered non-union collective agreements by the agency head; for more senior employees, it meant individual contracts.[33] For employers, it meant increasing employee dependence on managerial prerogative—referred to in 'soft' HRM language as 'building a culture based on trust'—and increasing the role of managerial prerogative in workplace agreements as well as in overall agency management practices.

One of the few analyses of the embedding of HRM principles in agencies is in a study of the Australian Taxation Office (ATO) conducted by Anderson, Griffin and Teicher between 1999 and 2002. By that time cultural change and the institutional arrangements required to support it were sufficiently mature to show the initial impact of HRM principles. The researchers found that although agency agreements had been formalised, the major policy defining the employment relationship at the ATO was its *People Strategy*: 'an HRM strategy that defines the employment relationship in terms of desired values and behaviours [and] ... seeks to achieve a cultural shift from a dependent workforce with an entitlement culture and requiring close supervision, to a self-managed workforce that exhibits flexibility and responds to continuous change within a performance culture'.[34] Consistent with the progressive management of that cultural shift, the Senior Executive Service were on individual contracts and executive level 2 employees were on a non-union collective agreement, while staff at lower classification levels remained on union-negotiated collective agreements. Overall, the authors concluded:

> There is some evidence of movement toward a managerially controlled employment relationship. Union representation and the degree to which staff are able to participate in decision-making have declined considerably. Decision-making has been centralised to senior managers, client responsive behaviours have been encouraged, performance

management has been initiated and temporary employees engaged to fulfil organisational requirements. Undoubtedly, the employment relation has moved from traditional industrial relations toward direct workplace relations.[35]

While APS human resource practices in agencies continued their nominal progress toward a unitarist, individual, high-trust model of employment relations, employees themselves did not find the transition so seamless. Apparently they were not all convinced that they really did want more direct relationships with their employers, or that the outcome of such relationships had always justified their trust: over time, numbers of non-union agency agreements in the APS fell. According to the Public Service Commissioner's *State of the Service* reports, the percentage of agency agreements made with unions under section 170LJ of the *Workplace Relations Act 1997* grew from 55 per cent in 1999 to almost 70 per cent in 2005,[36] including DEWR's own union agreement, made in that year after a considerable and high-profile struggle. For its part, DEWR's Secretary, Peter Boxall, sought to institute direct, high-trust relationships with his employees by making individual agreements compulsory for all promotions and for staff seeking to join the public service through that agency.[37]

After 2005, the *WorkChoices* legislation greatly strengthened secretaries' bargaining positions and their capacities to 'promote the Government's interests as the ultimate employer of APS employees'. By the time that legislation had been passed:

- agency heads had the power to dismiss any employees because of an operational requirement, or for reasons that include that ground;
- both union access to workplaces and industrial action had been further constrained,[38] decreasing employee access to protected industrial action to press any claim for a collective agreements;
- a range of matters had become 'prohibited content' for workplace agreements including those that dealt with: '… allowing for industrial action during the life of the agreement; deductions from an employee's pay or wages for union membership subscriptions … providing for paid leave to attend union training or union meetings; union bargaining fees; providing unions with information about employees bound by the agreement; … union right of entry; encouraging or discouraging union membership … mandating union involvement in dispute resolution';[39] and
- individual contracts could be required of anyone wishing to accept a promotion or transfer.

Furthermore, agency heads had the power at any time after the nominal expiry date of an agreement made under the *WorkChoices* framework to unilaterally terminate that agreement so that employees would fall back onto the new 'fair pay standard' drawing on old award classification rates as adjusted from time to time by the Fair Pay Commission.

Table 4 shows what this would have meant, on average, if it were to apply to APS employees based on 2004 APS award rates, and their actual rates of pay under agreements current as at 31 December 2005. Executive-level staff who had their individual or collective agreements terminated could lose nearly half of their annual income (and a number of conditions). The 'fair pay standard' would become the new benchmark for their next 'agreement'. Employers could choose not to settle a new collective agreement and leave employees on the 'fair pay standard' indefinitely, or until they were able to jump the new hurdles required to access protected industrial action, or until they accepted individual agreements.

Table 4: 2005 Non-SES Base salaries and Award Minimum Classification Rates

Classification	Base Salary	APS award minimum classification rates
Graduate	$41,000	$29,276
APS 1	$33,935	$27,099
APS 2	$39,028	$29,798
APS 3	$43,923	$32,791
APS 4	$48,944	$35,699
APS 5	$53,931	$38,964
APS 6	$62,775	$41,384
EL 1	$77,767	$47,539
EL 2	$96,063	$51,973

Sources: 2005 APS Remuneration Survey (current as at 31 Dec. 2005) at http://www.workplace.gov.au/workplace/Organisation/Government/Federal/Reports/2005APSRemunerationSurvey.htm, viewed 24 June 2006; Australian Public Service Award 1998 (AW766579) (varied to 16 Dec. 2004 (variation PR954310)) at http://www.wagenet.gov.au/WageNet/Search/View.asp?docid=259460&query=%28PUBLIC+SERVICE+AWARD+1998%29&quickview=Y&page=0#dochit1

The *2005–06 State of the Service Report* also indicated that the Public Service Act had been subject to a review that was likely to reinforce the *WorkChoices* changes listed above by 'liberalising non-ongoing arrangements'—by which was meant increasing the scope to employ non-permanent staff and to decline to convert them to permanent after a set period of employment. According to the report, this was one of the changes identified as worthy of consideration to ensure that the Act 'meets the future needs of agencies'.[40] Ongoing employment has traditionally been associated with a capacity for apolitical professionalism—which in turn is one of those Westminster-based values described in Chapter 1 as having a less than seamless intersection with the NPM-based APS Values. Other Westminster-based values may also have been on the table, including 'refining the [APS] values and Code of Conduct', although further information was deferred until after the 2007 election.[41]

Following that election, some of the powers made available to employers under *WorkChoices* will be rolled back. It was unlikely that APS employers would ever have deployed them in a wholesale way under the previous Government, although *WorkChoices* enhanced their capacity to target individuals who were no longer wanted in the workplace. But the fact remains that everyone would have known that the powers available under *WorkChoices* would have been there if they were wanted. It remains to be seen what will happen to the overall emphasis on management prerogative that has been strengthening progressively since the introduction of HRM principles into public service workplaces.

Organising principles

While organisational goals were meant to cascade down the direct line between employers and employees, as discussed in Chapter 3, 'soft' HRM expected day-to-day work to be organised from the 'bottom up'. 'Soft' HRM theorists envisaged committed, highly skilled employees with a capacity for teamwork and the flexibility to work out what needed to be done and to organise themselves to do it as well as it could be done—in return for ongoing high levels of job security, remuneration and skills investment. The new vision set out by the Secretary of the Department of the Prime Minister and Cabinet in 2005, was as follows:

> To the casual observer, walking around an office, it will be increasingly difficult to distinguish who is a public servant. Within departments there will be full-time, part-time and casual public servants. They will work with, and often sit alongside, contract providers and short-term consultants. They will be bound together by the work they do, not the conditions under which they are employed. The Australian Public Service, in the American language, will be 'a blended, multi-dimensional workforce'.[42]

It may be that the public servants concerned would find it almost as difficult as casual observers to distinguish who was or was not a public servant. This is devolution taken to extremes, resulting in a workplace without a common history or culture, supporting only the most impersonal and operational of interactions. Its organising principle is neither organic nor bottom up, as envisaged by 'soft' HRM, but top down like 'hard' HRM, reliant to a significant extent on management-initiated contracts with casuals, contractors and consultants. Any differences between ongoing staff and the rest would not, apparently, reflect any differences in the nature of 'the work they do'. This is not where 'soft' HRM was meant to be taking the APS—towards the Minister's 1996 vision of 'a quality job within a learning organisation, in which their creativity is actively sought [and they] have more autonomy over their work practices'.[43] Did something happen, or was it always just spin?

Policy goals

Remember that reforms conducted in the name of NPM varied from country to country and that in Australia, as elsewhere, 'the reform program shifted emphases according to political and administrative circumstances'.[44] A critical political circumstance relevant to HRM reforms in the public service was the Government's ongoing industrial agenda. On this, DEWR's guidance was very explicit:

> The government expects that APS agencies will lead the way in utilising the flexibilities and opportunities for reform available under the *Workplace Relations Act 1996* (*WR Act*). The Policy Parameters allow APS agencies the flexibility to develop agreements that are tailored to their particular needs and circumstances and are exemplars of the government's workplace reforms.[45]

The Government presented its industrial agenda to its employees in the same way that it presented that agenda to the workforce generally: as a matter of improving productivity by fostering direct relations between employees and employers that would have the effect of aligning their interests. What the Government delivered in the APS as elsewhere was an increase in employer control that would facilitate such alignment by eliminating 'third parties' (such as unions and industrial tribunals) from the workplace and enhancing the flexibility with which workplace relations could be conducted. As the ATO case study considered above suggests, this program had the effect of ratcheting up management prerogative and the systems (considered in Chapters 3 and 4) that make its presence felt. Australian research into private sector management has shown that the Australian experience has not varied significantly from that in the UK: in general, as an organisation's focus shifts from eliciting the commitment of workers to gaining control over them, 'soft' HRM practice hardens, although the rhetoric of 'soft' HRM tends to remain in place to ease the transition.[46] In addition to formal agreements and performance management arrangements, this emphasis can also be seen in the APS in the conduct of consultation processes more broadly. Evidence in the *2004–05 State of the Service Report* suggests that while managerial prerogative and management systems were being strengthened, the predicted cultural change was lagging behind:

> Time series data suggests that there has been a slight downward trend in employee data in a number of indicators that cluster around workplace relationships. Compared to 2003–04, public servants were somewhat less likely to feel that merit processes have been applied; less satisfied with the consultative mechanisms in their workplaces; less satisfied with their overall say in decisions that impacted on their work; and less likely to agree with most of the effectiveness indicators describing the impact of their agency's performance pay system.

...[In particular] this year employees reported being significantly less satisfied that the meetings they attended provided a forum in which to contribute their views on issues that impact on their work and with the overall say they have in decisions impacting on their work.[47]

The Government 'started from a fundamental proposition: namely that the industrial and staffing arrangements for the public service should be essentially the same as those of the private sector',[48] and, like the private sector, it moved on to the (re)assertion of 'management authority'. This involved a change in the psychological contract between employees, their employers, and, in the case of public servants, their 'ultimate employer', the Government.[49]

The psychological contract

The psychological contract has generated a significant literature. It been defined by Rousseau as the individual employee's subjective perceptions of the obligations binding both the employee and the employer.[50] Because it is subjective, it takes in matters outside a conventional formal contract, such as fair dealing, expectations of transparency, loyalty, and support in ethical decision making. The psychological contract 'both fills the perceptual gaps in the employment relationship and shapes day-to-day employee behaviour in ways that cannot necessarily be discerned from a written contract'.[51] Rousseau identifies a number of possible psychological contracts between employees and employers lying along a continuum, from 'relational contracts' at one end to 'transactional contracts' at the other. 'Relational' contracts look very like those governing employee expectations in a 'soft' HRM workplace; transactional contracts', on the other hand, look very like those governing employee expectations at 'hard' HRM workplaces. According to O'Donnell and Shields, the psychological contract for APS employment has been moving along the continuum away from relational and toward transactional contracts and 'hard' HRM since the early 1990s:

> Relational contracts are long-term, entailing considerable investment by both parties in training and development and a high degree of mutual interdependence, and involve rewards that are not explicitly performance contingent. Transactional contracts, by contrast, focus on short-term and monetised exchange, where rewards are explicitly tied to individual performance and low membership commitment by the employee (Rousseau and Ho 2000, 297-304). In general terms, the changes experienced by employees in the federal public sector since the early 1990s can be said to have involved a shift from a relational to a transactional employment regime.[52]

How this distinction applied in practice in the APS was examined in a study by O'Donnell and Shields of the operation of performance management in the

Departments of Finance and Administration (Finance) and Defence drawing on data gathered between 1998 and 2001. The study found that Defence—an atypical organisation in this respect—declined to move to transactional performance contracts with employees, opting instead, in the words of the then Secretary of the Department, Allan Hawke, to stay with a relational contract 'based on building performance through feedback and a developmental focus—without scores and ratings'.[53] He based this decision on the view that where the psychological contract is focused around short-term and monetised exchange, the process 'can lead to distorted results and raise issues of equity, ratings moderation and forced distributions'.[54]

The Department of Finance and Administration, in contrast, was characteristic of the growing majority of agencies that pursued transactional performance contracts.[55] In 2001, after several years without any access to collective bargaining, 62 per cent of its employees were already on individual AWAs and employees were being further motivated through an individual performance agreement and assessment system. While Finance's system called for a 'solid contribution to organisational objectives', the O'Donnell and Shields study found that, overall, it was weighted to reward certain 'behaviours' rather than particular outputs, effectively maximising management discretion over winners and losers. The behaviours sought by agency senior leadership were those defined by the senior leadership as characterising senior leadership, namely 'expertise in the field, creativity, will to win, ability to learn and people management'. Clearly the aim of the system was to align employee behaviour to the behaviour of their senior managers. Not surprisingly, individual outcomes—as judged by senior leadership—were believed by many individuals to be biased and subjective and, according to O'Donnell and Shields, resulted in considerable cynicism about the objectivity of the scheme.[56]

However, for the truly cynical, biased schemes are at least as effective in aligning employee behaviour to implicit management requirements as transparent schemes are in aligning employee behaviour to explicit requirements:

> Anthony (1990) argues that when a small senior management group attempts to superimpose a new set of espoused values upon subordinates that are discordant with the latter's sense of reality, the result may be that they act out the surface signals of the 'new culture' but cynically and without internalisation. Existing bureaucratic structures (hierarchy, appraisal, promotion ladders) ensure that negative, critical, even whistleblowing feedback is unlikely to occur. On the contrary, the skilled performance enacted by employees may confirm senior management in its view that the new culture has taken ...[57]

Whether compliance reflects conviction or cynicism, the awarding of a single rating point focuses employee attention at the same time that it focuses employer control. In the event, Peter Boxall, the then Secretary of Finance, was given by Government the management of DEWR and with it responsibility for policing all agencies' bargaining outcomes.

What does responsiveness mean in this framework? Is its meaning set through the broad APS Values in the *Public Service Act*, a narrow transactional performance contract with senior management, or 'the interests of the Government' as what DEWR calls the 'ultimate employer'? When these coincide, there is of course no issue. But if, *in practice*, they do not, transactional contracts will invite attention to managerial authority before service-wide ethos. If it is to the agency head that employees look, then responsiveness will be framed in terms of whatever employees think the senior management wants; if it is the 'ultimate employer', then responsiveness may be to whatever the employees think the Government wants.

The Community and Public Sector Union has repeatedly raised concerns about politicisation and about public servants who feel compromised and concerned about their roles and responsibilities in an increasingly politicised workplace. Of course the union as a third party does not have organisational alignment at heart; but we know directly from employees that nearly a third of them have not been prompted by their experience to agree that their senior management acts in accordance with the APS Values.[58] Many of them were also aware (following Senate consideration of 'A Certain Maritime Incident' and 'Staff Employed under the *Members of Parliament (Staff) Act 1984 (MoP(S) Act)*') that the then Government had no enthusiasm for ministerial advisers being bound by a code of conduct embodying a set of values of its own. And yet the system—not the law but the system—has focused them on the kind of responsiveness developed through alignment with both of these groups: senior management, and 'ultimate employers' and their advisers.

There are other problems with transactional contracts. Because they emphasise vertical relations, they tend to weaken attention outward, to the public. In effect they induce a performance orientation like that created at the then DIMIA, or at the ATO: '"do our work, do it well and pass back to the other business lines what is theirs, because we're not funded for it and all it does is make our performance look bad"'.[59] The problem is that there has been a common view among agency heads (and the ultimate employer) that:

> ... the Australian community now expects high quality, seamless, accessible and responsive service delivery that is tailored to individual needs, and where outcomes are transparent. They also expect a greater say in the development of policies and programmes.[60]

To do this, the public service needs employees who are licensed to take account of changing circumstances and to innovate, consistent with the rhetoric of 'soft'

HRM. Nevertheless, in 2005–06, 59 per cent of APS employees did not agree that their agency involved them in decisions about their work.[61] As early as 2002, the Prime Minister advised that his Government had 'put the partnership between government and the community at the heart of our policy making.'[62] Three and a half years later, 43 per cent of employees did not agree that their agency encouraged the public to participate in shaping and administering policy.[63] And, as will be seen in the next chapter, outsourced service deliverers also report themselves to be pretty firmly cast in the role of rowers and not steerers.

In theory, the government as employer, regardless of the party in power, needs to establish genuinely mutual relationships with the people with whom it works inside and outside the APS itself. This theory is publicly endorsed by the heads of government as well as heads of the public service and key agencies.[64] And yet, while government calls for exchange, creativity and innovation, it has wanted these to occur within a strictly controlled and increasingly asymmetrical power relationship based on transactional contracts. This issue is explored further in the next chapter.

ENDNOTES

[1] See, for example, Andrew Podger, 'What Really Happens: Department Secretary Appointments, Contracts and Performance Pay in the Australian Public Service', *Australian Journal of Public Administration* 66(2),(2007), and 'Looking Upwards and Downwards: Key Issues and Suggestions for Managing Board/Minister/Departmental Relations', University of Canberra Conference on Governance, Mar. 2006, pp.10ff.

[2] See Public Service Commissioner, *2003–04 State of the Service Report* (Canberra, 2004), Appendix 4, Jurisdictions' Arrangements for the Appointment of Secretaries, Chief Executives and Senior Executives.

[3] Public Service Commissioner, *2004–05 State of the Service Report* (Canberra, 2005), 98.

[4] Karen Legge, *Human Resource Management: Rhetorics and Realities* (Macmillan: London 1995), 247.

[5] See Jim Kitay and Russell Lansbury, 'Human Resource Management and Industrial Relations in an Era of Global Markets: Australian and International Trends', *Human Resource Management and Workplace Change*, Proceedings of an Economic Planning Advisory Commission roundtable, 6 Feb. 1995, pp. 31–2.

[6] See Legge, *Human Resource Management*, Ch. 9.

[7] Peter Reith, Public Service Bill 1997, Second Reading Speech, 30 June 1997, at http://www.apsc.gov.au/circulars/billadvice972.htm, viewed 24 Feb. 2008.

[8] See Kitay and Lansbury, 'Human Resource Management and Industrial Relations', 34.

[9] Catherine Truss, Lynda Gratton, Veronica Hope-Hailey, Patrick McGovern and Philip Stiles, 'Soft and Hard Models of Human Resource Management: A Reappraisal', *Journal of Management Studies* 34(1) (1997) 70.

[10] Legge, *Human Resource Management*, Ch. 8.

[11] Ibid. 330.

[12] Kitay and Lansbury, 'Human Resource Management and Industrial Relations', 36.

[13] See Department of Employment and Workplace Relations, 'APS—Supporting Guidance for the Workplace Relations Policy Parameters for Agreement Making in the Australian Public Service' (June 2004), 4.

[14] Department of Employment and Workplace Relations, 'APS—Workplace Relations Policy Parameters for Agreement Making in the Australian Public Service' (Dec. 2003).

[15] See Duncan Macdonald, 'Public Sector Industrial Relations under the Howard Government', *Labour and Industry* 9(2) (Dec. 1998), 43–59.

[16] Eve Anderson, Gerard Griffin and Julien Teicher, 'From Industrial Relations to Workplace Relations in the Australian Tax Office: An Incomplete but Strategic Transition', *Journal of Industrial Relations* 47(3) (Sept. 2005), 350.

[17] Tony Blunn, 'Public Service values in the New Millennium', *Canberra Bulletin of Public Administration* no 107 (Mar. 2003), 30.

[18] See John O'Brien, 'Workplace Productivity Bargaining in the Australian Public Sector', in Jenny Stewart (ed.), *From Hawke to Keating: Australian Commonwealth Administration 1990–1993* (Canberra, n.d.), 90.

[19] Management Advisory Board/Management Improvement Advisory Committee, *The Australian Public Service Reformed: An Evaluation of a Decade of Management Reform* (Task Force on Management Improvement: Canberra, 1992), 150.

[20] John O'Brien, 'Employment Relations and Agency Bargaining in the Australian Public Service, 1993–1996', in Gwynneth Singleton (ed.), *The Second Keating Government: Australian Commonwealth Administration 1993–1996* (Canberra, 1997), 178.

[21] Department of Industrial Relations, *1994 Annual Report Enterprise Bargaining in Australia: Developments under the Industrial Relations Reform Act* (AGPS: Canberra, 1995), 29.

[22] The Public Service Act and Parliamentary Service Act 1999 made provision for departmental secretaries to enter into collective and/or individual employment contracts and agreements.

[23] See Department of Employment and Workplace Relations, 'APS—Workplace Relations Policy Parameters for Agreement Making in the Australian Public Service' (Dec. 2003) on the need to 'lead the way.'

[24] Peter Reith, *Towards a Best Practice Australian Public Service: Discussion Paper Issued by the Minister for Industrial Relations and the Minister Assisting the Prime Minister for the Public Service* (Canberra, 1996), 5.

[25] Ibid. 2.

[26] Ibid. p. viii.

[27] See, for a characteristic example, Coalition arguments cited in the Parliamentary Library's *Workplace Relations Amendment (Secret Ballots for Protected Action) Bill 2000, Bills Digest No. 18 2000–01*, at http://www.aph.gov.au/library/pubs/bd/2000-01/01BD018.htm, viewed 24 July 2006.

[28] Reith, *Towards a Best Practice Australian Public Service*, 2.

[29] David Kemp MP, 'Reforming the Public Service to Meet the Global Challenge', address to the Committee for Economic Development of Australia, Melbourne, 25 Feb. 1998, at http://www.apsc.gov.au/publications98/apsreformminister.htm, viewed 15 Aug. 2007.

[30] Ibid.

[31] Reith, *Towards a Best Practice Australian Public Service*, p. viii.

[32] See Department of Employment and Workplace Relations, 'APS—Supporting Guidance for the Workplace Relations Policy Parameters for Agreement Making in the Australian Public Service' (June 2004), 12: 'The *WR Act* makes entry conditional on union representatives holding a permit issued by the Industrial Registrar and providing at least 24 hours notice to the employer (verbal notice is sufficient under the *WR Act*). It is important that agencies ensure that union representatives observe the provisions of the *WR Act*. Given the provisions of the *WR Act*, there is no need for agencies to include right of entry provisions in their agreements, nor would it be appropriate for enhanced right of entry arrangements to be established through agreements.'

[33] David Kemp, 'Agreement Making and Reforms in the APS', address to 'Agreement making and achieving corporate goals', Canberra, 26 Mar. 1998, Section on 'Achievements under the Workplace Relations Act.'

[34] Anderson et al., 'From Industrial Relations to Workplace Relations', 342–3.

[35] Ibid. 349.

[36] See the *2001–02 State of the Service Report*, Ch. 4, at http://www.apsc.gov.au/stateoftheservice/2002/chapter04.htm, viewed 4 Sept. 2006; and *2004–05 State of the Service Report*, 97.

[37] Stephen Smith, Shadow Minister for Industry, Infrastructure and Industrial Relations, media release: 'Andrews Caught Red-handed Forcing Staff onto Contracts', 21 June 2005.

[38] Kevin Andrews, media release, 9 Oct. 2005: 'The Australian Government recognises that abuse of right of entry has the potential to cause disruption and damage at the workplace and therefore changes will be made that: tighten the requirements for the granting of an entry permit, including the introduction

of a "fit and proper persons" test; make it clear there is no right of entry for discussion purposes where all the employees are on AWAs; only allow entry to investigate a breach of an AWA if the employee party to the AWA provides written consent; require a union official to provide particulars of a breach he or she is proposing to enter to investigate to the employer; confirm a union official can only access the records of union members when investigating a breach, unless an order is made by the AIRC that non-member records can be investigated; require a union official to comply with a reasonable request by an employer that the meeting or interview should be conducted in a particular room or areas of the premises and that a specified route should be taken to that venue; and allow right of entry for Occupational Health and Safety (OHS) purposes under state legislation where the union official has a federal right of entry permit and the official has complied with all requirements of the relevant state OHS legislation.' Available at http://www.apsc.gov.au/publications98/apsreformminister.htm.

39 Department of Employment and Workplace Relations, 'APS—Supporting Guidance for the Workplace Relations Policy Parameters for Agreement Making in the Australian Public Service' (Apr. 2006), 13, at http://www.workplace.gov.au/NR/rdonlyres/68451B6C-5FBD-4F53-B705-0A8B3C623031/0/SupportingGuidanceGovernmentsPolicyParametersApril2006.pdf, viewed 24 June 2006.

40 Public Service Commissioner, *2005–06 State of the Service Report*, 56.

41 Ibid.

42 Peter Shergold, 'The Australian Public Service in 2035: Back to the Future', speech to CPA Annual Conference, Melbourne, 18 May 2005, at http://www.pmc.gov.au/speeches/shergold/aps_2035_back_to_the_future_2005-05-18.cfm, viewed 23 June 2006.

43 Reith, *Towards a Best Practice Australian Public Service*, 22.

44 Glyn Davis and R. A. W. Rhodes, 'From Hierarchy to Contracts and Back Again: Reforming the Australian Public Service', in Michael Keating, John Wanna and Patrick Weller (eds), *Institutions on the Edge? Capacity for Governance* (Allen and Unwin: Sydney, 2000), 76ff.

45 Department of Employment and Workplace Relations, 'APS—Supporting Guidance for the Workplace Relations Policy Parameters for Agreement Making in the Australian Public Service' (June 2004), 4.

46 Carol Gill, 'Use of Hard and Soft Models of HRM to Illustrate the Gap between Rhetoric and Reality in Workforce Management', RMIT School of Management Working Paper no. 99/13 (Nov. 1999), 41–2.

47 Public Service Commissioner, *2004–05 State of the Service Report*, 5, 178. Note that employee satisfaction in their overall say returned to 2003 levels in 2006 while responses relating to performance pay were somewhat more positive than those in 2005. See Australian Public Service Commission, *2005–06 State of the Service Employee Survey Results*, 21, question 27, and 50, question 70.

48 Reith, *Towards a Best Practice Australian Public Service*, 5, cited above.

49 For an extended discussion, see M. O'Donnell and J. Shields, 'Performance Management and the Psychological Contract in the Australian Federal Public Sector', *Journal of Industrial Relations* 44(3) (2002), 435–57.

50 Denise Marie-Therese Rousseau, 'The "Problem" of the Psychological Contract Considered', *Journal of Organisational Behavior* 19 (1998), 665–6.

51 O'Donnell and Shields, 'Performance Management and the Psychological Contract', 439.

52 Ibid. 440.

53 Allan Hawke, then Secretary of Defence, quoted ibid. 445.

54 Ibid.

55 According to the Department of Employment, Workplace Relations and Small Business, *APS non-SES Remuneration Survey* of October 2001 and the 14 June 2002 *APS SES Remuneration Survey*, 55% of agencies surveyed indicated their non-SES employees were eligible to participate in performance payment plans and 85% of agencies provided pay incentives to their senior executives. See http://www.workplace.gov.au/workplace/Organisation/Government/Federal/Reports/OtherAPSRemunerationSurveys.htm, viewed 15 July 2007.

56 O'Donnell and Shields, 'Performance Management and the Psychological Contract', 446–9.

57 Legge, *Human Resource Management*, 200.

58 Agreement varied between 63% in 2003 and 73% in 2006. See Australian Public Service Commission, *2005–06 State of the Service Employee Survey Results*, 4.

59 Anderson et al., 'From Industrial Relations to Workplace Relations', 345.

60 Lynelle Briggs, 'The Australian Public Service: Looking to the Future', Department of Finance and Administration seminar series: Challenging Tomorrow, 24 Mar. 2006, p. 8. Cf Shergold, 'The Australian

Public Service in 2035'; and Management Advisory Committee, *Connecting Government: Whole of Government Responses to Australia's Priority Challenges* (Canberra, 2004), Chs 3 and 6.

[61] See Australian Public Service Commission, *2005–06 State of the Service Employee Survey Results*, 19, question 23.

[62] John Howard, 'Strategic Leadership for Australia: Policy Directions in a Complex World', Nov. 2002, at www.dpmc.gov.au/speeches/pm/leadership/contents.cfm, viewed 4 Sept. 2006

[63] See Australian Public Service Commission, *2005–06 State of the Service Employee Survey Results*, 20, question 23.

[64] See Management Advisory Committee, *Connecting Government*, Ch 6, especially pp. 93ff.

Chapter 6. To market, to market: outsourcing the public service

Outsourcing in Australia has a long history.[1] While governments long had a practice of supporting not-for-profit organisations delivering caring services, the outsourcing of services previously delivered directly by government also began in those areas with clear commercial analogues, as a means of simply substituting private for public provision. Initially this included such services as school bussing and school cleaning and postal and telecommunication services. Outside private health and education services, however, clear commercial analogues for activities in welfare services were not so much in evidence, and 'by definition this rule[d] out [outsourcing of] most human services, given that there were seemingly few if any alternative suppliers in the market'.[2]

In fact, the large-scale outsourcing of more complex and sensitive services was not on the table until the second stage of the public sector reform process broadly associated with NPM. In the late 1980s, the Hawke Government called for an increased focus on regulation and competition consistent with the broader micro-economic reform agenda. This was followed by the mandating of market testing for support functions through the Defence Commercial Support Program, and then the commercialisation of the Department of Administrative Services. In 1995, the agenda was extended to the market provision of services and choice for citizens with the National Competition Policy, although initially the focus there was on state-based services. The preference for competitive contracting for the delivery of Commonwealth services became official policy in the first term of the Howard Government.[3] During its first year, the Minister Assisting the Prime Minister for the Public Service made it clear that, in the Government's view:

> It is no longer appropriate for the APS to have a monopoly. It must prove that it can deliver government services as well as the private or non-profit sectors.[4]

Since the mid-1990s, NPM has taken contracting organisations into areas of government activity characterised by increasing risk, sensitivity and complexity. Where necessary, it has created 'a new, competitive market',[5] such as the Jobs Network, in order to do so. In the process it has turned a significant number of public servants—already on formal performance agreements themselves and increasingly being moved on to individual employment contracts—into contract managers. Thus, while public sector providers were being exhorted to behave more like those in the private and community sectors, the latter were being drawn into market relationships with each other as well as with the government.

Throughout the same period, the public has been learning to base its relations with the goverment sector on market models—to enter into implicit and explicit contracts, and to become clients and consumers of government services. According to the *2004–05 State of the Service* report, the Australian Customs Service has *clients* (p. 64), as does the Department of Veterans Affairs (p. 60); on the other hand, Centrelink has *customers* (p. 63)—6.5 million of them in 2003–4—as does AusIndustry (p. 60). Employees of these and other agencies undertake 'client-focused' training to assist them in meeting their 'client service responsibilities' (p. 65). Many agencies undertake client surveys and collect customer feedback. Customers and clients of the agencies enter into relations with their service providers that are modelled on contracts for services. Some have actual contracts setting out their mutual obligations. The contract model is becoming an organising principle for public life:

> The central motif of the contract has extended beyond organising and managing the public sector to embrace the link between government and citizens (Yeatman 1995, 1996a). What was once a political association now takes on an implied contractual form. Electors become clients, their rights and expectations encapsulated in a 'Citizens Charter' or, in some Australian states, a 'guarantee of service'. This contract binds the state to produce certain levels of services, and specifies penalties for failure to comply. The principal and agent model, in which mutual obligations are spelled out in writing, becomes an organising principle for public life.[6]

The material that follows examines how the transactional contract as an organising principle has been extended beyond public sector employees, blurring the distinction between the public, for-profit and not-for-profit sectors and between citizens and consumers of government services. The intention is to shed further light on how the institutional and cultural boundaries of the APS have been being dismantled, together with what was distinctive about the public service ethos. At same time, the analysis points to the emergence overseas of new models for relations between the public and its servants that could reshape the transactional contract.

Outsourcing in theory

Within the month of its election in 1996, the Coalition Government established a National Commission of Audit to examine aspects of what the Commonwealth government did, how it did it, and the implications of these for its financial position.[7] That Commission reported very quickly—within two months—recommending a more limited role for government, a greater emphasis on effectiveness and efficiency, and the separation of policy formation from program delivery. These recommendations were underpinned by the 'common view,' as the Auditor-General put it, that 'public services would be provided more efficiently and effectively, with greater client satisfaction, in a more market-oriented environment which provided greater flexibility for management decision-making and the discipline of competition.'[8] The 'common view' prevailed (if not many of the Commission of Audit's specific proposals), and two years later, in 1998, the Commonwealth Employment Service (CES) was replaced as a provider of employment services by 'a new, competitive market'[9] to be known as the Jobs Network.[10]

The Jobs Network had even more 'strings to its bow' than the superior efficiency and effectiveness that comes with market competition. The Prime Minister saw the new service delivery model as one of those initiatives 'that go to the values and culture of our society';[11] the then Minister for Employment and Workplace Relations and Minister Assisting the Prime Minister for the Public Service said (wearing both hats) that the model was founded on:

> ... the conviction that community-based agencies are better equipped than bureaucracies to deliver 'pastoral care', avoid treating unemployed people as faces in a queue or numbers in a file, and foster the web of personal engagements which unemployed people have often lost ... The constant lesson of the welfare state is that government agencies can never substitute for the complex human relationships which sustain a social fabric of individuals-in-community.[12]

The initial carve-up of CES services was evenly balanced, with about a third of the market going to each of the government, community and private sectors. Not surprisingly, given the Minister's *a priori* view that '[g]overnment agencies are much better at delivering identical services to whole populations than meeting the needs of individual people,' the government provider was rapidly phased out, and with it one of the most heavily unionised sectors of the APS. By March 2000 the public sector's market share of employment services had fallen from 33 per cent to 8 per cent.[13] By 2003 the figure was 3 per cent.[14]

The outsourcing of service delivery in employment services pursued a purchaser/provider model, with DEWR purchasing employment services from a competitive marketplace while welfare services were purchased from Centrelink by (initially) the Department of Family and Community Services and then DEWR. The efficiency argument underpinning the purchaser/provider model was that that the contractual arrangement itself would force the purchaser to take responsibility for policy implementation by defining the outputs being sought, enabling the provider to focus on responsiveness to the public and value for money more generally.[15] Responsiveness to the public would also be enhanced by competition between providers for jobseeking 'customers', as they came to be called.

Outsourcing in practice

The appeal of the purchaser/provider model was not just the enhancement of service quality that was anticipated,[16] it was also the retention of policy control by the public sector purchaser. The Government had no intention of hiving off its policy decision-making role. In practice, however, the contracts that were meant to settle the distinction between policy direction and service delivery were often unable to do that work reliably, and in some cases had the effect of distorting the services to be delivered—often in much the same way that similar accountability mechanisms had distorted services delivered by the CES. In Jobs Network there were early problems with 'creaming' of easily placed jobseekers (the practice of selectively admitting clients with the best prospects of positive outcomes and avoiding more 'difficult' clients) and recycling of others through short-term placements. Contractual performance indicators favoured measurable outputs (after considerable revision, outcomes measurement for Jobs Network service providers is now based on numbers of jobseekers employed rated against 16 factors including labour market conditions) or measurable inputs (such as the maximum number of minutes per caller that should be spent responding to public phone queries) rather than the service user's experience (for example, how long they had to wait in the queue, whether complex queries were actually resolved or referred on, and the extent to which the service provided actually corresponded to the needs of the person being serviced). In the case of the Jobs Network, contract provisions required providers to build good working relations with their customers while at the same time reporting on them if they failed set activity tests. 'Often there is no scope for agencies to develop their own unique service approach, because the contract is so specific,' complained the founding CEO of The Salvation Army Employment Plus.[17] Organisations began to find that, contrary to the minister's expectations, it was the accountability requirements governing the conduct of government business that led to people being treated as 'as faces in a queue or numbers in a file,' not just some perverse bureaucratic *zeitgeist*:

> Agencies are increasingly asked to deliver a range of pre-determined government services with 'program evaluation' increasingly focussed on issues of contract compliance rather than the effectiveness of programs for those people that they target. Agencies increasingly compete against other agencies for funding, often 'corporatised' agencies with no local connection to the community ... social services run the risk of being treated as commodities. In this context the 'product' becomes more important than the 'people' for whom it was intended.[18]

Problems of a similar nature emerged even more famously with services outsourced by DIMIA. According to Palmer, the detention services contract with GSL read 'purchaser/provider' literally as a "master–slave' relationship, not a partnership'[19] with the result that it:

> ... create[d] a culture where the specified performance measures become, by default, entrenched as maximum standards because the service provider's focus is on ensuring compliance so as to avoid financial sanction. The nature of the activity is created by the contract.[20]

Palmer took the view, already reached by the ANAO[21] and other analysts,[22] that purchaser/provider arrangements for the delivery of complex social services were doomed to fail if they were policed too rigorously, and that there should be increased scope for feedback and innovation between the contracting parties along the lines of a 'cooperative partnership'.

Consistent with this view, second-generation contracting tended to downplay the purchaser/provider dichotomy by placing greater emphasis on instruments and rhetoric along the lines of 'relational contracts', 'cooperative partnerships', 'collaborative partnerships', 'integrated service delivery' or 'integrated governance'. Such terms imply a greater degree of reciprocity between the purchasing agency and the service provider than would be characteristic of the more purely 'procurement' function of purchaser/provider contracts. The rhetoric of cooperative partnerships—as the specimen titles above indicate—is classic *bureaucratese*; all varieties and combinations of sharing are capable of being included under almost as broad a range of headings. A review of the research and practice literature focusing on partnerships in the welfare sector shows a blossoming of guidance material on the design of such partnership arrangements after 1997, with much of the early work examining the practice in Canada and the UK.[23] Despite their various forms, all of these new arrangements were intended to specify, contractually, a kind of interactive space between the parties which could be filled by some or all of: information sharing; the sharing of financial or other support; the sharing of the actual work being undertaken; or the sharing of decision making. Without fully examining individual contractual arrangements (which is not straightforward as they are largely commercial in confidence[24]) it is difficult to know just how much is to be shared by whom, with whom and how often. The Management Advisory Committee advised public servants that the 'nature of the partnership can range from the more traditional purchase of service approaches through to arrangements based on complementary or shared goals'[25] —which covers just about everything.

Thus, while the more intellectually tidy purchaser/provider distinction did not go away, it became subject to the rhetoric of partnership:

> All government contracts may be said to aim at responsiveness to government in the sense that all such contracts are intended to achieve government-determined objectives. In the great majority of cases, this

aim is achieved through careful stipulation of goods and services which the contractor is obliged to deliver rather than through explicit resort to the value of responsiveness as such. However, the value of responsiveness is implicit in contractual terms that require regular consultation between the contractor and government officials and allow for the contractor to take note of changing government priorities. Such clauses, for instance are standard in contracts for information technology and for human resources. All partnership or relational contracts may be said to imply some reliance on the contractor's general willingness to accommodate as yet unstated wishes of the government. However, no contracts appear to explicitly require contractors to exercise the same sensitivity to government directions that are expected of public servants.[26]

While their levels of sensitivity might differ, public servants and service deliverers were intended, in the interests of partnership, to 'share the same goals and vision'[27] and to do so before the work began, because 'pre-existing shared values or initiatives that effectively promote common values are … important for joint working arrangements, particularly given the difficulties of articulating all the values and behavioural standards expected of partners in formal accountability arrangement[s]'.[28] In plain English this means that to become useful partners, non-government providers should ideally share the government's policies as well as its contracts.[29] At the very least they should be able to share its agenda—a word nicely poised between values and policy implementation—and wear the badge of partnership while they do the government's work. Former Prime Minister John Howard certainly advised the Centre for Independent Studies that he saw no distinction between service delivery parameters and the reinforcement of desirable 'social norms and values':

> There are times when governments need to look seriously at policies which might appear paternalistic in the libertarian lecture hall, but which help to reinforce social norms and values that are under assault in various ways.
>
> … These [social policy changes, i.e. the tough on drugs strategy, entrenchment of 'mutual obligation', promotion of 'traditional' approaches to education, the replacement of the Commonwealth Employment Service with a private Jobs Network, a social coalition to tackle youth homelessness, a 'sea change' in Indigenous affairs policy, and the use of the tax system to 'support families with children'] are issues that go to the values and culture of our society, the institutions that support strong values and fundamental questions about the relationship between government and citizens when it comes to individual and civic responsibility.[30]

Can community organisations with views on 'fundamental questions about the relationship between government and citizens' that do not coincide with those of the government deliver its services for it? Can, for example, the Brotherhood of St Laurence implement a system that removes recipients' discretion over how their welfare payments are spent when 'the frontline experience of the Brotherhood of St Laurence points to a number of practical problems with the minister's proposal'?[31] Or can an agency that is delivering employment services for the government provide its own financial support to a client that it has been required to report to Centrelink for failing to meet activity tests? Can these groups make values choices without having made political choices as well? Experience suggests not, as the following story posted on the ABC's website suggests:

> The federal Minister for Human Services, Joe Hockey, has accused the Catholic Church of a political stunt by pulling out of the government's welfare-to-work management program.
>
> Catholic Social Services Australia no longer wants to be part of the program and says it is a harsh system that does not protect the vulnerable.
>
> Mr Hockey says the organisation is walking away from society's most vulnerable.
>
> 'Catholic Social Services Australia are choosing to use those people most vulnerable in order to score some political points in partnership with the Labor Party,' he said.
>
> 'We engage Catholic Social Services to help those people most vulnerable in the community.
>
> 'It is bizarre and quite contradictory behaviour to walk away from helping people who are vulnerable and it's very disappointing.'
>
> But the chief executive of the St Vincent de Paul Society, Dr John Falzon, says the welfare-to-work program demonises those in need.
>
> He says members of the organisation took a firm stand against the scheme right from the beginning.
>
> 'There is a desperate loss of hope that these people face,' he said.
>
> 'This program, instead of offering dignity, it would actually take away hope.
>
> 'We would dearly like to see the welfare reform as an opportunity for the Government to embrace the politics of hope rather than one of demonisation and punitive measures.'[32]

Clearly the terms of the debate have moved beyond purchaser/provider issues and into the area of values. If you are not with us you do not wish 'to help those people most vulnerable in the community'. This line of argument illustrates why it is important to government from a political perspective to have the community sector involved in delivering its welfare reforms. From inside the tent they are less likely to embarrass the Government by criticising its welfare delivery policies or, at least, they are more likely to choose their battles with considerable care. Among them might be those whom John Howard identified as, 'powerful vested interests with scant regard for the national interest [because they sit] outside the one mainstream'[33] but the public puts more faith in their commentary than it does in that of government.[34] Further, once community organisations that may have been critical of aspects of government policy have publicly become partners, they can be seen by their constituency to be actually delivering the service model they formerly questioned. At this point, community organisations are providing government with a further political benefit in addition to skilled service delivery. The government is able to use more than their familiarity with the community—it is also able to use their familiarity to the community. The medium becomes the message. The churches are supporting mutual obligation. The churches are adhering to the 'breaching' guidelines.

This means that community organisations (such as Hillsong Church[35]) which find their way into 'the one mainstream' are more likely to seek and to be found eligible to receive government service delivery contracts than those who do not. One analysis has noted, for example, that 'some emerging partnerships between government and community organisations may be the precursor of a new neo-corporatism that favours a selected few of what governments as contractors consider to be the more successful and reliable community organisations'.[36] They are likely to be joined as government partners by the private sector—which, in addition to being efficient, is largely exempt from values conflicts of this nature—and other service deliverers who also have claims on the government's service delivery money, such as an appropriate regional presence and well-placed referees. (Private sector companies that benefited from the initial carve-up of CES services 'were located at the rate of about four to one in Coalition-held regional electorates'[37]). None of these criteria for partnership was unique to the Howard Government. Nor was it the first to use social engineering to 'reinforce social norms and values that are under assault'. What is unique is the very significant quantitative and qualitative enhancement of direct public sector control over community sector activities represented by the extent of contracting for the delivery of social welfare programs, and its association with a growing emphasis on the rhetoric of partnership and a shared agenda—to the extent that, as one CEO complained, 'there is a risk in this outsourced world that the church simply becomes the government service'.[38]

In fact, some second-stage service delivery contracts—call them cooperative partnerships—ask more of service deliverers than simply sharing the government's agenda. Partners are required to actively think themselves into the policies they propose to deliver. This process is more complex than the straightforward withholding of resources from universities or service delivery organisations until they can see their way to implementing the government's preferred industrial relations arrangements.[39] These cooperative partnerships mean looking at the community through the government's values system and extrapolating along its policy lines to create new ways of implementing its views on 'fundamental questions about the relationship between government and citizens when it comes to individual and civic responsibility'. The very process of engaging in a cooperative partnership requires these community organisations to stop thinking critically about government policy and to start thinking of creative ways to implement it. Or, as one department's discussion paper on funding peak bodies has it, 'in return for funding, organisations are expected to contribute to government policies that support families and communities and to carry information between the community and the Government on important social issues'.[40] These cooperative partners are to stop thinking as outsiders and to start thinking as insiders: to become, in short, responsive at the level of policy as well as implementation.

While service deliverers are expected to implement the government's values agenda with the services they provide, the government, for its part, is not required to respond to values-based issues raised by providers. Or it may choose to respond, as the then federal Minister for Human Services, Joe Hockey, did, by claiming that the NGOs concerned were making political and not values-based points. There are any number of contradictions embedded in the rhetoric of partnerships between a monopoly purchaser such as government and a contracted provider, and beneath them all is the fundamental reality of who holds the purse strings. Chapter 3 referred to the use of contracts to control the advocacy activities of service providers through contract clauses that directly restrict or inhibit advocacy-related activities, the possible encouragement of inhibitions on 'biting the hand that feeds you', and the use of competitive grants to drive wedges between community organisations.[41] These constraints can be brought to bear through purchaser-provider arrangements as well as through grants—and under all the talk of partnerships, purchase/provider arrangements retain the mechanism of enforcement. It is a contradiction that is not lost on community organisations themselves:

> Associated with this is a form of managerialism, which involves out-sourcing the responsibility for specific issues away from the centre of government without, however, giving away the control. In other words, the contract holds the provider responsible for the achievement of the outcomes required by the purchaser but without giving the

provider the scope to develop and implement services that are consistent with the agency's philosophy or mission.[42]

That is one view. The view articulated by the former Secretary of the Department of the Prime Minister and Cabinet was more benign:

> My impression is that many of the non-government organisations that represent community interests are becoming more effective. Indeed an increasing number contract to deliver programmes on behalf of government. Critics highlight the risk that this will allow them to be co-opted by the State. My experience, by contrast, is that by becoming partners with government a mutual dependence grows and with it the influence of the advocate-provider. Dependence is increasingly mutual.[43]

What we have here may be a specimen of 'the contest for ideas' that the Management Advisory Committee advised public servants to expect as 'routinely associated with whole of government work'.[44] It is true that community organisations have some leverage with governments, and that 'network architects' are advised by experts to 'bear in mind that the benefits a well-known nonprofit brings to a government-run network can also prove an impediment if the network manager needs to change policy or impose consequences on such a high-profile participant'.[45] But it is also important to note that government does not fund 'advocate-providers'; it only funds outcomes; where outcomes are not delivered funding ceases to flow; and the amounts of funding involved are often considerable. The fact that providers can briefly embarrass government just makes it that much more important for public servants to make partnerships work and to make them look like partnerships, by becoming 'an effective intermediary between Ministers and advocacy groups'.[46]

Acting as an effective intermediary between ministers and advocacy groups delivering publicly funded programs is far from straightforward. On paper, at least, power-sharing 'is commonly seen as a defining feature of partnerships',[47] yet public servants are required to help 'stakeholders understand that the government remains the final decision maker.'[48] NGOs are not alone in finding the situation sometimes fraught: according to the *2005–06 State of the Service Report*, 35 per cent of employees who had dealt directly with stakeholders or with people from other levels of government over the preceding 12 months had faced a challenge in balancing the need to be fair and effective, impartial and courteous in delivering services to the Australian public, and responsive to the Government (as per the APS Values).[49] A Government that turned increasingly to 'a strong political executive with more political instruments for securing and sustaining control and direction' was not likely to let go of those instruments in the case of NGOs, especially a Government that wanted to increase its control over program implementation in particular[50] and the country's values in general.[51]

No wonder the Management Advisory Committee saw a need for public service skills to 'facilitate cooperation and partnerships, build commitment to a shared agenda, manage and share information, manage change, engage stakeholders, and resolve conflict'.[52] Public servants are expected to operate in the grey area in partnerships where professional equality meets decision-making inequality. In particular, they have to manage any perceived conflict between responsiveness to government and responsiveness to recipients of welfare services. Where these conflicts do not lie outside the government's agenda, they are not always resolved by the straightforward application of the legal requirements of the Social Security Act 1996 and administrative law. Public servants may respond by refocusing policy conflict as differences relating to practical decision making at a lower level, making it look procedural or technical and not ideological. They may argue for reporting requirements or performance indicators that constitute de facto compromises in terms of action (as occurred at Centrelink and at DIMIA) while at the same time vigorously maintaining the service deliverer's prerogative to tailor decision making to local client circumstances. Alternatively, they may begin by simply assuming (for example) that mutual obligation means work for the dole and comprehensive activity tests, so alternative values or higher level policies are organised out of the partnership agenda. It should be no matter for surprise that 'relationship management' is seen as an increasingly vital public service capability.[53] Public servants have to make cooperative partnerships work for the government in as seamless a way as can be managed, although the best place to start remains '[a] relentless attention to choosing participants with shared values'.[54]

As this background suggests, one interesting feature of the increase in market share of contracting for the delivery of social welfare programs is that there is something like a genuine convergence of the situations in which the partners are being placed.[55] Public servants have been learning, thanks to AWAs and performance assessment and pay systems, all about what it means to be on the receiving end of a transactional contractual relationship, and contractors are learning all about what it means to be responsive to the government agenda as part of their terms of engagement. Agencies are even advised by the Australian Public Service Commission to consider how the APS Values and *Code of Conduct* apply to their contractors, with especial attention to the APS Values relating to service delivery and to responsiveness to government in implementing its policies and programs.'[56] Accordingly:

> … private contractors, such as the members of the Jobs Network, can expect themselves to be dragged further and further into the government embrace. Outsourcing may weaken some aspects of public accountability,

especially over inputs and processes. But government accountability for results brings increased control over private organisations who contract to provide public services.[57]

The need for accountability persists, even although service deliverers change. But the form in which it persists has meant that both the public service and providers are being progressively repositioned as part of the 'new'—but still fundamentally managerialist—'governance network' that is anticipated to continue to replace traditional public administration. For the public service, this has meant increasing exposure to a contractual model of employment relations through individual performance 'agreements' often underpinned by individual employment contracts, with the same contractual model being reinforced and mirrored through relationships within and between agencies. Like community organisations whose activities have been marketised and who are 'encouraged … to take advantage of the other party'[58] in order to survive, the public service has been devolved and the individuals isolated and encouraged to compete.

Contestability has imposed a change of identity on both public servants and the organisations with whom they are competing for the patronage of government. The sectors, as Mulgan among others points out, are converging:

> A little more than a decade of extensive outsourcing public services has already seen considerable evolution, as classic contracts have given way to relational contracts and the importance of shared values between the contracting parties has been given greater weight. The line between public and private is likely to become even more blurred and the distinctiveness of public sector values even less clear-cut.[59]

Increasingly, community organisations that have entered into partnerships will be circumstanced very like public sector agencies, and the employees of both are likely to be drawn closer to the private sector model. It remains an open question as to whether their performance overall will improve as much as NPM theorists led governments to hope. Some academics have argued that the consequence of such convergence will be the loss of distinctive mechanisms of accountability particular to each sector (cooperative networking, hierarchy and competition, respectively), resulting in a net loss to the 'democratic accountability of social institutions as a whole'.[60] In *The Performing State: Reflections on an Idea whose Time Has Come but whose Implementation Has Not*, the Public Governance Committee of the OECD considered the same problem from a different angle:

> A public service ethic is the bedrock of governmental performance which depends at least as much on people as on machinery and process. This view clashes sharply with the principal-agent model popularised by new institutional economies (NIE) and imported into the public sector by

New Public Management. NIE and some versions of NPM teach that public employees are self interested, opportunistic agents, slackers who feather their own nest at the expense of the public interest. In this view, public agents can be made to perform only if they are actively monitored, given clear instructions as to what is expected of them, and strong incentives to do the job right. The notion that agents might do more than is formally expected of them because they have internalised public service values may be alien to NIE/NPM, but it is familiar to generations of students who overcame education handicaps because of teachers who stayed after class to help them, the police officer who coached the community sports team and never asked for pay, the visiting nurse who dropped by shut-ins after her daily rounds were done, and in countless other ways. Of course, this was never the whole story of public employment, or even the larger part, but it was the stuff out of which governments performed, earned the trust of their peoples and communities and states were built.[61]

While the argument sets alternatives at extremes, it retains a lesson for the APS. In the words of the Palmer Report (and as the churches have found), 'the nature of the activity is created by the contract'.[62] If the high-performing public servant requires private sector performance impedimenta to improve efficiency and effectiveness, then it should not be surprising if the efficient and effective public servant sheds some of the public service ethic along the way. Transactional contracts, after all, focus on short-term and monetised exchange, where rewards are explicitly tied to individual performance and low membership commitment by the employee. Under a psychological contract shaped by transactional relations, the APS Values are not about internalising an ethic, but about exhibiting certain behaviours, and the behaviours themselves include and privilege 'people with new skills who think more like businesspeople and … think in a whole new way about what it means to be a government employee'.[63] The 'whole new way' of thinking more like businesspeople flows through the contractual model:

> When public service is just a job, no special value is attached to having the work performed by government employees. With tasks specified in contracts, it would seem to make little difference whether the work is performed by people on the government's payroll or by firms which get the contract through competitive tenders. As long as the work process or output can be specified, public service and private employment are interchangeable.[64]

No wonder 'in most developed countries, the ethic of public service still exists, but not as robustly as in the past'.[65] At the same time, the OECD paper speculates, without reaching a settled conclusion, as to why, 'despite their positive ratings, most developed countries have been beset in recent decades by a decline of trust and confidence in government and political leaders'.[66] It posits the possibility that output measures make for ever shifting goal posts and ever higher expectations. But it is equally worth speculating on the loss to government of its particular relation to the governed as expressed through the belief in a public service ethos—even though this was 'rejected as simply a cover for inefficiency and empire building by bureaucrats'[67] by those at the more doctrinaire end of the NPM debate. It may be that people do not want to be governed by an entity that increasingly presents itself as a large corporate structure—or at least that their relationship to such an entity does not entail belief or gratitude or commitment.[68] It may be that while taxpayers like efficiency, they do not like people making profits out of delivering their services. It may be that citizens to not want to think of themselves as customers, or to have their communication with government take the form of 'formal market research to understand stakeholders' views or ... a structured campaign involving advertising, public relations or similar'.[69] Alternatively, it may be that while citizens do not have any problems with such an approach to being serviced, it comes at the expense of feeling governed. They may not find it as simple to swap their client hats and their citizen hats when confronting different functions of government as theorists may posit. In any event, if citizens are to have an enduring relationship with their government, for most of them it will have to be through the medium of those who work for that government. The terms of their engagement will determine the terms of that relationship:

> Contracts narrow accountability to matters expressly agreed to, in contrast to a normative sense of responsibility for serving the public. When contracts are used to formalise responsibilities and relationships, the specified items often become a checklist that informs the performing party of what it must do to fulfil its obligations. But just as a party to a private agreement is not bound to perform tasks not specified in the agreement, a party to an internal government contract cannot be called to account for failing to provide unspecified services. Managing by contract thus leads to managing by checklist, as managers take care to assure that itemised tasks are completed.[70]

Public value management

There is a school of thought which argues that in order to rebalance internal and external performance standards, internal and external commitment to the work of public service, NPM models need to evolve into a new practice. Public Value Management has taken root in the crevices opened by NPM—between government and governed, between purchaser and provider, between performance indicators and public services:[71]

... the practice of the new public management often emphasised narrow concepts of cost-efficiency over other considerations (i.e. the focus was on technical rather than allocative efficiency). Those things that were easy to measure tended to become objectives and those that couldn't were downplayed or ignored. Hence within some public services 'efficiency' measures represented the average cost of processing a given output (e.g. Finished Consultant Episodes in hospitals), regardless of what mattered to the public. In these circumstances it was possible for measures of efficiency to improve without there being a concomitant improvement in the service experienced by the user (as occurred under the internal market when measured outputs increased substantially but service quality did not). Improvements in efficiency in this narrow sense were not synonymous with increases in public value.[72]

Public Value Management is premised on a view of public value that is 'a broader measure than is conventionally used within the new public management literature, covering outcomes, the means used to deliver them as well as trust and legitimacy'.[73] This means equity, ethos and accountability are effectively part of the service delivered by government.[74] Insofar as it calls for the negotiation of community service priorities 'on the ground', Public Value Management is continuous with calls for local autonomy in configuring whole of government service delivery. The Management Advisory Committee did not hesitate, for example, to argue that 'from an implementation point of view it will also be critical, once the right people are in the right jobs, to give them the necessary flexibility and authority to deliver integration, particularly for whole of government service delivery'.[75] However, many theorists also see Public Value Management principles as applying at a higher level, where the authority to deliver service integration has become the authority to design policy within the limits set by a particular 'authorising environment'.[76] These proposals raise issues for Westminster systems in general[77] and for Australian arrangements in particular, because they assume a system in which the processes of devolution and outsourcing release rather than reconfigure power.

In Australia, however, as was argued in chapter 4, the government may have devolved managerial power but it retained and even recentralised policy control:

The Australian case provides a distinct change of direction from classic NPM features towards a multi-dimensional integrated model. The comprehensive change program covers the resurrection of the central agency as a major actor; enhancement of control over departments; central monitoring of delivery at agency level; implementation of a whole-of-government approach; and departmentalisation through absorbing statutory authorities and reclaiming control over independent agencies ... Underlying the redirection are political control and performance issues – the government that drove a neo-liberal variant of NPM has had to confront the impact of its own reforms …[78]

The Australian government has tightened rather than relaxed its controls over its public services—not just as a consequence of changed systems of management but also through the act of outsourcing itself used as a means of political agenda-setting. Australia may be no more than an outlier in the latter respect—other countries may be using whole-of-government issues as an opportunity for some recentralising—but the point is that despite the rhetoric around collaboration and negotiation with communities, the model continues to be surrounded by 'political control and performance issues'.

These issues are not easily resolved or reconciled. Public Value Management has considerable implications for the APS Values as a management tool, for responsiveness as a management driver, and for the ethos of public service. In particular, it suggests a means of rebalancing responsiveness as a value, returning to it a strong flavour of community orientation that was evident in the 1976 report of the RCAGA. However, it appears to do this by introducing a concept of public interest that is not determined by the government of the day, but by public servants in consultation with communities and providers. It has been argued that Public Value Management approaches give public service managers a capacity to shape policy and 'a degree of autonomy and entrepreneurialism that is not typical of public servants in Westminster systems',[79] and does not sit comfortably in those systems. While this is true, its emphases on values such as equity, ethics, public trust and legitimacy do sit comfortably in a Westminster system, as does its insistence that these are also part of the public's interest in public service decision making. That aspect of the public interest is the subject of the final chapter.

ENDNOTES

[1] See Kylie McIntosh, Jason Shauness, and Roger Wettenhall, *Contracting Out in Australia: An Indicative History*, Centre for Research in Public Sector Management, University of Canberra (Canberra, 1997), chapters 1 and 2.

[2] Jim Chalmers and Glyn Davis, 'Rediscovering Implementation: Public Sector Contracting and Human Services', *Australian Journal of Public Administration* 6(2) (June 2001), 77.

[3] Glyn Davis and R. A. W. Rhodes, 'From Hierarchy to Contracts and Back Again: Reforming the Australian Public Service', in Michael Keating, John Wanna and Patrick Weller (eds), *Institutions on the Edge? Capacity for Governance* (Allen and Unwin: Sydney, 2000), 83–4.

[4] Peter Reith, *Towards a Best Practice Australian Public Service*, Discussion paper, Nov. 1996, Canberra, AGPS, p. x.

[5] David Kemp, Minister for Education, Training and Youth Affairs, media release, 26 Feb.1998: announcement that employment services will be contracted out to a range of organisations (to be known as the Jobs Network), at http://www.detya.gov.au/ministers/kemp/K10_260298.htm.

[6] Davis and Rhodes, 'From Hierarchy to Contracts', 92.

[7] June 1996 National Commission of Audit (established Mar. 1996), Report to the Commonwealth Government, Canberra, AGPS, 1996, Executive Summary, at http://www.finance.gov.au/pubs/ncoa/execsum.htm#I1.

[8] Pat Barrett, 'Auditing in a Changing Government Environment', paper based on a lecture presented in the Department of the Senate Occasional Lecture Series, 21 June 2002, p. 8, at http://www.aph.gov.au/Senate/pubs/pops/pop39/c05.pdf, viewed 4 July 2007.

[9] See Peter Shergold, 'Two Cheers for the Bureaucracy: Public Service, Political Advice and Network Governance', Australian Public Service Commission Lunchtime Seminar, 13 June 2003: 'The CES, which enjoyed 50 years as a public service monopoly, is gone. It has been replaced by market competition', at http://www.pmc.gov.au/speeches/index.cfm.

[10] To some extent this development had been foreshadowed four years earlier, when *Working Nation* (May 1994) suggested the introduction of competitive delivery of the CES case management function through the use of both private and community-based case managers.

[11] See Michelle Grattan, 'Paternal Policies Protect Values under Threat: PM', reporting on a speech to the Centre for Independent Studies, *The Age*, 5 May 2006, p. 6, at http://www.theage.com.au/news/national/paternal-policies-protect-values-under-threat-pm/2006/05/04/1146335868659.html?page=fullpage.

[12] Tony Abbott, 'Against the Prodigal State', Centre for Independent Studies, *Policy* (Spring 2001), 38.

[13] David Abello and Helen MacDonald, 'Jobs Network: Changing Community Sector Values', *The Drawing Board: An Australian Review of Public Affairs* 3(1) (July 2002), 59.

[14] Julian Teicher, Quamrul Alam and Bernadine Van Gramberg, 'Managing Trust and Relationships in PPPs: Some Australian Experiences', *International Review of Administrative Sciences* 72(1) (Mar. 2006), 90.

[15] See Richard Mulgan, 'Public Accountability of Provider Agencies: The Case of the Australian "Centrelink"', *International Review of Administrative Sciences* 68(1) (2002), 48.

[16] See Abbott, 'Against the Prodigal State', 38.

[17] Wilma Gallet, 'What Sets Us Apart?', BriefCACE, no 32 (July 2006), 2.

[18] Catholic Welfare Australia, *Reading the Signs of the Times: Challenges to the Future of Social Services in Australia*, Jan. 2006 (draft made available to Background Briefing, 1 Oct. 2006), at http://www.abc.net.au/rn/backgroundbriefing/stories/2006/1748895.htm, viewed 5 July 2007. See also Teicher et al., 'Managing Trust and Relationships in PPPs', 90; Karen Legge, *Human Resource Management: Rhetorics and Realities* (Macmillan: London, 1995), 234–40.

[19] M. J. Palmer, *Inquiry into the Circumstances of the Immigration Detention of Cornelia Rau: Report* (July 2005), 176, at http://www.minister.immi.gov.au, viewed 13 Feb. 2006.

[20] Ibid. 176, 177–8.

[21] Ibid. 178. These comments were based on the ANAO's audit of the previous DIMIA contract with Australasian Correctional Management. The Inquiry was unable to access that part of the ANAO's report that dealt with the current contract, which was under embargo at the time of the Inquiry.

[22] See M. and P. Henderson, 'Partnerships for Service Delivery: Review of the Research and Practice Literature', Report to the Queensland Department of Communities (2004), 6–8, at http://www.getinvolved.qld.gov.au/share_your_knowledge/resources/documents/pdf/partnershipreview.pdf.

[23] See ibid. 13–29; and Jake Chapman, *System Failure* (Demos, 2002), at www.demos.co.uk, viewed 27 Sept. 2006.

[24] See Richard Mulgan, 'Government Accountability for Outsourced Services', *Australian Journal of Public Administration* 65(2) (2006), 50-51: '... once a service is outsourced, many aspects of the outsourcing arrangement are treated as commercially confidential and beyond the range of public inquiry. The actual details of the contracts themselves between government and provider may be protected from public scrutiny. Agencies are required to report to Parliament about all contracts over $100,000 but the information sought is restricted to a few key aspects of the contract, such as the name of the contractor, the general subject matter of the contract, the term and price of the contract, and whether the contract contains any specific confidentiality clauses. Such information, while significant, falls well short of full disclosure. Individual Jobs Network contracts, for instance, are not available to parliamentary committees or the public.'

[25] Management Advisory Committee, *Connecting Government: Whole of Government Responses to Australia's Priority Challenges* (Canberra, 2004), 100.

[26] Richard Mulgan, 'Outsourcing and Public Service Values: The Australian Experience', *International Review of Administrative Sciences* 71(1) (2005), 63.

[27] Henderson, 'Partnerships for Service Delivery', 6.

[28] Ibid.

[29] See also Stephen Goldsmith and William D. Eggers, *Governing by Network: The New Shape of the Public Sector* (Brookings Institution Press: Washington, DC, 2004), 40 ('Goal Congruence') and 65 ('Cultural Compatibility').

[30] Grattan, 'Paternal Policies Protect Values under Threat', 6.

[31] Tony Nicholson [Executive Director of the Brotherhood of St Laurence], 'Poverty Is Not an Item in a Press Release', *The Age*, 8 May 2006, p. 15.

[32] ABC News, 'Church's Welfare-to-work Pullout a Stunt: Hockey,' 18 Aug. 2006, at http://www.abc.net.au/news/stories/2006/08/18/1718019.htm, viewed 18 Aug. 2006.

[33] John Howard, 'The Role of Government: A Modern Liberal Approach', Menzies Research Centre 1995 National Lecture Series, p. 4, at http://www.ozpolitics.info/election2004/1995-rolegovt.htm, cited in Ch. 2.

[34] See results of a Globescan survey reported by World Economic Forum, 'Update: Public Trust Is Recovering', press release, Geneva, 31 Mar. 2004. Full results of the survey (data and tables) are at http://www.weforum.org/trustsurvey2004.

[35] Adele Horin, 'Hillsong Thinks Again on Welfare', 24 Aug. 2006, at http://www.smh.com.au/articles/2006/08/23/1156012614378.html, viewed 30 Aug. 2006. 'Hillsong Emerge, the only church charity in NSW to participate in a controversial welfare-to-work program ...' and see also 'The church is known not just for its style of Christian worship, but for its links to the burgeoning political influence of the 'religious right' through politicians associated with it ... Prime Minister John Howard opened Hillsong's Baulkham Hills convention centre in October 2002 and Treasurer Peter Costello spoke to thousands at the SuperDome conference this year': 'Hillsong's true believers', 7 Nov. 2004, at The Sun-Herald http://www.smh.com.au/articles/2004/11/06/1099547435083.html, viewed 30 Aug. 2006.

[36] John Casey and Bronwen Dalton, 'Ties that Bind? The Impact of Contracting and Project-based Funding Regimes on Advocacy', paper presented to Australian Political Studies Association Conference, University of Adelaide, 2004, p.18.

[37] Geoffrey Barker, 'The Public Service', in Sarah Maddison, Richard Dennis and Clive Hamilton (eds), *Silencing Dissent: How the Australian government is controlling public opinion and stifling debate* (Crows Nest: Allen and Unwin, 2007), 145.

[38] Gallet, 'What Sets Us Apart?', 2.

[39] 'Governmental funding of community organisations commonly requires them to place employees onto AWAs without any alternate option being offered': National Foundation for Australian Women, 'What Women Want: Consultations on Welfare to Work and Work Choices', p. 5, para 6, at http://www.nfaw.org/social/www/what-women-want.pdf, viewed 27 July 2007.

[40] Department of Family and Community Services, *Funding Peak Bodies* (2002), quoted in Bernadine Van Gramberg and Penny Bassett, 'Neoliberalism and the Third Sector in Australia', Victoria University Working Paper Series (May 2005), pp. 8–9.

[41] See Casey and Dalton, 'Ties that Bind?', 12; and Van Gramberg and Bassett, 'Neoliberalism and the Third Sector', 7: 'Efficiency measures such as competitive tendering, at the same time as the implementation of collaborative policies, have simultaneously exposed nonprofits to partnership arrangements while ensuring they are also pitted against each other in competition for funding opportunities.'

[42] See, for example, Teicher et al., 'Managing Trust and Relationships in PPPs', 92: 'For instance, Catholic welfare Australia (CFA) (Submission DR70 cited in Productivity Commission 2002) argued that compliance burdens have increased, and that DEWR makes unilateral decisions on contract variations and emphasises processes rather than outcomes. According to CFA the Jobs Network is on track to becoming a 'totally one-way partnership'. Similarly, another submission argued that DEWR imposes changes on providers with a 'take it or leave it attitude' leaving the providers to bear the cost (Submission 20, cited in Productivity Commission, 2002: 12.9). It could be argued that competition, quality, trust and participation have become peripheral matters for PPPs in the Jobs Network.'

[43] Peter Shergold, 'Government and Communities in Partnership: Sharing Responsibility', speech to Government and Communities in Partnership Conference, Melbourne, 18 May 2005, at http://www.dpmc.gov.au/speeches/shergold/sharing_responsibility_2005-05-18.cfm, viewed 25 Apr. 2006.

[44] Management Advisory Committee, *Connecting Government*, 106.

[45] Goldsmith and Eggers, *Governing by Network*, 139.

46 See Shergold, 'Two Cheers for the Bureaucracy'.

47 Henderson, 'Partnerships for Service Delivery', 9.

48 Management Advisory Committee, *Connecting Government*, 96.

49 Australian Public Service Commission, *State of the Service Employee Survey Results 2005–06* (Canberra, 2006), 35, question 50.

50 See discussion in Ch. 4; and John Halligan, 'The Integrated Performance Model in the Australian Public Sector and its Consequences for Public Sector Organisations', Paper for presentation at Panel on Autonomy and Steering Models of Public Sector Organisations, 9th International Research Symposium on Public Management, SDA Bocconi, Milan, 6–8 Apr. 2005, pp. 7ff.

51 Including in the teaching of English literature and of history, the values required of migrants and the presence of chaplains in all schools. See the then Prime Minister's 'A Sense of Balance: The Australian Achievement in 2006', Address to the National Press Club, Parliament House, at http://www.pm.gov.au/News/Speeches/speech1754.html, viewed 6 Mar. 2007.

52 Management Advisory Committee, *Connecting Government*, 53.

53 Ibid. 43-4.

54 Goldsmith and Eggers, *Governing by Network*, 130.

55 This is an issue that engages academics as well as practitioners. See for example, Mulgan, 'Outsourcing and Public Service Values', cited above; and Robert E. Goodin, 'Democratic Accountability: The Third Sector and All', Paper presented to a Seminar series on 'Institutional Analysis of Law, Politics, and Society' at the Baldy Center for Law & Social Policy State University of New York Law School, 12 Mar. 2004, at http://www.law.buffalo.edu/baldycenter/pdfs/goodinpaper04.pdf, viewed 16 Aug. 2007.

56 See Australian Public Service Commission, *Embedding the APS Value,* (Canberra, 2003), Sections 2 and 6, at http://www.apsc.gov.au/values, viewed 16 Apr. 2006. Values applying to the internal APS workplace relationships are not, however, considered relevant to contractors' own employment practices, although other Commonwealth employment legislation, such that covering occupational health and safety and anti-discrimination, is.

57 Mulgan 2006, 'Government Accountability for Outsourced Services', 57.

58 Teicher et al., 'Managing Trust and Relationships in PPPs', 88. See also Gallet, 'What Sets Us Apart?'; and Catholic Welfare Australia 2006, *Reading the Signs of the Times*, cited above.

59 Mulgan 2005, 'Outsourcing and Public Service Values', 69.

60 Goodin, 'Democratic Accountability', 48.

61 Organisation for Economic Cooperation and Development, *The Performing State: Reflection on an Idea whose Time Has Come but whose Implementation Has Not*, paper for 23rd Session of the Public Governance Committee, GOV/PGC/ (2006), 7, para 27.

62 Palmer, *Inquiry*, 177–8. See also OECD, *Performing State*, 13.

63 Deirdre Lee, acquisition director, US Department of Defence, quoted by Goldsmith and Eggers, *Governing by Network*, 157.

64 OECD, *Performing State*, 7, para 28.

65 Ibid.

66 Ibid. 4, para 14.

67 Gerry Stoker, 'Public Value Management: A New Narrative for Networked Governance?', *American Review of Public Administration* 36(1) (2006), 46.

68 See, e.g., Teicher et al., 'Managing Trust and Relationships in PPPs', 91: 'The Jobs Network offers choices but no evidence exists that choices have any impact on service outcomes. Recipients reportedly feel that government plays a minimal role and seeks to shift the accountability to service providers.'

69 Management Advisory Committee, *Connecting Government*, 106.

70 OECD, 13, para 58.

71 For a full account of openings created by NPM for PVM, see Gerry Stoker, 'Public Value Management: A New Narrative for Networked Governance?', *American Review of Public Administration* 36(1) (Mar. 2006), 41–57; Gavin Kelly, Geoff Mulgan and Stephen Muers, 'Creating Public Value: An Analytical Framework for Public Service Reform', Strategy Unit, UK Cabinet Office (2002), at www.strategy.gov.uk, viewed 6 Mar. 2007; 'Citizens, Government, Democracy: A New Deal?', Saskatchewan Institute of Public Policy, University of Regina, no. 1 (2000), 6, at http://www.uregina.ca/sipp/documents/pdf/may.pdf, viewed 3 July 2007 (extracting material from a speech to the Institute by Jocelyn Bourgon); and sources

in Martin Marcussen and Jacob Torfing, 'Grasping Governance Networks', Centre for Democratic Network Governance, Roskilde University Working Paper Series no 5 (2003), 4–5.

[72] Kelly et al., 'Creating Public Value', 9.

[73] Ibid. 3.

[74] Ibid.

[75] Management Advisory Committee, *Connecting Government*, 52. See also p. 101.

[76] R. A. W. Rhodes and John Wanna, 'The Limits to Public Value, or Rescuing Responsible Governments from the Platonic Guardians', *Australian Journal of Public Administration* 66(4) (2007), 409.

[77] See ibid. 406–21.

[78] Halligan, 'The Integrated Performance Model', 1. See also similar comments from Podger, 'Looking Upwards and Downwards'.

[79] Rhodes and Wanna, 'Limits to Public Value', 409.

Chapter 7. Reforming the reforms?

The 'public interest' is a term with many meanings, some of them legislative and many contested.[1] According to the Australian Public Service Commission's *Supporting Ministers, Upholding the Values*, so far as Australian public servants are concerned, 'the elected Government alone has the authority to determine the public interest in terms of policies and programmes, while public servants assist Governments to deliver that policy agenda and those priorities'.[2] This makes the public interest look very like the policy and program interests of Government. The Commission does, however, introduce a broader notion of public interest when it advises that public servants also:

> … have a responsibility for protecting the public interest in terms of ensuring the integrity of government processes, including compliance with the law and fair and impartial decision-making in accordance with approved guidelines.[3]

This is the point—the integrity of government processes—at which the public service has to make decisions about the public interest that have not already been made in government policy objectives. Some of those decisions are being made for public servants, inappropriately, by the systems implementing the NPM drivers of contestability, performance management, devolution, human resource management and outsourcing. These systems serve to increase the risk of over-responsiveness and a predisposition to identify and serve political as well as policy ends—what Mulgan calls 'the unforced eagerness of officials to assist their government's case'.[4] This is not to argue that the public service as a whole has been politicised—in the sense considered in Chapter 1 of having crossed the 'line between proper responsiveness to the elected government and undue involvement in the government's electoral fortunes'—just that the systems themselves, in their operation, do not strike a balance between managing for the government's desired outcomes and 'performing its functions in an impartial and professional manner', as public servants are required to do under s. 10(1)(a)of the Act.

The systems implementing NPM also underpin substantial gains in efficiency[5] and sometimes in effectiveness. Not only is it impossible to return to the arrangements of the 1980s and early 1990s, it is also undesirable. Some aspects of NPM are now uncontested—for example, the reduction in internal regulation and the focus on organisational performance more generally. The problem, then—at least the problem from the point of view of a sustainable public service in a Westminster system—is to retain the flexibility and performance orientation of NPM but to reduce the negative impact of existing drivers or to introduce more balanced drivers. These are not mutually exclusive alternatives.

There is certainly scope to review the systems considered in the course of this monograph for their impact on the capacity of the public service to perform its functions in a way that is apolitical, avoiding 'the crossing of a line between proper responsiveness to the elected government and undue involvement in the government's electoral fortunes'.[6] In the case of contestability, such change would have to be driven mainly from the political level, and aimed at moderating the use of contestability to landscape the level playing field. Change at this level is proposed following the 2007 election, including the issuing of guidance on the relationship between ministers and lobbyists,[7] and changes to the independence of advisory bodies such as the Australian Research Council.[8] How these changes work in practice over time remains to be seen. From the public service end, however, there is still a need to increase the consistency and the transparency of portfolio-wide practices around appointments and grants. The same general observations apply to outsourcing. Again, changes have been foreshadowed at the political level to contract provisions gagging service providers or requiring government clearance of media releases, government submissions and reports[9]—undoubtedly a critical step in making contestability work as a means of democratising policy advice. From the public service end, some administrative practices could also be revisited, including guidance discouraging advocacy or encouraging competition between providers rather than collaboration between them. In addition, Public Value Management strategies applied to operational decision making may provide a means of enriching service delivery relationships at the purchaser/provider and provider/delivery interfaces.

Agency workplace relations arrangements are both political and bureaucratic in design and change needs to be driven at both levels. At the industrial relations level this means reviewing the balance between individualised and collective arrangements in the workplace; at the human resource management (now often called 'employee relations') level, it means revising the strategies for employee alignment that are likely to contribute to the development of an assumption culture. Following the 2007 election the AWAs are to be phased out,[10] but it would also be worth examining broader 'psychological contract', including the current over-emphasis on the role of managerial prerogative, and the under-emphasis on workplace consultation around the conduct of work and the exercise of discretion in public service decision making.

In terms of individual performance assessment and pay arrangements themselves, system design is mainly driven at bureaucratic level and could be reviewed at that level against a whole range of rhetoric/reality issues. These should include those thrown up by 'soft HRM' assurances and 'hard HRM' practices, and the overarching question asked by Allan Hawke about whether rhetoric/reality concerns are endemic to any system of linking pay to performance management in a public service employment framework. It would be worth beginning with a new question, namely, what performance review mechanism would help maintain the balance between conflicting values, so that 'being apolitical does not remove an employee's obligation to be responsive to the Government and to implement its policies and programs, nor does responsiveness permit partisan decisions or decisions that are not impartial'.[11] The answer might involve some form of performance agreement, but it is likely to be one 'based on building performance through feedback and a developmental focus—without scores and ratings'.[12]

The impact of devolution is also determined partly at the political level and partly by agency executive. Recent studies have already identified a number of system changes at the government/ministerial level that promise to reduce the impact of drivers encouraging over-responsiveness. Anne Tiernan has put forward some proposals relating to the conduct of ministerial advisers.[13] Andrew Podger has put forward others in relation to the duration of secretarial appointments and the performance management arrangements associated with them.[14] The new Government has signalled its intention to act on both of these areas, putting in place a ministerial code,[15] appointing agency heads and department secretaries for fixed five-year periods unless the appointee has a preference for a shorter period,[16] and requiring full merit-based appointment processes for most non-secretarial agency heads.[17] In addition, it has foreshadowed moving away from performance-based pay arrangements for agency heads and departmental secretaries, and restoring the jurisdiction of the Remuneration Tribunal to fix their pay and conditions.[18] Depending on how these policies are implemented over time, these changes could have considerable flow-on implications for public servants down the line in particular agencies. For many of the agency systems currently in place, there would be new assumptions underpinning their operation. Public servants would be less likely to believe that political statements, or even political intimations, were to be understood as informal policy directives.

Another means of addressing the downside of devolution would be the introduction of more public forms of accountability, particularly at senior levels, than those currently provided for through devolved systems and individual performance agreements. These would have the effect of increasing the leverage of public servants who are resisting expectations of politically motivated behaviour from ministers' offices or from their own senior managers. Agency heads could, for example, be required to outline in annual reports what they have done to publish, promote and support the use of agency protocols in dealing with ministers and their advisers. They could also be asked to outline the nature and regularity of guidance provided to agency staff on due process and the exercise of individual discretion—particularly what they have done at times when such decision making is the subject of high profile political and media attention. For many agency heads, such a requirement would mean no more than formalising existing practice. For others, it might call for considerable changes to existing practice. Agency heads, like most senior public servants, are accomplished at selective reporting, but such a requirement would also have the benefit of routinely exposing them to relevant questioning at Senate Estimates.

More broadly, agency heads could be required to collect data from employees on the implementation of the APS Values in agency management practices. Public servants could be asked whether, in their view, middle and senior managers behave ethically and in ways that are consistent with the APS Values. The *State of the Service Employee Survey*s cannot gather statistically reliable data from smaller agencies, and in any event the continuance of the surveys would be threatened if they were made the vehicle for possibly invidious comparisons of this nature. The outcomes of these agency-specific surveys could also be made part of an agency's annual reporting process. Such an approach may be subjective, but it is no less so than the downward performance ratings currently enforced through performance assessment and pay systems.

Finally, there is the issue of enforcement. If the *State of the Service* reports are a good indicator, agencies do not—with the one exception of pursuing leaks—appear to have identified or investigated misconduct that is particularly associated with APS Values relating to subsections 10(1)(a) and (f) of the Public Service Act ('the APS is apolitical, performing its functions in an impartial and professional manner'; and 'the APS is responsive to the Government in providing frank, honest, comprehensive, accurate and timely advice and in implementing the Government's policies and programs'). The types of conduct pursued in 2005–06—and in the two other years for which such data was gathered—are laid out in Table 5. Although these types of misconduct are clearly important, they do not go to the difficult issues of politicisation and responsiveness.[19] The type of misconduct included here that is most likely to intersect with subsections 10(1)(a) and (f) of the Public Service Act is 'unauthorised disclosure of information', which is not a difficult matter to isolate and pursue, being usually contrary to the government's political interests rather than inappropriately aligned with them. But as this study has argued, over-responsiveness is at least as much of an issue for the public service, and for effective government, as disaffection.

Table 5. Number of employees by types of misconduct in investigations finalised during 2005–6

Type of misconduct	Employees investigated for this type of misconduct (Number) [1]	Cases where a breach was found (%)	Agencies with finalised investigations (Number)
Improper access to personal information (e.g. browsing)	792	82	10
Conflict of interest	755	80	9
Improper use of Internet/email	283	78	29
Inappropriate behaviour of employees (other than harassment or bullying) during working hours (e.g. treating clients or stakeholders disrespectfully)	133	70	33
Harassment and/or bullying	72	53	27
Improper use of resources other than Internet/email (e.g. vehicles)	52	75	13
Unauthorised disclosure of information (e.g. leaks)	41	20	12
Fraud other than theft (e.g. identity fraud)	40	80	13
Improper use of position status (e.g. abuse of power, exceeding delegations)	28	50	10
Private behaviour of employees (e.g. at social functions outside working hours)	21	57	12
Theft	20	60	11
Misuse of drugs or alcohol	9	78	6

[1] An individual employee may be counted against more than one type of misconduct.

Note: Agencies were asked for data on employees who were the subject of formal investigations, and were specifically asked not to include data on initial investigations that did not proceed to formal misconduct procedures. However, it is possible that some agencies may have provided information on elements of the Code that were suspected of being breached in both formal and informal investigations.

Source: *2005–06 State of the Service Report*, Table 4.5.

There is, however, new guidance from the Australian Public Service Commission that has been issued to 'implement the Government's policy commitment not to use public servants in government advertising'. It probably should be asked whether or not guidance on the application of the APS Values should vary with the policy commitments of new Governments, but in this case the change is not one of meaning but of the seriousness with which the APS Values are to be applied. The guidance cites Chapter 6 of the previous Government's *Guide on Key Elements of Ministerial Responsibility*, which stipulates that 'Ministers should be scrupulous in avoiding asking public servants to do anything that the APS principles do not permit, and in particular should not ask them to engage in activities which could call into question their political impartiality'. The Ministerial guidance is then applied by the Commission to public servants as follows:

If such a request were ever made of a public servant by a Minister or his/her staff, the public servant must refuse. This is a legal obligation deriving from sections 10 and 13 of the *Public Service Act*, which set out the APS Values and the APS Code of Conduct respectively.[20]

This has always been a legal obligation, but the *State of the Service* data does not suggest that any agencies have ever had such a breach brought to their attention, or, if they have, have ever decided to pursue it.[21] Nevertheless, the guidance means that public servants have explicit grounds for refusing to engage in activities which could call into question their political impartiality. They also have explicit grounds for questioning whether or not particular activities are likely to call into question their political impartiality. They have reason to ask for formal advice and to ensure that senior managers have formal responsibility for any advice that they provide. They have grounds to ask, in critical and difficult circumstances, for written protocols. What is new is that they now also have grounds to expect that where the activities of individuals appear to call into question their political impartiality, those matters will be pursued with at least as much seriousness as fraud and improper use of the internet.

Breaches of subsections 10(1)(a) and (f) of the Public Service Act are likely to come in shades of grey, but the penalties for misconduct are equally variable; and if these values are to have any meaning then they should be enforced as well as promoted. In fact, to continue promoting the APS Values, as agencies are exhorted to do, will only bring them into disrepute if public servants see that they are not taken seriously, or only selectively so.

Because the public service cannot, in Westminster systems, determine the public interest, its capacity to serve that interest is vested in the integrity of its own processes. Institutional change is partly in the hands of government, but it is also partly in the hands of public servants. Over time, Governments settle in and begin to see institutions from the perspective of incumbency rather than of Opposition. This being the case, the public service should take whatever measures are open to it to maintain the integrity of its own processes.

ENDNOTES

[1] See, for example, R. A. W. Rhodes and John Wanna, 'The Limits to Public Value, or Rescuing Responsible Governments from the Platonic Guardians', *Australian Journal of Public Administration* 66(4) (2007), 415ff.

[2] Australian Public Service Commission, *Supporting Ministers, Upholding the Values* (Canberra, 2006), 11.

[3] Ibid.

[4] Richard Mulgan, 'Truth in Government and the Politicisation of Public Service Advice', *Public Administration* 85(3) (2007), 578.

[5] See Ch. 4, notes 17, 18, 19.

[6] Mulgan, 'Truth in Government', 570.

[7] Penny Wong, 'Labor's Approach to the Australian Public Service', speech to the Institute of Public Administration Australia, 20 Sept. 2007, p. 5.

[8] Senator Kim Carr, Labor Senator for Victoria and Shadow Minister for Industry, Innovation, Science and Research, 'Building a Strong Future for Australian Research', 15 Nov. 2007, at http://www.chass.org.au/media/MED20071115KC.php.

[9] Matthew Franklin, 'Labor to Lift Gag on Critics', *Australian*, 9 Jan. 2008, at http://www.theaustralian.news.com.au/story/0,25197,23026526-12332,00.html, viewed 28 Feb. 2008.

[10] ABC News, 'Govt "Leading by Example" in AWA Abolition', 13 Feb., at http://www.abc.net.au/news/stories/2008/02/13/2162103.htm, viewed 28 Feb. 2008.

[11] Public Service Commission, *APS Values and Code of Conduct in Practice: Guide to Official Conduct for APS Employees and Agency Heads* (revised 2005), Ch. 1, at http://www.apsc.gov.au/values/conductguidelines3.htm, viewed 22 June 2007.

[12] Allan Hawke, then Secretary of Defence, quoted in Michael O'Donnell and John Shields, 'Performance Management and the Psychological Contract inthe Australian Federal Public Sector', *Journal of Industrial Relations* 44(3) (2002), 445.

[13] See Anne Tiernan, *Power without Responsibility* (University of New South Wales Press: Sydney, 2007).

[14] See Andrew Podger, 'What Really Happens: Department Secretary Appointments, Contracts and Performance Pay in the Australian Public Service', *Australian Journal of Public Administration* 66(2) (2007), 145.

[15] See Senate Finance and Public Administration Committee, Hansard, 18 Feb. 2008, pp. 48ff.

[16] Wong, 'Labor's Approach to the Australian Public Service', 7.

[17] Australian Public Service Commission, 'Merit and Transparency: Merit-based Selection of APS Agency Heads and Statutory Office Holders', 5 Feb. 2008, at http://www.apsc.gov.au/publications08/meritandtransparency.htm, viewed 25 Feb. 2008.

[18] Wong, 'Labor's Approach to the Australian Public Service', 7.

[19] Section 13 of the Act sets out the Code of Conduct. Section s.13(11) of the Act explicitly links the Code to the APS Values by specifying that 'an APS employee must at all times behave in a way that upholds the APS Values and the integrity and good reputation of the APS'. This provision is often applied in concert with other provisions to because it broadens coverage (see the *2004–05 State of the Service Report*, p. 128); nevertheless, the types of misconduct found are as set out in Table 4.5.

[20] Australian Public Service Commission, 'Guidelines on the Involvement of Public Servants in Public Information and Awareness Initiatives',12 Dec. 2007, at http://www.apsc.gov.au/publications07/publicinformation.htm, viewed 27 Feb. 2008.

[21] The 2004–05 and 2005–06 reports provide comparable data against the same 12 types of misconduct.

References

Abbott, Tony, 'Against the Prodigal State', Centre for Independent Studies, *Policy* (Spring 2001), 37–9.

———— Transcript of *Four Corners*, 'Going Backwards', ABC, 2001, at http://www.abc.net.au/4corners/stories/s326017.htm, viewed 31 Aug. 2006.

ABC News, 'Church's Welfare-to-work Pullout a Stunt: Hockey', 18 Aug. 2006, at http://www.abc.net.au/news/stories/2006/08/18/1718019.htm, viewed 18 Aug. 2006

———— 'Govt "Leading by Example" in AWA Abolition', 13 Feb. 2008, at http://www.abc.net.au/news/stories/2008/02/13/2162103.htm, viewed 28 Feb. 2008.

Abello, David and Helen MacDonald, 'Jobs Network: Changing Community Sector Values', *The Drawing Board: An Australian Review of Public Affairs* 3(1) (2002), 51–63.

The Age, editorial, 20 July 2005, at http://www.theage.com.au/news/editorial/nelson-calls-the-research-tune/2005/07/19/1121538971011.htm, viewed 3 Sept. 2006.

Allen, Geoffrey, 'A Different Agenda: The Changing Meaning of Public Service Efficiency and Responsiveness in Australia's Public Services', Doctoral Dissertation, Griffith University, 2005.

Anderson, Eve, Gerard Griffin and Julien Teicher, 'From Industrial Relations to Workplace Relations in the Australian Tax Office: An Incomplete but Strategic Transition', *Journal of Industrial Relations* 47(3) (2005), 339–52.

Andrews, Kevin, 'Right of Entry', media release, 9 Oct. 2005, at http://www.apsc.gov.au/publications98/apsreformminister.htm, viewed 15 Aug. 2007.

Australian National Audit Office, *Developing Policy Advice*, ANAO Audit Report no. 21, 2001–2 (Canberra, 2001).

———— *Managing People for Business Outcomes: Year Two, Across Agency*, ANAO Audit Report no. 50, 2002–3 (Canberra, 2003).

———— *Performance Management in the Australian Public Service*, ANAO Audit Report no. 6, 2004–5 (Canberra, 2004).

Australian Public Service Commission, *The Australian Experience of Public Sector Reform* (Canberra, 2003).

———— *Australian Public Service Statistical Bulletin*, 2001–02 (Canberra, 2002).

———— *Australian Public Service Statistical Bulletin*, 2002–03 (Canberra, 2003).

———— *Australian Public Service Statistical Bulletin*, 2003–04 (Canberra, 2004).

———— *Australian Public Service Statistical Bulletin*, 2004–05 (Canberra, 2005).

———— *Values and Code of Conduct in Practice: Guide to Official Conduct for APS Employees and Agency Heads,* revised (Canberra, 2005), at http://www.apsc.gov.au/values/conductguidelines.htm, viewed 22 June 2007.

———— *Embedding the APS Values* (Canberra, 2003), at http://www.apsc.gov.au/values/, viewed 16 Apr. 2006.

———— 'Guidelines on the Involvement of Public Servants in Public Information and Awareness Initiatives', 12 Dec. 2007, at http://www.apsc.gov.au/publications07/publicinformation.htm., viewed 27 Feb. 2008.

———— 'Merit and Transparency: Merit-based Selection of APS Agency Heads and Statutory Office Holders', 5 Feb. 2008, at http://www.apsc.gov.au/publications08/meritandtransparency.htm., viewed 25 Feb. 2008.

———— *State of the Service Employee Survey Results 2002–03* (Canberra, 2003).

———— *State of the Service Employee Survey Results 2003–04* (Canberra, 2004).

———— *State of the Service Employee Survey Results 2004–05* (Canberra, 2005).

———— *State of the Service Employee Survey Results 2005–06* (Canberra, 2006).

———— *Supporting Ministers, Upholding the Values* (Canberra. 2006).

Ayer, Kavita, 'Poor Choices: Cicero, Tony Abbott and the Agency of Poverty', Monash University, School of Historical Studies (2004), at http://www.arts.monash.edu.au/eras/edition_6/ayerarticle.htm, viewed 3 Mar. 2007.

Barrett, Pat, 'Auditing in a Changing Government Environment', paper based on a lecture in Department of the Senate Occasional Lecture Series, 21 June 2002, at http://www.aph.gov.au/Senate/pubs/pops/pop39/c05.pdf, viewed 4 July 2007.

———— 'Results Based Management and Performance Reporting—An Australian Perspective', 5 Oct. 2004, at http://www.anao.gov.au/uploads/documents/Results_Based_Management_and_Performance_Reporting1.pdf, viewed 16 Feb.2006.

Bartos, Stephen, 'The AWB Affair—Matters of Governance', National Institute for Governance, 1 May 2006, at http://governance.canberra.edu.au/our_work/recent_events/Seminars/The%20AWB%20Affair.pdf1, viewed 1 Mar. 2007.

Behm, Allan, Lynne Bennington and James Cummane, 'A Value-creating Model for Effective Policy Services', *Journal of Management Development* 19(3) (2000), 162–78.

Bevir, Mark and R.A.W. Rhodes, 'A Decentered Theory of Governance: Rational Choice, Institutionalism and Interpretation', University of California Institute of Governmental Studies working paper (2001), at http://www.igs.berkeley.edu/publications/workingpapers/WP2001-10.pdf, viewed 3 Mar. 2007.

Blunn, Tony, 'Public Service values in the New Millennium', *Canberra Bulletin of Public Administration* 107 (2003), 28–31.

Bourgon, Jocelyn, 'Citizens, Government, Democracy: A New Deal?', Saskatchewan Institute of Public Policy, University of Regina, no. 1 (2000), 1, 6, at http://www.uregina.ca/sipp/documents/pdf/may.pdf, viewed 3 July 2007.

Brawley, Sean, 'A Comfortable and Relaxed Past: John Howard and the "Battle of History": The First Phase—February 1992 to March 1996', *Electronic Journal of Australian and New Zealand History*, (1997), at http://www.jcu.edu.au/aff/history/articles/brawley.htm, viewed 31 Aug. 2006.

Briggs, Lynelle, 'Public Service Reform', SES breakfast, 12 May 2005, at http://www.apsc.gov.au/media/briggs120505.htm, viewed 25 June 2007.

———— 'A Passion for Policy?', ANZSOG/ANU Public Lecture Series, 29 June 2005, at http://www.apsc.gov.au/media/briggs290605.htm viewed 30 Aug. 2006.

———— 'APS Governance', keynote address to DEWR Governance Workshop, 22 Feb. 2005, at http://www.apsc.gov.au/media/briggs220205a.htm, viewed 16 Feb. 2008.

———— 'The Australian Public Service: Looking to the Future', Department of Finance and Administration seminar series: Challenging Tomorrow, 24 Mar. 2006.

———— '*Supporting Ministers, Upholding the APS Values*: A Good Practice Guide—Public Service Commissioner's Launch', 9 Mar. 2006, at http://www.apsc.gov.au/media/briggs090306.htm, viewed 20 June 2006.

Casey, John and Bronwen Dalton, 'Ties that Bind? The Impact of Contracting and Project-based Funding Regimes on Advocacy', paper presented to Australian Political Studies Association Conference, University of Adelaide, 2004.

Catholic Welfare Australia, *Reading the Signs of the Times: Challenges to the Future of Social Services in Australia*, Jan. 2006 (draft made available to ABC

Background Briefing, 1 Oct. 2006), at http://www.abc.net.au/rn/backgroundbriefing/stories/2006/1748895.htm, viewed 5 July 2007.

Chalmers, Jim and Glyn Davis, 'Rediscovering Implementation: Public Sector Contracting and Human Services', *Australian Journal of Public Administration* 6(2) (2001) 74–85.

Chapman, Jake, *System Failure* (Demos, 2002), at www.demos.co.uk, viewed 27 Sept. 2006.

Cleary, M., 'The Role and Influence of the Nonprofit Sector in Australia', APPC Conference on Governance, Organisational Effectiveness and the Nonprofit Sector, 5–7 Sept. 2003.

Cole, Terence, *Report of the Inquiry into Certain Australian Companies in Relation to the UN Oil-for-Food Programme*, vol. 1. (2006).

Comrie, Neil, *Report of the Inquiry into the Circumstances of the Vivian Alvarez Matter* (Sept. 2005).

Davis, Glyn and R. A. W. Rhodes, 'From Hierarchy to Contracts and Back Again: Reforming the Australian Public Service', in M. Keating, J. Wanna and P. Weller (eds), *Institutions on the Edge? Capacity for Governance* (Allen & Unwin: Sydney, 2000), 74–98.

Davis, Mark, 'Workplace Ad May Breach Public Service Code, Says Gillard', *Brisbane Times*, 17 July 2007, at http://www.brisbanetimes.com.au/news/national/workplace-ad-may-breach-public-service-code-says-gillard/2007/07/16/1184559705331.html, viewed 17 July 2007.

Department of Education, Employment and Workplace Relations, Submission to the Senate Inquiry into the *Workplace Relations Amendment (Transition to Forward with Fairness) Bill 2008*, 29 Feb. 2008, at http://www.aph.gov.au/Senate/committee/eet_ctte/wr_tff08/submissions/sub27.pdf, viewed 7 Mar. 2008.

Department of Employment, Workplace Relations and Small Business, 2001 APS non-SES Remuneration Survey (2002), at http://www.workplace.gov.au/workplace/Organisation/Government/Federal/Reports/OtherAPSRemunerationSurveys.htm, viewed 15 July 2007.

Department of Employment and Workplace Relations, 2002 APS SES Remuneration Survey (2003), at http://www.workplace.gov.au/workplace/Organisation/Government/Federal/Reports/OtherAPSRemunerationSurveys.htm, viewed 15 July 2007.

——— *Annual Report 2002–03* (2003), at http://www.dewr.gov.au/dewr/Publications/AnnualReports/2002-03/, viewed 23 July 2007.

———— 'APS—Workplace Relations Policy Parameters for Agreement Making in the Australian Public Service' (Dec. 2003).

———— 'APS—Supporting Guidance for the Policy Parameters for Agreement making in the Australian Public Service' (June 2004).

———— *2005 APS Remuneration Survey* (current at 31 Dec. 2005) (2006), at http://www.workplace.gov.au/workplace/Organisation/Government/Federal/Reports/2005APSRemunerationSurvey.htm, viewed 24 June 2006.

———— 'APS—Supporting Guidance for the Workplace Relations Policy Parameters for Agreement Making in the Australian Public Service' (2006), at http://www.workplace.gov.au/NR/rdonlyres/68451B6C-5FBD-4F53-B705-0A8B3C623031/0/SupportingGuidanceGovernmentsPolicyParametersApril2006.pdf, viewed 24 June 2006.

Department of Immigration and Multicultural and Indigenous Affairs, *2002–03 Annual Report* (Canberra, 2003), at http://www.immi.gov.au/annual_report/annrep03/report03.htm, viewed 21 Feb. 2006.

Department of Industrial Relations, *1994 Annual Report on Enterprise Bargaining in Australia: Developments under the Industrial Relations Reform Act* (AGPS: Canberra, 1995).

———— *1995 Annual Report on Enterprise Bargaining in Australia: Developments under the Industrial Relations Reform Act* (AGPS: Canberra, 1996).

Edwards, Meredith, 'Social Science Research and Public Policy: Narrowing the Divide', Academy of Social Sciences in Australia: Policy Paper no. 2 (Canberra, 2004).

Fortier, Isabelle, 'From Skepticism to Cynicism: Paradoxes of Administrative Reform', *Choices: Journal of the Institute for Research on Public Policy* 9(6) (Aug. 2003), 13ff.

Franklin, Matthew, 'Workplace Authority Boss in Clear over Ads', *The Australian*, 1 Aug. 2007, p. 2.

———— , 'Labor to Lift Gag on Critics', *Australian*, 9 Jan. 2008, at <http://www.theaustralian.news.com.au/story/0,25197,23026526-12332,00.html, viewed 28 Feb. 2008.

Gallet, Wilma, 'What Sets Us Apart?', *BriefCACE*, no. 32, July 2006, pp. 1–4.

Goldsmith, Stephen and William D.Eggers, *Governing by Network: The New Shape of the Public Sector* (The Brookings Institution Press, Washington D.C., 2004).

Goodin, Robert E., 'Democratic Accountability: The Third Sector and All', paper presented to seminar series on 'Institutional Analysis of Law, Politics, and Society' at the Baldy Center for Law and Social Policy, State University of New York Law School, 12 Mar. 2004, at http://www.law.buf-falo.edu/baldycenter/pdfs/goodinpaper04.pdf, viewed 16 Aug. 2007.

Grattan, Michelle, 'Paternal Policies Protect values under Threat: PM', reporting on a speech to the Centre for Independent Studies, *The Age*, 5 May 2006, p. 6, at http://www.theage.com.au/news/national/paternal-policies-protect-values-under-threat-pm/2006/05/04/1146335868659.html?page=fullpage, viewed 6 Mar. 2007.

Halligan, John, 'Labor, the Keating Term and the Senior Public Service', in Gwynneth Singleton (ed.), *The Second Keating Government: Australian Commonwealth Administration 1993–1996* (Canberra, 1997), 50–62.

——— 'The Integrated Performance Model in the Australian Public Sector and its Consequences for Public Sector Organisations', paper for Panel on Autonomy and Steering Models of Public Sector Organisations, 9th International Research Symposium on Public Management, Milan, 2005, at http://scholar.google.com/scholar?hl=en&lr=&q=cache:s-dZ71LFftQJ:www.blis.canberra.edu.au/crpsm/activities/documents/JohnHalliganpaper.doc+Halligan+Integrated+performance+model, viewed Mar. 2007.

Hamilton, Clive, 'The Dirty Politics of Climate Change', speech to Climate Change and Business Conference, Adelaide, 20 Feb. 2006, at http://www.tai.org.au/, viewed 30 Aug. 2006.

Hamilton, Clive and Sarah Maddison, *Silencing Dissent* (Allen and Unwin: Sydney, 2007).

Hannan, Ewin and Shaun Carney, 'Thinkers of Influence', *The Age*, 10 Dec. 2005, p. 6.

Hazelhurst, Cameron and John Nethercote (eds.), *Reforming Australian Government: The Coombs Report and Beyond* (Royal Institute of Public Administration/Australian National University Press: Canberra, 1997).

Henderson, M. and P., 'Partnerships for Service Delivery: Review of the Research and Practice Literature', Report to the Queensland Department of Communities (2004), at http://www.getinvolved.qld.gov.au/share_yourknowledge/resources/documents/pdf/partnershipreview.pdf, viewed 5 Mar. 2007.

Hockey, Joe, 'Appointment of Director and Deputy Director, Workplace Authority, and Workplace Ombudsman', press conference, 21 June 2007, at http://www.joehockey.com/mediahub/transcriptDetail.aspx?prID=, viewed 17 Aug. 2007.

Horin, Adele, 'Hillsong Thinks Again on Welfare', *Sydney Morning Herald*, 24 Aug. 2006, at http://www.smh.com.au/articles/2006/08/23/1156012614378.html, viewed 30 Aug. 2006.

Howard, John, 'The Role of Government: A Modern Liberal Approach', Menzies Research Centre National Lecture Series (1995), at http://www.ozpolitics.info/election2004/1995-rolegovt.htm, viewed 1 Mar. 2007.

———— 'Ethical Standards and values in the Australian Public Service', *Canberra Bulletin of Public Administration*, no. 80 (1996), 1–3.

———— Transcript of the Prime Minister the Hon John Howard MP interview with Kerri-Anne Kennerley, Radio 2GB, 1 Nov. 2001, at http://www.pm.gov.au/news/interviews/2001/interview1434.htm, viewed 31 Aug. 2006.

———— 'Strategic Leadership for Australia: Policy Directions in a Complex World', Nov. 2002, www.dpmc.gov.au/speeches/pm/leadership/contents.cfm, viewed 4 Sept. 2006.

———— 'A Sense of Balance: The Australian Achievement in 2006', address to National Press Club, Parliament House, Jan. 2006, at http://www.pm.gov.au/media/Speech/2006/speech1754.cfm, viewed 6 Mar. 2007.

James, Carolynne, 'Economic Rationalism and Public Sector Ethics—Conflicts and Catalysts', *Australian Journal of Public Administration* 62(1) (2003), 95–108.

Kayrooz, Carole, Pamela Kinnear and Paul Preston, 'Academic Freedom and Commercialisation of Australian Universities: Perceptions and Experiences of Social Scientists', The Australia Institute discussion paper no. 37 (2001), at http://www.tai.org.au/documents/dp_fulltext/DP37.pdf., viewed 1 Mar. 2007.

Keating, Paul, 'Performance and Accountability in the Public Service: A Statement by the Prime Minister', Parliament House, 1 July 1993.

Kelly, Gavin, Geoff Mulgan and Stephen Muers, 'Creating Public Value: An Analytical Framework for Public Service Reform', Strategy Unit, UK Cabinet Office, (2002), at http://www.cabinetoffice.gov.uk/strategy/downloads/files/public_value2.pdf, viewed 6 Mar. 2007.

Kemp, David, 'Reforming the Public Service to Meet the Global Challenge', address to Committee for Economic Development of Australia, Melbourne, 25 Feb. 1998, at http://www.apsc.gov.au/publications98/apsreformminister.htm, viewed15 Aug. 2007

———— announcement that employment services will be contracted out to a range of organisations (to be known as the Jobs Network), media release,

26 Feb. 1998, at http://www.detya.gov.au/ministers/kemp/K10_260298.htm, viewed 5 Mar. 2007.

———— 'Agreement Making and Reforms in the APS', conference on agreement making and achieving corporate goals, Canberra, 26 Mar. 1998. .

Kitay, Jim and Russell Lansbury, 'Human Resource Management and Industrial Relations in an Era of Global Markets: Australian and International Trends', *Human Resource Management and Workplace Change*, Proceedings of an Economic Planning Advisory Commission roundtable, Canberra, 6 Feb. 1995, pp. 17–70.

Langford, John, 'Acting on values: An Ethical Dead End for Public Servants', *Canadian Public Administration* 47(4) (2004), 429–50.

Lawrence, David, 'Calls for Govt to Drop Latest Workplace Ads', *Lateline*, broadcast 1 Aug. 2007, at http://www.abc.net.au/lateline/content/2007/s1994498.htm, viewed 17 Aug. 2007.

Legge, Karen, *Human Resource Management: Rhetorics and Realities* (Macmillan: London, 1995).

Macdonald, Duncan, 'Public Sector Industrial Relations under the Howard Government', *Labour and Industry* 9(2) (1998), 43–59.

McGuinness, P. P., 'A Politicised Public Service?', *Quadrant* editorial, no 93, Apr. 2007, at http://www.henrythornton.com/article.asp?article_id=4647, viewed 28 Feb. 2008.

McIntosh, Kylie, Jason Shauness and Roger Wettenhall, *Contracting out in Australia: An Indicative History*, University of Canberra Centre for Research in Public Sector Management (Canberra, 1997).

Maddison, Sarah, Richard Denniss and Clive Hamilton, (eds), 'Silencing Dissent: Non-government Organisations and Australian Democracy', The Australia Institute, discussion paper no 65 (2004), at http://www.tai.org.au/documents/dp_fulltext/DP65.pdf, viewed 1 Mar. 2007.

Management Advisory Board/Management Improvement Advisory Committee, *The Australian Public Service Reformed: An Evaluation of a Decade of Management Reform* Task Force on Management Improvement (Canberra, 1992).

Management Advisory Board, *Building a Better Public Service* (AGPS: Canberra, 1993).

Management Advisory Committee, *Performance Management in the Australian Public Service: A Strategic Framework* (Canberra, 2001).

———— *Connecting Government: Whole of Government Responses to Australia's Priority Challenges* (Canberra, 2004).

Manne, Robert, 'The Nation Reviewed', *The Monthly*, no. 12, May 2006,

Marcussen, Martin and Jacob Torfing, 'Grasping Governance Networks', Centre for Democratic Network Governance Roskilde University Working Paper Series, no. 5 (2003).

Marr, David and Miriam Wilkinson, *Dark Victory* (Allen and Unwin: Sydney, 2003).

Mulgan, Richard, 'Public Accountability of Provider Agencies: The Case of the Australian "Centrelink"', *International Review of Administrative Sciences* 68(1) (2002), 45–59.

————— 'Government Accountability for Outsourced Services', *Australian Journal of Public Administration* 65(2) (2006), 48-58. and Government discussion papers, 2005, at http://www.crawford.anu.edu.au/de-grees/pogo/discussion_papers/PDP05-6.pdf, viewed 5 Mar. 2007.

————— 'Outsourcing and Public Service Values: The Australian Experience', *International Review of Administrative Sciences* 71(1) (2005), 55-70.

————— 'Truth in Government and the Politicisation of Public Service Advice', *Public Administration* 85(3) (2007), 569–86.

Munro, Paul 'The *WorkChoices* Legislation: A Factor in the Rationale for Founding the Australian Institute for Employment Rights', 30 Nov. 2005, at http://www.buseco.monash.edu.au/mgt/re-search/aier/speeches.php, viewed 30 Aug. 2006.

National Commission of Audit, *Report to the Commonwealth Government* (AGPS: Canberra, 1996), at http://www.finance.gov.au/pubs/ncoa/exec-sum.htm#I1, viewed 5 Mar. 2007.

National Foundation for Australian Women, 'What Women Want: Consultations on Welfare to Work and Work Choices', at http://www.nfaw.org/so-cial/www/what-women-want.pdf, viewed 27 July 2007.

Nethercote, John 1997, 'New Public Service Legislation: The *Public Service Bill 1997*', Parliamentary Library Background Paper no. 2, 1997–8, 22 Sept. 1997, http://www.aph.gov.au/Library/pubs/bp/1997-98/98bp02.htm, viewed 8 Jan. 2008.

Nicholson, Tony, 'Poverty Is Not an Item in a Press Pelease', *The Age*, 8 May 2006, p. 15.

O'Brien, John, 'Workplace Productivity Bargaining in the Australian Public Sector', in Jenny Stewart (ed.), *From Hawke to Keating, Australian Commonwealth Administration 1990–1993*, University of Canberra Centre for Research in Public Sector Management with the Royal Institute of Public Administration Australia (RIPAA) (Canberra, 1995), 85–102.

———— 'Employment Relations and Agency Bargaining in the Australian Public Service, 1993–1996', in Gwynneth Singleton (ed.), *The Second Keating Government: Australian Commonwealth Administration 1993–1996* (Canberra, 1997), 175–94.

O'Donnell, Michael and John O'Brien, 'Performance-based Pay in the Australian Public Service: Employee Perspectives', *Review of Public Personnel Administration* 20 (2000), 20–34.

O'Donnell, Michael and John Shields, 'Performance Management and the Psychological Contract in the Australian Federal Public Sector', *Journal of Industrial Relations* 44(3) (2002), 435–57.

Organisation for Economic Cooperation and Development, 'Governance in Transition: Public Management Reforms in OECD Countries', OECD/PUMA (Paris, 1995).

———— 'In Search of Results: Perfomance Management Practices', Feb. 1997, at http://www.oecd.org/dataoecd/18/12/36144694.pdf, viewed 16 Feb. 2008.

———— *The Performing State: Reflection on an Idea whose Time Has Come but whose Implementation Has Not*, Paper for the 23rd Session of the Public Governance Committee GOV/PGC/ (2006).

Osbourne, David and Ted Gabler, *Reinventing Government: How the Entrepreneurial Spirit Is Transforming the Public Sector* (Addison-Wesley Publishing: Reading, Mass, 1992).

Osbourne, David and Peter Plastrik, *Banishing Bureaucracy: The Five Strategies for Reinventing Government* (Addison-Wesley Publishing: Reading, Mass, 1997).

Palmer, M. J., *Inquiry into the Circumstances of the Immigration Detention of Cornelia Rau: Report* (Canberra, 2005), at http://www.minister.immi.gov.au, viewed 13 Feb. 2006.

Parliament of Australia, *Senate Report on a Certain Maritime Incident* (Canberra, 2002), at http://www.aph.gov.au/senate/committee/maritime_incident_ctte/report/a06.htm, viewed 20 Apr. 2006.

Parliamentary Library, 'Changes in the Australian Public Service 1975–2003', Chronology no. 1, 2002–3, at http://www.aph.gov.au/library/pubs/chron/2002-03/03chr01.htm, viewed 1 Mar. 2007.

———— *Workplace Relations Amendment (Secret Ballots for Protected Action) Bill 2000, Bills Digest no. 18, 2000–01*, at http://www.aph.gov.au/library/pubs/bd/2000-01/01BD018.htm, viewed 24 July 2006.

——— 'Workplace Relations Reforms: A Chronology of Business, Community and Government Responses', Chronologies Online, last updated 6 Dec. 2007, at http://www.aph.gov.au/library/pubs/BN/2007-08/Workplace_Relations_chron.htm, viewed 17 Feb. 2008.

Patapan, Haig, John Wanna and Patrick Weller (eds), *Westminster Legacies* (University of New South Wales Press: Sydney, 2005).

Pearce, Dennis, Julian Disney and Heather Ridout, 'The Report of the Independent Review of Breaches and Penalties in the Social Security System' (2002), at http://eprints.anu.edu.au/archive/00001515/01/index-8.html, viewed 31 Aug. 2006,

Podger, Andrew, 'The Australian Public Service: A values-based Service', presentation to IIPE Biennial Conference on 'Reconstructing "The Public Interest" in a Globalising World: Business, the Professions and the Public Sector, Brisbane, 5 Oct. 2002, at www.apsc.gov.au/media/podger051002.htm, viewed 16 Feb. 2008.

——— 'Citizen Involvement—The Australian Experience', presentation to the CAPAM Malaysia High Level Seminar, Kuala Lumpur, 8 Oct. 2003, at http://www.apsc.gov.au/media/podger081003.htm, viewed 17 Feb. 2008.

——— 'Beyond Westminster: Defining an Australian Approach to the Roles and values of the Public Service in the 21st Century', address to IPAA Seminar, 2 May 2002, at http://www.apsc.gov.au/media/podger020502.htm, viewed 25 June 2007.

——— 'Looking Upwards and Downwards: Key Issues and Suggestions for Managing Board/Minister/Departmental Relations', paper for University of Canberra Conference on Governance, Mar. 2006.

——— 'What Really Happens: Department Secretary Appointments, Contracts and Performance Pay in the Australian Public Service', *Australian Journal of Public Administration* 66(2) (2007), 131–46.

——— 'Pride and Prejudice: Ms Bennett as the New Face of a Very Public Service', *Public Sector Informant*, 7 Aug. 2007, p. 6.

Prime Minister and Cabinet (Miscellaneous Provisions) Act 1994, at http://scaletext.law.gov.au/html/comact/8/4321/top.htm, viewed 1 Mar. 2007.

Public Service Commissioner, *2002–03 State of the Service Report* (Canberra, 2003).

——— *2003–04 State of the Service Report* (Canberra, 2004).

——— *2004–05 State of the Service Report* (Canberra, 2005).

——— *2005–06 State of the Service Report* (Canberra, 2006).

Public Service Commissioner's Directions 1999, viewed 1 March 2007, <http://scaleplus.law.gov.au/html/instruments/0/26/top.htm>

Public Service and Merit Protection Commission, *Re-engineering People Management: From Good Intentions to Good Practice* (Canberra, 1997), at http://www.apsc.gov.au/publications96/reengineering.htm, viewed 14 Feb. 2008.

Public Service Reform Act 1984, at http://www.austlii.edu.au, viewed 1 Mar. 2007.

Quiggin, John, 'The Enron Approach Masks Hidden Dangers', Evatt Foundation, 15 Apr. 2002, at http://evatt.org.au/news/23.html, viewed 2 Mar. 2007.

Reith, Peter, *Towards a Best Practice Australian Public Service: A Discussion Paper Issued by the Minister for Industrial Relations and the Minister Assisting the Prime Minister for the Public Service* (Canberra, 1996).

———— 'Public Service Bill 1997: Second Reading Speech', 30 June 1997, at http://www.apsc.gov.au/circulars/billadvice972.htm, viewed 24 Feb. 2008.

Rhodes, R. A. W., and John Wanna, 'The Limits to Public Value, or Rescuing Responsible Governments from the Platonic Guardians', *Australian Journal of Public Administration* 66(4) (2007), 406–421.

Rowse, Tim, 'The "Responsive"Public Servant: Coombes the Man, Coombes the Report', *Australian Journal of Public Administration* 61(1) (Mar. 2002), 99–102.

Royal Commission on Australian Government Administration, *Report*, AGPS (Canberra, 1976).

Seketee, Mike, 'Service out of Order', *Weekend Australian*, 22–3 Apr. 2006, p. 18.

Shergold, Peter, 'Administrative Law and Public Service', Australian Institute of Administrative Law Opening Address, 3 July 2003, at www.pmc.gov.au/speeches/shergold/administrative_law_2003-07-03.cfm, viewed 27 June 2006.

———— 'Two Cheers for the Bureaucracy: Public Service, Political Advice and Network Governance', Australian Public Service Commission Lunchtime Seminar, 13 June 2003, at http://www.pmc.gov.au/speeches/index.cfm, viewed 27 June 2006.

———— 'Regeneration: New Structures, New Leaders, New Traditions', speech to Institute of Public Administration Australia National Conference, Canberra, 11 Nov. 2004, at http://www.pmc.gov.au/speeches/shergold/regeneration_2004-11-11.cfm, viewed 26 June 2006.

———— 'Plan and Deliver: Avoiding Bureaucratic Hold-up', speech to Australian Graduate School of Management/Harvard Club of Australia, National Press Club, Canberra, 17 Nov. 2004, at http://www.dp-mc.gov.au/speeches/shergold/plan_and_deliver_2004-11-17.cfm, viewed 27 June 2006.

———— 'Once was Camelot in Canberra? Reflections of Public Service Leadership', Sir Roland Wilson Lecture, Canberra, 23 June 2004, at www.pmc.gov.au/speeches/shergold/public_service_leadership_2004-06-23.cfm> viewed 19 June 2006.

———— 'The Australian Public Service in 2035: Back to the Future', speech to CPA Annual Conference, Melbourne, 18 May 2005, at http://www.pmc.gov.au/speeches/shergold/aps_2035_back_to_the_future_2005-05-18.cfm, viewed 25 Apr. 2006.

———— '"The Need to Wield a Crowbar": Political Will and Public Service: A Short Historical Discourse on Attempts to Overcome the Perceived Ossification and Inertia of Buttoned-up Public Servants (and Why They're Now the Better for It)', Dunstan Oration, Adelaide, 7 Apr. 2005, at http://www.dpmc.gov.au/speeches/shergold/political_will_2005-04-07.cf, viewed 23 Nov. 2005.

———— 'Goodbye to All that Power', *Public Sector Informant*, Apr. 2005, p. 2.

———— 'Government and Communities in Partnership: Sharing Responsibility', speech to Government and Communities in Partnership Conference, Melbourne, 18 May 2005, at http://www.dpmc.gov.au/speeches/shergold/sharing_responsibility_2005-05-18.cfm, viewed 25 Apr. 2006.

———— 'Pride in Public Service', speech to National Press Club, Canberra, 15 Feb. 2006, at http://www.pmc.gov.au/speeches/index.cfm, viewed 15 Mar. 2006.

Sinclair, Lara, 'Voters Fearful of IR Laws', *The Australian*, 3 Aug. 2007, at http://www.theaustralian.news.com.au/story/0,25197,22180820-5013404,00.html, viewed 17 Aug. 2007.

Smith, Stephen, 'Andrews Caught Red-handed Forcing Staff onto Contracts', media release, 21 June 2005.

Spry, Max, 'Executive and High Court Appointments', Parliamentary Library Research Paper 7, 2000–1, at http://www.aph.gov.au/library2000,/pubs/rp/2000-01/01RP07.htm#appointments, viewed 17 Feb. 2008.

Stewart, Jenny, 'Value Conflict and Policy Change', *Review of Policy Research* 23(1) (2006) 183–95.

Stoker, Gerry, 'Public Value Management: A New Narrative for Networked Governance?', *American Review of Public Administration* 36(1) (2006), 41–57.

Teicher, Julian, Quamrul Alam and Bernadine Van Gramberg, 'Managing Trust and Relationships in PPPs: Some Australian Experiences', *International Review of Administrative Sciences* 72(1) (2006), pp. 83–98.

Truss, Catherine, Lynda Gratton, Veronica Hope-Haily, Patrick McGovern and Philip Stiles, 'Soft and Hard Models of Human Resource Management: A Reappraisal', *Journal of Management Studies* 34(1) (1997), 53–73.

Van Gramberg, Bernadine and Penny Bassett, 'Neoliberalism and the Third Sector in Australia', Victoria University School of Management Working Paper Series (Melbourne, 2005), at http://eprints.vu.edu.au/archive/00000120/01/wp5_2005_bassett_gramberg.pdf., viewed 1 Mar. 2007.

Wanna, John, 'Public Service, Public Values: The Implementation of a Charter of Values in the Australian Public Service', Australasian Political Studies Association Conference, Dunedin, 2005.

Weekend Australian, 'Time to Account for AWB Scandal', editorial, 30 Sept.–1 Oct. 2006, p. 18.

Weller, Patrick, *Australia's Mandarins: The Frank and the Fearless?* (Allen & Unwin: Sydney, 2001).

———— *Don't Tell the Prime Minister* (Scribe Publications: Melbourne, 2002).

Willacy, Mark, 'Govt Says Even "Job Snobs" Can Find Work in Olympic Year', *The World Today* Archive, 28 June 2000, at http://www.abc.net.au/worldtoday/stories/s146078.htm, viewed 31 Aug. 2006.

Wong, Penny, 'Labor's Approach to the Australian Public Service', speech to the Institute of Public Administration Australia, 20 Sept. 2007.

World Bank, *Governance and Development* (Washington, D.C., 1992).

Zussman, David, 'Engaging Stakeholders: Why, When and How?', National Institute for Governance (Canberra, 2003).

Appendix: Extract from Chronology no. 1 2002-03 — Changes in the Australian Public Service 1975-2003[1]

Chronology

Milestones	Details	Source Documents
1975	Equal Employment Opportunity (EEO) Section is established in the Public Service Board to address employment inequities facing women, indigenous Australians, people with disabilities and people from a non-English speaking background.	Public Service Board, Annual Report 1974–75.
1975	Administrative Appeals Tribunal is established to provide independent review of a wide range of administrative decisions made by the Commonwealth Government and some non-government bodies.	Administrative Appeals Tribunal Act 1975.[1]
July 1975	Confrontation between the Government and the Opposition-controlled Senate over the appearance of public servants as witnesses to give evidence. Government ministers instruct public servants 'to claim privilege in respect of answers to all questions' with which the Senate was concerned. This conflict leads ultimately to the formalisation of guidelines for public service witnesses in 1978.	Senate Debates, 15 July 1975, pp. 272930. Odgers' Australian Senate Practice (10th edition), section 19.6 House of Representatives Debates, 28 September 1978, pp. 150409.
1976	Report into government administration (Coombs Commission) supports: • more accountability for public servants; • mechanisms to improve the relationship between officials and the community; • an emphasis on managerial skills; • more efficient and responsive service delivery; • devolution of responsibility, as well as greater flexibility and diversity in organisational styles; • more efficient and economical use of human resources; and • a more open public service.	Royal Commission on Australian Government Administration, Report, AGPS, Canberra, 1976.
1976	Commonwealth Ombudsman is established to consider complaints from people who believe they have been adversely affected by the defective administration of Commonwealth departments or agencies.	Ombudsman Act 1976. http://www.austlii.edu.au/
1977	Legislation to facilitate judicial review by the Federal Court of some exercises of Commonwealth power (came into operation 1 October 1980).	Administrative Decisions (Judicial Review) Act 1977.
1977	Legislation to allow for the dismissal of staff who engage in industrial action and the suspension without pay of staff who cannot work as a result of industrial action (repealed with effect from November 1983).	Commonwealth Employees (Employment Provisions) Act 1977 (now defunct).
1979	Facilitation of the retrenchment of public servants surplus to requirements and a requirement for the permanent head to ensure the efficient, effective and economical use of the department's staff.	Commonwealth Employees Redeployment and Retirement Act 1979 (now defunct).

[1] The text of legislation is available at www.austlii.edu.au and http://scaleplus.law.gov.au/

Milestones	Details	Source Documents
1980	Public Service Board advises departments to adopt the common law principle of 'No work as directed, no pay'. This is ruled not to be legal, leading to the amendment of the *Public Service Act 1922* to provide for the principle (repealed in 1983).	
1982	Extension of the right of the community to access information in the possession of the Commonwealth Government.	*Freedom of Information Act 1982.*
January 1983	Reid Report (review announced 23 September 1982) emphasises the importance of quality management (including financial management and personnel management), as well as issues relating to machinery of government, ministerial responsibility and administrative review.	Review of Commonwealth Administration report, AGPS, Canberra, 1983.
December 1983	Statement by the Prime Minister emphasises efficiency, effectiveness, equity and responsiveness to Ministers and the Parliament (leads to the *Public Service Reform Act 1984*).	R. J. L. Hawke, Reforming the Australian Public Service: A Statement of the Government's Intentions, AGPS, Canberra, 1983.
1984	Merit Protection and Review Agency established to ensure that actions taken in relation to Commonwealth employees are fair and equitable.	Merit Protection (Australian Government Employees) Act 1984.
1984	Public Service Reform Act 1984: • enshrinement of the merit principle; • equal employment opportunity; • industrial democracy; • permanent part-time work; • opening up of opportunities at lower levels; • formation of Senior Executive Service (effective 1 October 1984); • provision for consultants to be appointed by ministers; and • greater political role in appointing and managing departmental secretaries (no longer 'Permanent Heads').	*Public Service Reform Act 1984* (now defunct).
1984	Abolition of the Public Service Arbitrator.	Conciliation and Arbitration Amendment Act 1983.
February 1984	Financial Management Improvement Program emphasises a shift away from compliance towards performance control (including program budgeting which is phased in during the mid-1980s).	Australian Public Service Board and Department of Finance, *Financial Management Improvement ProgramDiagnostic Study*, 1984.
21 March 1984	Announcement that a working party will monitor EEO practices in the Department of Employment and Industrial Relations and develop a management plan (other departments to follow).	
26 March 1984	Cabinet agrees to proceed with changes outlined in Reforming the Australian Public Service: A Statement of the Government's Intentions.	
April 1984	*Budget Reform* paper sets out the Government's reform priorities: • better means of identifying and setting budget priorities; • more emphasis on the goals and objectives of programs; • improved performance and efficiency; and • effective review mechanisms.	Department of Finance, Budget ReformA Statement of the Government's Achievements and Intentions in Reforming Australian Government Financial Administration, AGPS, Canberra, 1984.
June 1984	The *Members of Parliament (Staff) Act 1984* takes effect. This legislation creates a separate, formal legislative basis for the employment of staff by members of parliament, making such employment potentially independent from public service employment.	Members of Parliament (Staff) Act 1984

Milestones	Details	Source Documents
1985	Public Service Board develops a model Occupational Health and Safety (OH&S) agreement.	
11 June 1986	Prime Minister announces the streamlining and rationalisation of some functions and agencies in response to difficult economic circumstances.	R. J. L. Hawke, Address to the Nation on the Economic Situation, 11 June 1986.
25 September 1986	Prime Minister's statement to Parliament announces: • establishment of Efficiency Scrutiny Unit to investigate cost-saving opportunities; • measures to enhance financial efficiency; and • changes to personnel management.	R. J. L. Hawke, *Statement to the House of Representatives on Reform of the Australian Public Service*, 25 September 1986.
1987	Restructuring and Efficiency Principle rationalises job classifications for clerical and support staff.	
July 1987	Efficiency Scrutiny Unit recommends the replacement of the Public Service Board with a Public Service Commission (holding a reduced role), the devolution of some functions to departments and the transfer of some functions to the Department of Employment and Industrial Relations and to the Department of Finance.	D. Bock, Report by Efficiency Scrutiny Unit on proposed successor. arrangements to the Public Service Board, Canberra, 1987.
14 July 1987	Announcement of the formation of 'mega departments', generally headed by a senior minister assisted by junior ministers (number of departments reduced from 28 to 18).	Prime Minister's media release, 14 July 1987.
18 September 1987	Replacement of Public Service Board with smaller Public Service Commission (some responsibilities transferred to the Department of Finance or the Department of Industrial Relations, or devolved to departments). Establishment of Australian Public Service Management Advisory Board, to advise the Government on significant management issues and act as a forum for consideration of major management activities (replaced by the Management Advisory Committee in 1999).	*Administrative Arrangements Act 1987* (now defunct).
April 1988	The Parliamentary Joint Committee on Public Accounts (JCPA) commences a review of the Audit Office. The Committee's report, delivered in 1989, would lead ultimately to the introduction of the Auditor-General Bill 1994, and finally the passage of the *Auditor-General Act 1997*, which would establish the Auditor-General as an officer of the Parliament (see also 1 January 1998, below).	JCPA, The Auditor- General: Ally of the People and the ParliamentReform of the Audit Office, Report no. 296.
August 1988	Adoption of the Structural Efficiency Principle leads to rationalisation of job classifications for professional, technical and blue collar grades.	
8 December 1988	*Privacy Act 1988* passed, regulating the collection, handling and use of personal information by the Commonwealth, and also establishing the Privacy Commissioner within the Human Rights and Equal Opportunity Commission.	*Privacy Act 1988*
December 1989	Management Improvement Advisory Committee established to support the Management Advisory Board.	
March 1990	Aboriginal and Torres Strait Islander Commission replaces the Commonwealth's Department of Aboriginal Affairs and Aboriginal Development Commission, taking over responsibility for many of the Commonwealth's indigenous programs.	Aboriginal and Torres Strait Islander Commission Act 1989
12 June 1990	Privacy Commissioner releases a directory detailing the amount and type of records of a personal nature held by the Commonwealth.	*Personal Information Digest*, Human Rights and Equal Opportunity Commission, Sydney, 1989.

Milestones	Details	Source Documents
August 1990	Decision to restructure the Commonwealth Bank in preparation for a partial public float heralds a series of major full or partial privatisations, including: • Commonwealth Bank; • Qantas and Australian Airlines; • Telstra (announced October 1997); • Major airports; • Moomba-Sydney gas pipeline; • National electricity transmission network; and • DASFLEET.	Department of Finance and Administration, *Asset Sales: Past Projects* Commonwealth Bank Restructuring Bill 1990, *Bills Digest* 8 November 1990.
13 November 1990	Economic Planning and Advisory Council (EPAC) report concludes that productivity improvements in the public sector have generally outpaced those in the private sector.	The size and efficiency of the public sector, Canberra, EPAC, 1990.
1991	Occupational Health and Safety programs required in agencies, to be developed in consultation with unions.	Occupational Health and Safety Act 1991
July 1991	Agencies are allowed to use property service providers other than the Department of Administrative Services, and a 1.25 per cent Efficiency Dividend clawback is applied to the running costs of all agencies.	John Wanna, Christine Ryan and Chew Ng, From Accounting to Accountability. A Centenary History of the Australian National Audit Office, Allen & Unwin, 2001, p. 136.
15 July 1992	Announcement that the Refugee Review Tribunal will replace the Refugee Status Review Committee, resulting in more limited avenues of appeal.	
9 September 1992	Announcement that all new contracts with the Department of Administrative Services will include a clause requiring suppliers to comply with the EEO requirements of the Government.	
6 November 1992	Announcement of a workplace agreement allowing for productivity reforms and agency-level bargaining.	
December 1992	An evaluation of a decade of management changes concludes: • the direction of change was correct; • changes were well accepted, and had many; positive effects as well as some costs; and • further changes needed to be undertaken.	Task Force on Management Improvement, The Australian Public Service Reformed: An evaluation of a decade of management reform, AGPS, 1992.
December 1992	Service-wide *APS Agreement 199294* (extended to 1995) includes: • some funded wage increases; • further pay negotiations at agency level; and • equalisation of pay on expiry of agreement.	Improving productivity, jobs and pay in the Australian Public Service 199294, Department of Industrial Relations, December 1992.
December 1992	Performance pay introduced for SES and senior officers in order to encourage productivity growth (later wound back for senior officers).	Improving productivity, jobs and pay in the Australian Public Service 199294Agreement between the Commonwealth Government and public sector unions, Canberra, 1992.
1993	Audit Office (ANAO) undertakes an audit of the 1992 performance pay agreement. The audit finds almost all senior staff were given pay increases under the scheme, and that the scheme was a *de facto* system for awarding significant pay increases.	ANAO, 'Performance Pay: Performance Appraisal and Pay in the Australian Public Service', *Audit Report* no. 16, 1993, ANAO, Canberra. John Wanna, Christine Ryan and Chew Ng, From Accounting to Accountability. A Centenary History of the Australian National Audit Office, Allen & Unwin, 2001, pp. 14246.

Milestones	Details	Source Documents
1994	Provision of fixed term appointments for departmental Secretaries.	Prime Minister and Cabinet (Miscellaneous Provisions) Act 1994.
June 1994	In response to the 1989 Joint Committee on Public Accounts' (JCPA) report on the Audit Office, the Government introduces new financial accountability legislation, and announces its intention that the Auditor-General be funded directly from the Budget and that a parliamentary Audit Committee be established. (Ultimately, no separate committee is set up. Instead, the JCPA is changed to the Joint Committee on Public Accounts and Audit).	House of Representatives Debates, 29 June 1994, p. 5796. 'Auditor plans are good, not ideal', *Canberra Times*, 22 June 1994.
7 October 1994	Cabinet introduces measures to enforce equal representation of women on public boards and committees.	
1995	Report of the Public Service Act Review Group recommends that the *Public Service Act 1922* be replaced by a new Act that will be 'built around the principles and values which stress the centrality of an apolitical public service with merit-based staffing, high standards of honesty and integrity, a strong focus on efficiency and results, and responsiveness and accountability to the government of the day while maintaining a capacity to provide quality and impartial advice.'	R. McLeod, Report of the Public Service Act Review Group, AGPS, Canberra, 1994.
1995	Public Service and Merit Protection Commission (PSMPC) established through the amalgamation of the Public Service Commission and the Merit Protection and Review Agency.	
4 May 1995	Government announces plans to replace the Public Service Act 1922 in response to Report of the Public Service Act Review Group.	
July 1995	Government and unions agree to a service-wide enterprise agreement for 1995–96.	
14 September 1995	Administrative Review Council's report into the effectiveness of the merits review tribunals makes a number of recommendations, including the consolidation of five tribunals into a single new tribunal.	Administrative Review Council, Better decisions: review of Commonwealth Merits Review Tribunals, Canberra, AGPS, 1995.
September 1995	Service-wide APS agreement 1995–96 includes a strategy for securing further efficiencies.	*Continuous Improvement in the APS*, Agreement between the Commonwealth Government and public sector unions, September 1995.
1996	Six departmental secretaries' appointments terminated following the change of government. The departures were: • Christopher Conybeare (Immigration); • Peter Core (Transport); • Michael Costello (Foreign Affairs and Trade); • Stephen Duckett (Health); • Stuart Hamilton (Environment); and • Derek Volker (Employment Education and Training).	'Top bureaucrats victims of purge', *Sydney Morning Herald*, 9 March 1996.
1996	Industry Commission, Bureau of Industry Economics and Economic Planning Advisory Commission amalgamate on an administrative basis. In 1998 they become the Productivity Commission.	*Productivity Commission Act 1998* Productivity Commission website: *History of the Productivity Commission*
June 1996	National Commission of Audit (established March 1996) recommends a more limited role for government, a greater emphasis on effectiveness and efficiency, and the separation of policy formation from program delivery.	National Commission of Audit, *Report to the Commonwealth Government*, Canberra, AGPS, 1996.

Milestones	Details	Source Documents
November 1996	Discussion paper issued by The Hon Peter Reith MP, leads to the *Public Service Act 1999* and the *Parliamentary Service Act 1999*. It points to the potential benefits of flexibility, streamlining and cultural change.	P. Reith, *Towards a Best Practice Australian Public Service*, November 1996.
November 1996	Small Business Deregulation Task Force reports to the Government on ways to reduce the compliance burden on small businesses (e.g. single entry point for collection of information and effective use of information technology).	Small Business Deregulation Task Force, *Time for Business*, 1996.
December 1996	Under the Workplace Relations Act 1996: • illegal for agencies to pay employees while on strike, or using bans or limitations; • limitations on union officials' access to workplaces; • provision for agencies to make individual agreements with staff; • award simplification, removing some rights that had been negotiated under previous awards; and • move from paid rate awards to minimum rate awards (eroding pay over time).	Workplace Relations Act 1996.
1997	Government introduces Public Service Bill (amended Bill passed in 1999).	
March 1997	Agencies to be responsible for agreement making, using certified agreements and/or Australian Workplace Agreements, and subject to the Government's policy parameters.	Media release, Minister for Industrial Relations, 5 March 1997.
March 1997	All government departments, agencies and business enterprises dealing with the public to be required to develop customer service charters.	Media release, *Putting service first in the public service*, Minister for Small Business and Consumer Affairs, 26 March 1997.
20 March 1997	Attorney-General announces that the Government proposes to amalgamate the Administrative Appeals Tribunal, the Social Security Appeals Tribunal, the Immigration Review Tribunal and the Refugee Review Tribunal to create a single review body to be called the Administrative Review Tribunal (expected to commence operations in February 2001). Originally, the Veterans' Review Board was also to be amalgamated but this was reversed in February 1992.	Media release, *Reform of merits tribunal*, Attorney-General, 20 March 1997. Media release, *Establishment of the Administrative Review Tribunal*, Attorney-General, 9 May 2000.
24 March 1997	Prime Minister responds to the *Time for Business* report, agreeing to a range of measures including the electronic facility, www.business.gov.au	J. Howard, *More Time for Business*, Canberra, AGPS, 1997.
25 April 1997	Announcement that departments' information technology infrastructure will be outsourced to the private sector.	Media release, *Outsourcing of Information Technology infrastructure*, Minister for Finance, 25 April 1997.
July 1997	First Australian Workplace Agreement in the APS.	The Hon. Dr David Kemp MP, 'An Overview of APS ReformsWhat we are doing', 25 February 1998.
24 September 1997	Launch of Centrelink, a statutory authority that provides customer services on behalf of several government agencies (a significant example of split between purchaser and provider of services).	*Commonwealth Service Delivery Act 1997.* http://www.centrelink.gov.au/
26 November 1997	First Certified Agreements in the APS (agreements at department or agency level)Public Service and Merit Protection Commission.	
8 December 1997	Commitment that all appropriate government services will be Internet-deliverable by 2001.	Media release, *OGIT to play leading role bringing Australia online*, Minister for Finance and Administration, 8 December 1997.

Milestones	Details	Source Documents
11 December 1997	Announcement of new purchasing arrangements, including the establishment of a new Purchasing Advisory and Complaints Service.	Media release, *Government purchasing: a better deal for business*, Minister for Finance and Administration and Minister for Industry, Science and Tourism, 11 December 1997. Media release, *New Purchasing Advisory and Complaints Service*, Minister for Finance and Administration, 9 March 1998.
1998	*Charter of Budget Honesty Act 1998* is passed, providing for the publication of: • regular reports setting out fiscal strategy; • an intergenerational report at least once every five years assessing the long term sustainability of government policies; • a pre-election economic and fiscal outlook report; and • costing of election commitments.	Charter of Budget Honesty Act 1998.
1 January 1998	Package of new financial management legislation comes into effect:	
	• responsibilities of agency heads in such areas as record keeping, fraud control and borrowing;	*Financial Management and Accountability Act 1997.*
	• reporting and auditing requirements for Commonwealth authorities, as well as standards of conduct;and	Commonwealth Authorities and Companies Act 1997.
	• more independence for the Auditor-General and a greater role for Parliament in advising of its audit priorities, approving the appointment of the Auditor-General and reviewing the budget of the Auditor-General.	Auditor-General Act 1997.
26 February 1998	Announcement that employment services will be contracted out to a range of organisations (to be known as the Job Network).	Media release, *New Job Network to replace the CES*, Minister for Education, Training and Youth Affairs, 26 February 1998.
March 1998	Regulations are introduced into Parliament requiring the Public Service Commissioner to present an annual *State of the Service Report* to Parliament.	Regulation 12 of the Public Service Regulations.
11 March 1998	First fully audited accrual financial statements for the Commonwealth.	Media release, *Milestone reached in shift to accrual-based budget*, Minister for Finance and Administration, 11 March 1998.
April 1998	Productivity Commission established as the Government's principal review and advisory body on microeconomic policy and regulation.	Productivity Commission Act 1998.
May 1998	New procurement guidelines provide 'core policies and principles intended to strike a balance between prescription and empowerment so as to encourage agencies to obtain the best value from procurement, on a whole of life basis'.	*Procurement Guidelinescore policies and principles*, Department of Finance and Administration, 1998.
1 July 1998	Commonwealth's policy of non-insurance is replaced with a policy of self-insurance, providing more incentive to manage risk.	Media release, *Responsible Risk Management for the Commonwealth Government*, Minister for Finance and Administration, 30 June 1998.
3 July 1998	Business Entry Point is launched (an electronic information and transaction facility for businesses).	www.business.gov.au

Milestones	Details	Source Documents
3 August 1998	Launch of a booklet outlining the Government's expectations of the APS in areas such as customer focus, agreement making and performance measurement.	*APS Reform: Building on Good Practice,* Public Service and Merit Protection Commission, 1998.
4 March 1999	Remuneration Tribunal determines a new approach to setting the remuneration levels for departmental secretaries which includes provision for an annual performance bonus, to become available during 1999-2000 (the Prime Minister to make a recommendation to the Tribunal on the performance of a secretary after considering a report prepared by the Secretary to the Department of Prime Minister and Cabinet and the Public Service Commissioner).	
11 May 1999	First accrual Budget delivered (an agency is funded for an agreed price for its outputs, including non-cash items such as depreciation). The accrual budgeting framework includes the introduction of the Capital Use Charge and the Agency Banking Incentive Scheme. The first requires agencies to include the costs to their operations of capital use; the second requires agencies to conduct their own banking and manage their annual appropriations.	Media release, *First accrual-based Budget in 1999*, Minister for Finance and Administration, 24 November 1998.
19 May 1999	Senior Executive Leadership Capability Framework, prioritises: • shaping strategic thinking; • achieving results; • cultivating productive working relationships; • exemplifying personal drive and integrity; and • communicating with influence.	Media release, *Launch of the Senior Executive Leadership Capability Framework, Canberra*, Minister Assisting the Prime Minister for the Public Service, 19 May 1999.
1 July 1999	Agencies able to operate bank accounts with private sector banks, opening the Reserve Bank of Australia to competition.	Media release, *Government to open its transactional banking to competition*, Minister for Finance and Administration, 31 July 1998.
19 August 1999	Dismissal of Paul Barratt (Secretary of Defence) upheld by the Federal Court: • Prime Minister does not require cause to dismiss a secretary; and • a dismissed secretary is entitled to hear the grounds on which they are to be dismissed, and to put their case to the Secretary of the Department of Prime Minister and Cabinet.	Barratt v Howard [1999] FCA 1183
1 September 1999	SES selection changed to be based on the Senior Executive Leadership Capability Framework.	*PSMPC Circular 1999/11*, 25 August 1999.
5 December 1999	*Public Service Act 1999* and *Parliamentary Service Act 1999* take effect, establishing the separation of parliamentary departments from public service departments and enshrining a range of features, including: • values and codes of conduct; • protection for whistleblowers; • employment equity; • prohibition on patronage and favouritism; • streamlining of employment powers (including those of dismissal) of departmental secretaries; and • making provisions for departmental secretaries to enter into collective and/or individual employment contracts and agreements. The Act also replaces the Management Advisory Board with the Management Advisory Committee.	Public Service Act 1999. Parliamentary Service Act 1999.